RHETORICAL
ANALYSIS
of SPEECHES

D1202659

RHETORICAL ANALYSIS of SPEECHES

LIONEL CROCKER

Professor and Chairman,
Department of Speech
Denison University

ALLYN AND BACON, INC.   BOSTON

PN4142
C7

© Copyright, 1967, by Allyn and Bacon, Inc., 150 Tremont Street, Boston. All rights reserved. No part of this book may be reproduced in any form, or by any means, without permission in writing from the publisher.

Printed in the United States of America.

Library of Congress catalog card number: 67–17709

PREFACE

THE SELECTIONS THAT make up this text are fairly representative of the concerns of the American people with war and peace during the past forty years. The address by Franklin D. Roosevelt reveals the diplomatic skill of one of America's greatest Presidents. Before we entered the war officially President Roosevelt recognized the need of supporting Great Britain in her struggle with the Axis powers. This lend-lease speech is followed by Winston Churchill's address delivered to the Congress of the United States within a few weeks after the declaration of war by the United States. There are no doubt greater speeches by both statesmen but these two represent the culmination of a decision that undoubtedly won the war.

For the war speeches and its aftermath it was felt necessary to dwell upon the historical occasions. But for the speeches by the other orators the occasions are familiar to the student.

The speeches by the two spokesmen for the Far East are included because more and more the United States finds itself involved in the Far Pacific. The recent Manila Conference and the annual rejection of Red China from the United Nations are evidence of our concern in this area.

The speeches of Brutus and Antony are studied from the rhetorical rather than the literary point of view. Shakespeare lived in a period of rhetorical renaissance. The oration is a common device in his plays.[1]

This is not just another compilation of speeches. This is a word-by-word, sentence-by-sentence, paragraph-by-paragraph rhetorical analysis, always keeping the speaker, the speech, the audience and the occasion in mind.

The speakers included in this volume are all important people who have helped to shape the world we live in. Preceding each speech

---

[1] See, for example, Milton Boone Kennedy, *The Oration in Shakespeare* (Chapel Hill: The University of North Carolina Press, 1942).

is a brief biographical sketch. In almost every instance there are full length biographies of the speakers that the student might like to consult as he studies in depth the rhetorical impact of these people.

Lionel Crocker

CONTENTS

71277

RHETORICAL
ANALYSIS
of SPEECHES

FOREWORD

CASE STUDIES

This text, a compilation of studies in speech making, is for the use of students of public speaking in such classes as persuasion, rhetoric, speech composition and the history of public speaking. From many of his other courses the student should be well acquainted with the case study approach. In the liberal arts college many courses such as sociology, economics, English literature and history depend upon concrete studies to develop and deduce principles. Similarly, in the professional schools such as business administration, medicine, law, dentistry and engineering students analyze individual cases to discover the underlying principles that may apply to other cases. This volume of analyzed speeches uses various types of public address to illustrate principles of rhetoric.

DEFINITION OF RHETORIC

Through long usage rhetoric is one of those words, like art, that can mean anything the user intends to have it mean. One or two familiar definitions will help us get near what we mean when we use the term. Aristotle's definition, "The faculty of finding all the available means of persuasion in a given case" is well known to students of classical rhetoric. Genung defined rhetoric as "the art of adapting discourse, in harmony with its subject and occasion, to the requirements of a reader or hearer." I. A. Richards declared, "Rhetoric should be the study of misunderstandings and its remedies." These attempts at definition can be stated in Aristotle's dictum, "of the three elements in speech making —the speaker, the subject, and the person addressed, it is the last one, the hearer that determines the speaker's end and object."

THE NATURE OF SPEECH

Why study public speaking? What place does the study of speech making play in the student's course of study? One speaks long before one learns to write. Most ideas that find their way into writing are the outgrowth of discussion. Behind every one of the speeches contained in this text is much discussion.

Speaking deals with minds that are present and listening. The writer of an article cannot be sure who his readers will be. The speaker has his audience before him. Out of this difference in audiences many problems arise.

The American Speech Association is the outgrowth of the attempt to give speech the importance in the curriculum it deserves. Before 1914 most speech courses, if any, were taught in departments of English. But the problems of speaking are different from those of writing or of literature. Literature deals with subjects that have more or less permanency. Speaking, like journalism, deals with the fleeting present. Speaking must be immediately intelligible; writing may be abstruse.

Personality plays an important part in the speech situation. Every speaker in this study is a personality; no two of these people express themselves in the same way. In no other activity in college does the personality of a student count for so much.

THE FUNCTION OF SPEECH

Dictatorships shun public speaking. Tongues are silenced in a closed society because there must be no discordant voices along the party line. Personality and personal opinion must be smothered. In a democracy, on the other hand, everyone has an opportunity to be heard. Each member of such a society must make the most of this opportunity and responsibility by studying the techniques of getting ideas across to an audience.

Through speaking the leader motivates, suggests, guides and organizes others to do their work. He does not handle *people*. He handles *ideas*, so the tool to help him in his work is the spoken and written word. The speaker's effectiveness depends upon his ability to get his thinking across to other people and upon his skill in finding out what other people need.

Lincoln in the debates with Douglas declared that in a democracy public opinion is everything. Public opinion is shaped by public speaking. Mme. Chiang Kai-shek is still speaking to American audiences. An AP dispatch of October 5, 1966 indicates that the Chairman of the

Foreign Relations Committee is worried about her activities. "Chairman J. W. Fulbright of the Senate Foreign Relations Committee has asked the State Department to explain 'under what auspices' Mme. Chiang Kai-shek is attempting to influence foreign policy. The Arkansas Democrat told the Senate Monday that the wife of the president of Nationalist China is making a one-year tour of the United States and is delivering speeches he said that call 'upon the United States to use its power to overthrow Red China.' "

HOW TO USE THE TOOLS OF RHETORIC

Purpose

At the outset the public speaker must know his purpose in speaking to an audience, whether that audience be one person or many. The general ends have been set forth as to instruct, to impress or stimulate, to actuate or persuade, to entertain and to convince. In approaching a given situation the speaker must know what he wants to do with a particular audience. A. Whitney Griswold wanted to actuate his audience to use discussion. Wendell Willkie wanted to impress his audience with the value of education.

Support

After a speaker has chosen his thesis he has to know what tools he must summon to make it acceptable to the particular audience he is addressing. The number and extent of support will depend upon the willingness of the audience to accept what he says.

Audience Analysis

An audience can be, to some degree, analyzed by a speaker. Some questions that will help diagnose an audience are: What has been the experience of the audience, both direct and indirect? What set of values determines the conduct of the audience? How do age, sex and occupation influence decisions?

Motivation

Attention and interest must be held by the speaker. He can do this by appealing to the needs, wants, concerns, beliefs, judgment and emotions of his audience. What appeals can be made to self-interest, patriotism, sense of belonging, idealism, taste, sentiment, affection, property or reputation?

Identification

A speaker attempts to get on common ground with his audience. How can the speaker make his audience feel he is one with them? How can he win their confidence? Lyndon B. Johnson is skilled in identifying himself with his audience, the Congress of the United States.

Language

One rhetorical tool a speaker must master is his manner of expressing himself orally. The speaker deals with sound that impinges on the ear. A speaker must choose words and language that will be meaningful to those he addresses. What words will get the response desired? Not only word choice but phrase and sentence choice must be mastered. Franklin D. Roosevelt and Winston Churchill were masters of the word, the phrase and the sentence in public discourse.

Arrangement

Another rhetorical tool is the arrangement of ideas. What should come first, and what last? Some subjects lend themselves to one order and some to another. A speaker may use the chronological, the logical, place order or the topical as occasion demands. Usually a speech has three parts—the introduction, the discussion and the conclusion. Each of these divisions must accomplish its mission for the speaker as he tries to get into the experience of his audience.

DISTINGUISHED MOLDERS OF OPINION

These case studies are focused on men, and one woman, who were known for their unusual speaking abilities and for their control of an audience. Roosevelt and Churchill kept the morale of the western world high by means of their speeches in World War II. Harry Emerson Fosdick, the greatest preacher of the twentieth century, is a conscious user of rhetorical tools of persuasion and makes a perfect specimen for study. Three brilliant educators, speaking under different circumstances, are analyzed to find out if possible how they achieved their results: Robert M. Hutchins, formerly President of the University of Chicago, A. Whitney Griswold of Yale University and Virgil

Hancher of the State University of Iowa. A celebrated liberal, Wendell Willkie, with a one-world vision, is used as a case study for briefing to show logical arrangement of ideas. A Filipino statesman, Carlos P. Romulo, gave a historical speech at Bandung under difficult circumstances which yields many insights into the composition of a speech. Mme. Chiang Kai-shek is an Oriental woman with an American education pleading the cause of her native land. Her methods of persuasion can be studied with profit. President Lyndon B. Johnson illustrates many of the principles of rhetoric in his justly acclaimed speech on Negro voting rights. And, finally, a classic example of the use and abuse of persuasive techniques is found in the speeches of Brutus and Antony in *Julius Caesar*.

All these speeches are studied with the hope that the college student will learn principles he himself can employ in his own speech making.

CONCEPTS USED IN THE RHETORICAL ANALYSIS OF SPEECHES

These concepts of invention, arrangement and style have been gleaned from the rhetoricians of many centuries. Plato and Aristotle, Cicero and Quintilian, Campbell and Whately, A. E. Phillips and James A. Winans, Kenneth Burke and I. A. Richards, and many others, have contributed to our knowledge of what effective discourse should be. For example, Aristotle gave us the three concepts of proof: personal, logical and emotional. Quintilian gave us the four concepts of an effective introduction: to secure good will, to secure attention, to prepare the audience and to suggest the speech purpose. Following are 33 categories of rhetorical concepts.

A. INTRODUCTION

1. Purposes: To secure good will, to secure attention, to prepare audience, to suggest speech purpose. (Quintilian)

2. Material: May emphasize speaker, theme, audience, occasion.

3. Faults: False assumption, excuses and apologies, ill-advised funny stories, false leads. (O'Neill and Weaver)

B. DISCUSSION

4. Steps in composition: Formation of the idea, consideration of the idea, immediate preparation, delivery of the idea. (Spearman)

5. Selection of subject: Fit the speaker, the audience, the occasion.

6. Kinds of materials: Facts, reasons, opinions, examples.

7. Uses of illustrations: Provides clearness, proof, memory, imagination, rests the audience, provides for various hearers, presents argument differently, employs tact, educates audience to use illustrations, ornaments the address, introduces narrative element, introduces humor. (Beecher)

8. Factors of interest: Animate, antagonistic, concrete, unusual, similar, vital, uncertain. (Phillips)

9. Impelling motives: Self-preservation, property, power, reputation, taste, sentiment, affection. (Phillips)

10. General ends: To inform, actuate, entertain, impress, convince. (O'Neill and Weaver)

11. Outlines: Topical, simple list, causal relation, time order.

12. Patterns of speech structure: Extended analogy, string of beads, partition of a text, repetition of a pattern, problem-solution, motivated sequence, exclusion, deduction, induction, negation and affirmation.

13. Reference to experience: *Principle:* the more the speaker brings his idea within the vivid experience of the audience the more likely will he be to attain his end, and obversely. (Phillips)

14. Factors governing reference to experience: Originally intense, experienced frequently, frequently recollected, recent. (Phillips)

15. Imagination: Helps with construction, helps speaker to invent or discover, produces images, realizes the invisible, stimulates the imagination of the audience. (Dale)

16. Humor: Disappointment theory, derision theory. Exaggeration, understatement, parody, satire, grotesquery, ridicule, irreverence, sarcasm.

17. Figures of speech: Synecdoche, metonymy, simile, metaphor, personification, apostrophe.

18. Three fundamentals of composition: Coherence, unity, emphasis.

19. Language: Choice of words, phrases, slogans, repetition, rhythm, imagery.

20. Principles of style: Clearness, energy, ease.

21. Types of reasoning: Inductive, deductive, causal relation.

22. Definition: Negation, example, application, etymology, context, authority, function.

23. Development of theme: Definition, particulars and details, comparison and contrast, illustration, presentation of reasons, application of a principle, cause and effect.

24. Three kinds of proof: Logical, emotional and personal. (Aristotle)

25. Ways of getting material: Observing, corresponding, talking, reading, thinking. (O'Neill and Weaver)

26. Analysis of audience: What does the audience know about you? about your subject? what influence do occasions have on audience? youth? homogeneity? sex? status? affiliations?

27. Patterns of persuasion: Competition, cooperation, immediacy, delay, precedent, ideals, conformity, adventure, status quo, exclusiveness.

28. Suggestion: Confidence in speaker, elementary impulses, convention, prejudices. (Scott and Howard)

29. Deliberation: Important matters, unusual talking points, new ideas, complicated ideas.

30. Sentences: Short, long, antithetical, interrogatory, declarative, simple, complex.

31. Identification with theme, audience and occasion.

C. CONCLUSION

32. Types: Summary, recapitulation, application. (Broadus)

33. Warnings: Brevity, simplicity, unity, energy.

The student of communication will find these concepts and others treated in his basic text. In the rhetorical analyses of the speeches in this text, these concepts will be referred to time and again.

CHIEF SOURCES OF
RHETORICAL CONCEPTS

Aristotle. *Rhetoric.* (Lane Cooper, tr. and ed.) New York: Appleton-Century-Crofts, Inc., 1932.

Beecher, Henry Ward. *Yale Lectures on Preaching* (1st ser.). New York: J. B. Ford & Co., 1872.

Broadus, J. A. *Preparation and Delivery of Sermons,* 3rd Ed. New York: Sheldon & Co., 1872.

Burke, Kenneth. *A Rhetoric of Motives.* Englewood Cliffs, N.J.: Prentice-Hall, Inc., 1950.

Cicero. *On Oratory and Orators.* (J. S. Watson, tr. and ed.) London: H. G. Bohn, 1855.

Crocker, Lionel and Hildebrandt, Herbert W. *Public Speaking for College Students,* 4th Ed. New York: American Book Company, 1965.

Dale, R. W. *Nine Lectures on Preaching.* New York: E. P. Dutton & Co., Inc., 1878.

Montague, W. P. *The Ways of Knowing.* New York: The Macmillan Co., 1925.

O'Neill, J. M. and Weaver, A. T. *Elements of Speech.* New York: Longmans, Green & Co., Inc., 1926.

Phillips, A. E. *Effective Speaking.* Chicago: The Newton Company, 1908.

Quintilian. *Institutes of Oratory.* (J. S. Watson, tr. and ed.) London: H. G. Bohn, 1856.

Scott, W. D. and Howard, D. T. *Influencing Men in Business*. New York: The Ronald Press Company, 1928.

Spearman, C. E. *The Abilities of Man*. New York: The Macmillan Co., 1927.

AID TO THE DEMOCRACIES[1]

Our Country Is Going to Play Its Part

President FRANKLIN D. ROOSEVELT

Delivered at the dinner of the White House Correspondents'
Association, Washington, D.C., March 15, 1941.

AT THE DECEMBER 1942 conference of the National Association of Teachers of Speech, President Franklin D. Roosevelt was named the greatest public speaker of all the contemporary orators and the most effective in estimating audience reaction.

No one can overestimate the value of the Fireside Chats in keeping the United States steady during the depression. Wherever one was, in a restaurant, in an automobile, or at a public meeting, action was stopped to listen to the confident words of the President. His magnificent voice and skill in delivery made everything he said seem important and inspiring. He had a gift of conversational directness.

Many think that Roosevelt was the supreme politician. In 1914, he ran for the Democratic nomination for United States Senator from New York and lost. In 1920, he aimed at a still higher position, and he was nominated for the Vice-Presidency of the United States on the same ticket with James M. Cox. Roosevelt resigned from the Navy and campaigned vigorously. He made more speeches than any other Vice-Presidential candidate in history. In spite of the help of his wife Eleanor, Cox and Roosevelt were defeated by the biggest margin in

---

[1] *Vital Speeches*, Vol. VII, No. 12.

the history of the Republic up to that time, even losing Hyde Park, Roosevelt's home town. Eleven times Roosevelt tried his luck at the polls; he was successful in nine of them. Once he lost in a primary, not a general election; the other time he lost when Harding won over Cox.

Defeated in the political arena, he turned his attention to business. He also took an active part in the world about him. He was active in the Boy Scout movement, in the affairs of Harvard, which made him an overseer in 1917, and as chairman of the committee to raise funds for the Woodrow Wilson Foundation.

Then, in 1921, he was stricken with infantile paralysis while vacationing at Campobello Island. The heroic struggle against this dreaded disease was told in the play *Sunrise at Campobello* with Ralph Bellamy in the starring role. With the help of Eleanor Roosevelt and his secretary, Margaret Le Hand, and his friend and personal secretary, the late Louis Howe, he fought for recovery. Mrs. Roosevelt read to him for long hours. Many think that it was during this period that he developed the social sense that led later to the enactment of the Welfare State.

By 1924, he was able to get around on crutches and to take an active part in Democratic politics, to place Al Smith's name before the Democratic Convention in that year. By 1928, he was walking with two canes and had ceased to lead the life of an invalid. Al Smith insisted on Roosevelt's running for Governor of New York State. He conducted a strenuous campaign and was elected by a majority of 25,564. During his two terms as Governor (1929–33), he got through much legislation.

This emphasis on social legislation is seen in his remark, "I believe that in the future the State . . . will assume a much larger role in the lives of its citizens. . . . Now some people are going to say this is socialistic. My answer to them is that it is 'social,' not 'socialistic.' "[2]

In 1932, he was elected President of the United States during the depths of the depression. He promptly declared a general bank holiday. The New Deal was born. Government agencies were set up to revive business by pumping vast sums into the economy, by developing natural resources, by offering work to the unemployed. Following his re-election in 1936, Roosevelt encountered increasing opposition. The Supreme Court declared several New Deal measures invalid. Then followed Roosevelt's attempt to pack the Supreme Court in 1937, which failed. The attempt to purge New Deal opponents in Congress also failed. In foreign affairs, Roosevelt furthered a "good neighbor" policy toward Latin America. He was re-elected to a third term in 1940.

---

2 *New York Times,* December 30, 1928.

He helped to align the United States more and more with Great Britain, while the first peacetime Selective Service Act came into being.

The Isolationists were temporarily stopped in their attack on his policies aimed at helping Britain when, on December 7, 1941, Japanese bombs fell on Pearl Harbor. The next day Congress declared war on Japan, and on December 11 Roosevelt asked Congress for a declaration of war against Germany and Italy. Congress voted it unanimously, as it later voted requests for tremendous appropriations. And in January the Senate passed the Second War Powers Bill, which expanded the Government's authority to expedite production and the movement of supplies. A normally anti-Administration Congress was apparently doing its best to implement Roosevelt's words after Pearl Harbor: "No matter how long it may take us to overcome this unpremeditated invasion, the American people in their righteous might will win through to absolute victory."

During his fourth administration he engaged in international conferences: Casablanca, Quebec, Teheran and Yalta. He labored for perpetual peace through the United Nations. He died suddenly on April 12, 1945 at Warm Springs, Georgia and was buried at Hyde Park.

Roosevelt's speeches were prepared with great care. He surrounded himself with people with unusual talent for putting words into the right shape. Robert E. Sherwood, the playwright, gives us an insight into the composite manner of drafting his speeches. "When he wanted to give a speech for some important purpose, whether it was connected with a special occasion or not, he would discuss it first at length with Hopkins, Rosenman, and me, telling what particular points he wanted to make, what sort of audience he wished primarily to reach and what the maximum limit was to be. He would dictate pages and pages, approaching his main topic, sometimes rambling so far away from it that he couldn't get back, in which case he would say, 'Well—something along those lines—you boys can fix it up.' "[3]

How fortunate the two English-speaking nations, Great Britain and the United States, were to have two men so gifted with pen and voice to lead them! Churchill's great sentences and phrases reverberated in the minds and hearts of the British and gave them strength; Roosevelt's effective use of the radio carried his voice into every American home. He was the first American President to use the radio with such power. One but wonders what the effect might have been had television been available. What a picture he would have made! Seated

---

[3] Robert E. Sherwood, *Roosevelt and Hopkins: an Intimate History*, Rev. Ed. (New York: Harper & Row, Publishers, 1950), pp. 371-2.

at his desk with his self-assurance, his flashing smile, his well modu-
lated voice, his aristocratic accent, the toss of his head, his eloquent
gestures! All would have produced an electric effect on the American
public. But lacking television he used radio to the fullest.

THE SETTING

Congress unlocked the keys to the arsenal of democracy and handed
them to President Roosevelt on March 8, 1941. The debate over the
Lend-Lease bill took 58 days. Unlimited billions were to be given to
the nations battling the Axis powers. The Senate passed the bill 60 to
31 and the House passed it 260 to 165. From such a voting record one
can see that there was opposition on the part of the isolationist leaders
such as Burton K. Wheeler, who had been a leading New Deal backer
but turned isolationist. After Wheeler realized he was beaten, he
warned that he would "take to the stump" to prevent Mr. Roosevelt
from exercising the powers of the act in such a way as to "lead this
country into war."

After disposing of amendments, such as no American Expeditionary
Force, prohibition of United States convoys outside the Western
Hemisphere and restriction of the further transfer of naval units, the
Administration leaders rolled on to a final vote of 49 Democrats, one
Independent and ten Republicans for Lend-Lease.

The Lend-Lease Act gave the President power to sell, transfer, lend
or lease necessary war supplies to nations whose defense was vital to
the United States in World War II. By the end of the war most of the
United Nations had been declared eligible for lend-lease aid, though
not all demanded or received it. The end of lend-lease was announced
on August 31, 1945. The total aid given exceeded $50,600,000,000.

1. *Many of these people are undoubtedly known to the speaker. Watch
how the speaker addresses the seen audience and the unseen audience throughout
the speech. This is a difficult art.*

1. My Friends: This dinner of the
White House Correspondents' Association is unique. It is the first one at which
I have made a speech in all these eight
years. It differs from the press conferences that you and I hold twice a week.
For you cannot ask me any questions
tonight; and everything I have to say is
word for word "on the record."

2.   For eight years you and I have been helping each other. I have been trying to keep you informed of the news of Washington, and of the nation, and of the world, from the point of view of the Presidency. You, more than you realize, have been giving me a great deal of information about what the people of this country are thinking and saying. In our press conferences, as at this dinner tonight, we include reporters representing papers and news agencies of many other lands. To most of them it is a matter of constant amazement that press conferences such as ours can exist in any nation in the world.

2.   *The speaker establishes good will by complimenting the audience on their part in government.*

3.   That is especially true in those lands where freedoms do not exist— where the purposes of our democracy and the characteristics of our country and of our people have been seriously distorted.

3.   *The audience gives the speaker an excellent opportunity to stress one of the freedoms of a democracy.*

4.   Such misunderstandings are not new. I remember a quarter of a century ago that in the early days of the first World War, the German Government received solemn assurances from their representatives in the United States that the people of America were disunited; that they cared more for peace at any price than for the preservation of ideals and freedom; that there would even be riots and revolutions in the United States if this nation ever asserted its own interests.

4.   *The speaker makes the transition to the main theme of his address, which is unanimity of the nation, by means of an illustration. Note the skillful transitions throughout the speech.*

5.   Let not dictators of Europe or Asia doubt our unanimity now.

5.   *This sentence paragraph states the theme of the address. This is the end of the introduction.*

A UNITED NATION IN ACTION

6. *Here we have a revelation of the speaker, personal proof. Note that the speaker uses the common word* worried, *not concerned or troubled. Roosevelt's vocabulary is filled with common words. There are no unusual words in this address.*

6. Before the present war broke out on September 1, 1939, I was more worried, more worried about the future than many people—indeed than most people. The record shows that I was not worried enough.

7. *Here we have a figure from everyday life, "water over the dam." Note how the speaker limits his subject. He is not going to talk about the past.*

7. That, however, is water over the dam. Do not let us waste time in reviewing the past, or fixing or dodging the blame for it. History cannot be rewritten by wishful thinking. We, the American people, are writing new history today.

8. *"The big news story . . ." Here is an example of the speaker using the language of his immediate audience, an example of addressing the seen and the unseen audience at the same time. The speaker's ability to phrase is seen in such words as "democracy has gone into action."*

8. The big news story of this week is this: The world has been told that we, as a united nation, realize the danger that confronts us—and that to meet that danger our democracy has gone into action.

9. *Here the speaker is using the topic of degree, Nazism is worse than Prussianism.*

9. We know that although Prussian autocracy was bad enough in the first war, Nazism is far worse in this.

10. *This paragraph is an amplification of paragraph 9. For the convenience of reading before a microphone the material is put in short paragraphs. In composition for reading many of the paragraphs would be put together. This mechanical device is worth noting.*

10. Nazi forces are not seeking mere modifications in colonial maps or in minor European boundaries. They openly seek the destruction of all elective systems of government on every continent—including our own; they seek to establish systems of government based on the regimentation of all human beings by a handful of individual rulers who have seized power by force.

11. *Watch the employment of conversational devices, "Yes, these men . . ." The adjective* hypnotized *seems to be the exact word. Note the refutation of the claim of a new order—how the speaker tears it apart.*

11. Yes, these men and their hypnotized followers call this a new order. It is not new and it is not order. For order among nations presupposes something enduring—some system of justice under which individuals over a long period of time, are willing to live. Humanity will never permanently accept a system imposed by conquest and based on slavery.

12. These modern tyrants find it necessary to their plans to eliminate all democracies—eliminate them one by one. The nations of Europe, and indeed we ourselves, did not appreciate that purpose. We do now. The process of the elimination of the European nations proceeded according to plan through 1939 and well into 1940 until the schedule was shot to pieces by the unbeatable defenders of Britain.

12. *Note the use of the general term "modern tyrants" rather than Hitler and Mussolini. Note the use of the word eliminate three times in this paragraph. Roosevelt is skilled in the use of this device: words, phrases, sentence structure are repeated with effect. Other instances in this address are numerous. The short, pithy sentence "We do now" should be noted.*

DEMOCRACY MAKES A DECISION

13. The enemies of democracy were wrong in their calculations for a very simple reason. They were wrong because they believed that democracy could not adjust itself to the terrible reality of a world at war.

13. *The listener is aware of a struggle, a fight—"The enemies of democracy." This is a factor of interest.*

14. They believed that democracy because of its profound respect for the rights of man would never arm itself to fight.

14. *Look at the repetition of the same words in these three paragraphs. There are several such passages which are reminiscent of Walt Whitman or Carl Sandburg or Amy Lowell. Here is a repetition of the idea of the rights of a democracy.*

15. They believed that democracy because of its will to live at peace with its neighbors, could not mobilize its energies even in its own defense.

14–15. *Note repetition of sentence form, "They believed . . ."*

16. They know now that democracy can still remain democracy and speak and reach conclusions and arm itself adequately for defense.

17. Note the use of the vernacular of the gangster. By implication he calls the enemies gangsters. Note the amplification of the phrase.

17. From the bureaus of propaganda of the Axis powers came the confident prophecy that the conquest of our country would be "an inside job"—a job accomplished not by over-powering invasion from without, but by disrupting confusion and disunion and moral disintegration from within.

18. Here is a reiteration of the ideal of freedom of speech. Again note the phrase "the backstairs manufacturers of panic." Roosevelt is a phrase-maker of unusual power.

18. Those who believed that knew little of our history. America is not a country which can be confounded by the appeasers, the defeatists, the backstairs manufacturers of panic. It is a country that talks out its problems in the open, where any man can hear them.

19. Note the vividness. He does not say radio but every wave length; He does not say discussed at length but over every cracker barrel in all the land.

19. We have just now engaged in a great debate. It was not limited to the halls of Congress. It was argued, argued in every newspaper, on every wave length—over every cracker barrel in all the land. It was finally settled and decided by the American people themselves.

20. Here, again, is this device of the Yes . . . Roosevelt does not hesitate to end a sentence with a preposition. This paragraph is well composed. This is democracy. The rhythm of this paragraph is remarkable; it helps bring out the thought.

20. Yes, the decisions of our democracy may be slowly arrived at. But when that decision is made, it is proclaimed, not with the voice of any one man, but with the voice of one hundred and thirty millions. It is binding on us, all of us. And the world is no longer left in doubt.

21. Roosevelt clears the air. Like a knife his words cut and make the thought clear. He says the same thing in three different ways.

21. This decision is the end of any attempts at appeasement in our land; the end of urging us to get along with dictators; the end of compromise with tyranny and the forces of oppression.

22. The use of the word And is an example of his use of the conversational mode in his composition. The technical composition for radio should be noted. The speaker's eye sees that this sentence is important in that it is set off by itself. The voice would emphasize it accordingly.

22. And the urgency is now.

23. We believe firmly that when our production output is in full swing, the democracies of the world will be able to prove that dictatorships cannot win.

23. *Note the contrast of* We believe *with* They believed *in paragraphs 14 and 15. Roosevelt's style is streamlined, there are no surplus words. The thought "Dictators cannot win" is an echo of a thought in a previous speech.*

RUSHING AID TO BATTLE LINES

24. But, now the time element is of supreme importance. Every plane, every other instrument of war, old and new, every instrument that we can spare now, we will send overseas because that is the common sense of strategy.

24. *A new concept is to be dealt with and that is speed. Action seems to be breathed into the very words. The former concept of* unity *is brought in and linked to the concept of* speed. *In paragraph 32 note how the word* speed *is repeated four times and in the next paragraph it is repeated again.*

25. The great task of this day, the deep duty which rests upon each and every one of us is to move products from the assembly lines of our factories to the battle lines of democracy—now!

25. *"Battle lines of democracy": the speaker does not let the listener forget that it is a fight between democracy and tyranny.*

26. We can have speed. We can have effectiveness if we maintain our existing unity. We do not have and never will have the false unity of a people browbeaten by threats and misled by propaganda. Ours is a unity that is possible only among free men and women who recognize the truth, and face reality with intelligence and courage.

26. *Note the echo of the idea of unity, one of the keywords of the address.*

27. Today, at last, today at long last, ours is not a partial effort. It is a total effort and that is the only way to guarantee ultimate safety.

27. *In this section note such words as* now, today, at long last. *Is this phrase reminiscent of Edward VI?*

28. Beginning a year ago, we started the erection of hundreds of plants, and we started the training of millions of men.

28–29. *These paragraphs reveal the mind of the speaker. They build up the audience's confidence in the speaker, they show planning and forethought. The speaker recommends himself by what he says to the audience. Note the new title* *given the Lend-Lease bill; this skill in the use of words is one of Roosevelt's greatest powers of composition. Note the timeliness: "This week."*

29. Then, at the moment that the aid-to-democracies bill was passed this week we were ready, ready to recommend the seven-billion-dollar appropriation on the basis of capacity production as now planned.

30. *Note the conversational why.*

30. The articles themselves, why, they cover the whole range of munitions of war and of the facilities for transporting them across the sea.

31. *A factor of interest is the animate. Note how it is used here. The listener is left almost breathless. The commodity of which the dictators seem to have plenty is speed. Here the democracies are matching them. Speed is a keyword of the address.*

31. That aid-to-democracies bill was agreed to by both houses of the Congress on Tuesday afternoon last. I signed it one-half hour later. Five minutes after that I approved a list of articles for immediate shipment. And today, Saturday night, many of them are on their way. On Wednesday, I recommended an appropriation for new material to the extent of seven billion dollars; and the Congress is making patriotic speed in making the money available.

32. *The speaker carries his words to the fireside, "that watchword will find its way into every home in the nation." Repetition: "Speed and speed now, speed and speed now."*

32. Here in Washington, we are thinking in terms of speed and speed now, speed and speed now. And I hope that that watchword will find its way into every home in the nation.

33. *Note this beautiful transitional paragraph leading up to the next concept of sacrifices of privileges but not of rights. This is linked to the concept of immediacy.*

33. We shall have to make sacrifices —every one of us. The final extent of those sacrifices will depend on the speed with which we act now!

SACRIFICE OF PRIVILEGES, NOT RIGHTS

34. *The speaker is direct. His language is you, I, we, our. Here is the leader rallying his people to a great cause.*

34. I must tell you tonight in plain language what this undertaking means to you—to you and your daily life.

35. Whether you are in the armed services; whether you are a steel worker or a stevedore; a machinist or a house-wife; a farmer or a banker; a storekeeper or a manufacturer—to all of you it will mean sacrifice in behalf of your country and your liberties. Yes, you will feel the impact of this gigantic effort in your daily lives. You will feel it in a way that will cause to you many inconveniences.

35.   Note the specific reference to occupations. The points are driven home. Note the composition of the balanced phrases.

36. You will have to be content with lower profits, lower profits from business, from business because obviously your taxes will be higher.

36.   Unwelcome truths are spoken with candor—"taxes will be higher."

37. You will have to work longer at your bench, or your plow, or your machine, or your desk.

37.   A less skillful speaker would have left out this paragraph. But President Roosevelt wants to be sure that his audience gets the point.

38. Let me make it clear that the nation is calling for the sacrifice of some privileges, not for the sacrifice of fundamental rights. And most of us will do it willingly. That kind of sacrifice is for the common national protection and welfare; for our defense against the most ruthless brutality in all history; for the ultimate victory of a way of life now so violently menaced.

38.   The distinction between rights and privileges is well made. Note the three parts of this sentence. This device is often used by the speaker.

39. A half-hearted effort on our part will lead to failure. This is no part-time job. The concepts of "business as usual" of "normalcy" must be forgotten until the task is finished. Yes, it's an all-out effort and nothing short of an all-out effort will win.

39.   Note the alternation of the long and short sentences. Note the repetition within a sentence. Again note the conversational "Yes."

40. Therefore, we are dedicated, from hereon, to a constantly increasing tempo of production—a production greater than we now know or have ever known before—a production that does not stop and should not pause.

40.   The concept of speed is again linked to that of sacrifice.

JOINING TO PRESERVE FREEDOMS

41. *Note the timely character of the "Tonight . . ." Note the personal appeal, and respect for the leader. The appeal to unity is again repeated.*

41. Tonight, I am appealing to the heart and to the mind of every man and every woman within our borders who love liberty. I ask you to consider the needs of our nation at this hour, put aside all personal differences until the victory is won.

42. *Here is the use of the metaphor. Note how he handles the figure throughout the paragraph. Again, he carries the message to each individual.*

42. The light of democracy must be kept burning. To the perpetuation of this light, each of us must do his own share. The single effort of one individual may seem small. But there are 130 million individuals over here, and there are many more millions in Britain and elsewhere bravely shielding the great flame of democracy from the blackout of barbarism. It is not enough for us merely to trim the wick, or polish the glass. The time has come when we must provide the fuel in ever-increasing amounts to keep that flame alight.

43. *The speaker stays with the thought of individual response. He is after a response from each listener.*

43. There will be no divisions of party or section or race, no divisions of nationality or religion. There is not one among us who does not have a stake in the outcome of the effort in which we are now engaged.

44. *By recalling these four freedoms the speaker ties up his thought with previous utterances. There is a fundamental philosophy back of what he says. These ideals can be obtained only through the democratic process.*

44. A few weeks ago I spoke of four freedoms—freedom of speech and expression, freedom of every person to worship God in his own way, freedom from want, freedom from fear. They are the ultimate stake. They may not be immediately attainable throughout the world, but humanity does move toward those glorious ideals through democratic processes.

45. And if we fail—if democracy is superseded by slavery—then those four freedoms or even the mention of them will become forbidden things. Centuries will pass before they can be revived.

45. The alternative . . . The debater shows what will happen. Here is an appeal to self-preservation.

46. By winning now, we strengthen the meaning of those freedoms, we increase the stature of mankind, we establish the dignity of human life.

46. Here is another example of the sentence with the three parts.

LOYALTY AND WILL OF NATION

47. I have often thought that there is a vast difference between the word "loyalty" and the word "obedience." Obedience can be obtained and enforced in a dictatorship by the use of threat or extortion or blackmail, or it can be obtained by a failure on the part of government to tell the truth to its citizens.

47. Just as the speaker developed the difference between privileges and rights, he develops the difference between loyalty and obedience. We have a good example of development of the theme by definition. The leader calls to his followers to be loyal. Here is appeal to love of country.

48. Loyalty is different. It springs from the mind that is given the facts, that retains ancient ideals and proceeds without coercion to give support to its own government.

48. These four paragraphs "bleed" with the thought of loyalty. The listener who dialed in at this point would know at once what the speaker was talking about.

49. That is true in England and in Greece and in China and in the United States today. And in many other countries millions of men and women are praying for the return of a day when they can give that kind of loyalty.

49. Contrast the rhythm of this paragraph with the abrupt rhythm of the next paragraph.

50. Loyalty cannot be bought. Dollars alone will not win this war. Let us not delude ourselves as to that.

51. Today, nearly a million and a half American citizens are hard at work in our armed forces. The spirit, the determination of these men and our Army

51. Note the calling upon the names of past heroes. The tactful reference to Lee is an echo of the unity of the country. We have an example of emotional proof.

and Navy are worthy of the highest traditions of our country. No better men ever served under Washington, or John Paul Jones, or Grant, or Lee, or Pershing. That is a boast, I admit—but it is not an idle one.

52. *The next four paragraphs are especially well written. This device is used in almost every Roosevelt speech. Together they constitute what might be called a prose poem. "Upon that . . ."*

52. Upon the national will to sacrifice and to work depends the output of our industry and our agriculture.

53. *"Fighting the good fight." Biblical:* I Timothy 6:12.

53. Upon that will depends the survival of the vital bridge across the ocean —the bridge of ships that carry the arms and the food for those who are fighting the good fight.

54. Upon that will depends our ability to aid other nations which may determine to offer resistance.

55. *Hope is expressed.*

55. Upon that will may depend practical assistance to people now living in nations that have been overrun, should they find the opportunity to strike back in an effort to regain their liberties, and may that day come soon.

WARNING AGAINST OBSTRUCTION

56. *The speaker develops his theme by particulars and details. Note the appeals to self-preservation.*

56. This will of the American people will not be frustrated either by threats from powerful enemies abroad or by small, selfish groups or individuals at home.

57. The determination of America must not and will not be obstructed by war profiteering.

58. It must not be obstructed by unnecessary strikes of workers, by short-sighted management or by the third danger—deliberate sabotage.

59. For, unless we win, there will be no freedom for either management or labor.

60. Wise labor leaders and wise business managers will realize how necessary it is to their own existence to make common sacrifice for this great cause.

61. There is no longer the slightest question or doubt that the American people recognize the extreme seriousness of the present situation. That is why they have demanded, and got, a policy of unqualified, immediate, all-out aid for Britain, for Greece, for China and for all the governments in exile whose homelands are temporarily occupied by the aggressors.

62. And from now on that aid will be increased—and yet again increased—until total victory has been won.

MORALE OF VALIANT BRITAIN

63. The British are stronger than ever in the magnificent morale that has enabled them to endure all the dark days and the shattered nights of the past 10 months. They have the full support and help of Canada, of the other dominions, of the rest of their Empire, and the full aid and support of non-British people throughout the world who still think in terms of the great freedoms.

55–60. Another concept developed in the address is that of difficulties in the way. Specific means of obstruction are mentioned.

59. Again the debater tells what the alternative is.

60. Echo of the idea of sacrifice.

62. Emphasis by repetition.

63–65. The speaker echoes the admiration of the common man for the British. The speaker will not let the audience forget that this is a fight for "the great freedoms." Note the use of adjectives in these paragraphs: dark, shattered, brilliant, stirring, superb, valiant.

64. The British people are braced for invasion whenever such attempt may come—tomorrow—next week—next month.

65. *The speaker personifies the British in Winston Churchill. By implication Roosevelt tells his audience that he expects them to be as brave as the British. Note the use of antithesis "rather die as free men than live as slaves." Roosevelt is mindful of that portion of his audience which is the British Empire.*

65. In this historic crisis, Britain is blessed with a brilliant and great leader in Winston Churchill. But, knowing him, no one knows better than Mr. Churchill himself that it is not alone his stirring words and valiant deeds that give the British their superb morale. The essence of that morale is in the masses of plain people who are completely clear in their minds about the one essential fact—that they would rather die as free men than live as slaves.

BRITISH TO GET ALL THEY NEED

66. *Note the transitional phrase "These plain people."*

66–71. *Here again is a prose poem. Note the refrain: "From America, they will get . . ." The speaker is talking to plain people all over the world. The speech was broadcast in seven languages and was rebroadcast from London by the B.B.C. in 30 languages.*

67. *In these paragraphs note the oral style. This passage is like the free verse of Sandburg.*

66. These plain people—civilians as well as soldiers and sailors and airmen—women and girls as well as men and boys—they are fighting in the front line of civilization at this moment, and they are holding that line with a fortitude that will forever be the pride and the inspiration of all free men on every continent, on every isle of the sea.

67. The British people and their Grecian Allies need ships. From America, they will get ships.

68. They need planes. From America, they will get planes.

69. Yes, from America they need food and from America, they will get food.

70. They need tanks and guns and ammunition and supplies of all kinds.

From America, they will get tanks and guns and ammunition and supplies of all kinds.

71. China likewise expresses the magnificent will of millions of plain people to resist the dismemberment of their historic nation. China, through the Generalissimo Chiang Kai-shek asks our help. America has said that China shall have our help.

71. *Because the Chinese people have never been as close to the American people as the British the speaker does not devote as much space to China as he does to Britain. Suppose the speaker had reversed the amount of space in his treatment of the two nations—that would have been faulty audience adaptation.*

OUR PART IN SHAPING A NEW WORLD

72. And so, our country is going to be what our people have proclaimed it must be—the arsenal of democracy.

72–78. *This is the conclusion. Note the transitional phrase "And so . . ." The conclusion looks into the future. It is an appeal to action. Note the use of the phrase "arsenal of democracy." Did not Vandenburg, the isolationist, use this term? There is a demand by the opposition that peace terms be stated. Is this not a general attempt in that direction? Note emphasis by repetition: "I said when."*

73. Our country is going to play its full part.

74. And, when dictatorships—no I didn't say if, I said when dictatorships disintegrate—and pray God that will be sooner than any of us now dare to hope —then our country must continue to play its great part in the period of world reconstruction for the good of humanity.

75. We believe that the rallying cry of the dictators, their boasting about a master race, will prove to be pure stuff and nonsense. There never has been, there isn't now, and there never will be any race of people on the earth fit to serve as masters over their fellow men.

75–76. *The speaker boldly denies the claims of the opposition.*

76. *Note the masterful use of the verb "to goosestep . . ."*

76. The world has no use for any nation which, because of size or because of military might, asserts the right to goosestep to world power over the bodies of other nations and other races. We believe that any nationality, no matter how small, has the inherent right to its own nationhood.

77. *"We believe . . ." Here is a program. Such paragraphs as these form the treasury of the eloquency of the ages. Application type of conclusion. Note use of commonly used phrase "man's inhumanity to man."*

77. We believe that the men and women of such nations, no matter what size, can, through the processes of peace, serve themselves and serve the world by protecting the common man's security; improve the standards of healthful living; provide markets for manufacture and for agriculture. Through that kind of peaceful service every nation can increase its happiness, banish the terrors of war, and abandon man's inhumanity to man.

78. *The final paragraph is a prayer. Note its Biblical reference: Proverbs 31:28.*

78. Never in all our history, have Americans faced a job so well worthwhile. May it be said of us in the days to come that our children and our children's children rise up and call us blessed.

HERE WE ARE TOGETHER[1]

Defending All That to Free Men Is Dear

WINSTON S. CHURCHILL,

Prime Minister of Great Britain

Delivered to a Joint Session of the Congress of the United States of America, Washington, D.C., December 26, 1941.

WINSTON CHURCHILL (1874–1965) rallied the fighting spirit of Great Britain during the air blitz in 1940 with such fighting words as, "I have nothing to offer but blood, toil, tears, and sweat." Historians will have to reckon with what Great Britain and the civilized world owe to the magnificent oratory of this man. His mastery of the spoken word, along with other gifts, elevated him to a position of power seldom equaled in history. *Time* proclaimed Churchill to be one of England's "profoundest initiates into the artifices of rhetoric."[2] Churchill confesses that as a schoolboy he was not very good in Latin and Greek but that he did manage to master the English sentence.

Of interest to Americans is the fact that his mother was the American beauty, Jennie Jerome, daughter of Leonard Jerome, part owner of the *New York Times*. He made several lecture tours in this country. He received the highest fee ever paid to any lecturer at any time in

---

[1] *Vital Speeches*, Vol. VIII, No. 7.

[2] *Time*, XXXVI, Part II (Oct. 21, 1940), p. 36.

any country. On one of these tours he spoke on three subjects: "The Destiny of the English Speaking Peoples," "The War Debts" and "The Problem of Gold." And of most interest is the fact that he is an honorary American citizen, this honor having been conferred on him by President John F. Kennedy.

He had his ups and downs in British politics, changing parties when it suited him. The following is a brief sketch of his career. He was First Lord of the Admiralty in World War I (1911–15), until discredited by failure of the Dardanelles campaign. He was returned to office in Lloyd George's Liberal government (1917–21). He was conservative Chancellor of the Exchequer (1924–29). He replaced Neville Chamberlain as Prime Minister of a coalition government seven months after the outbreak of World War II, when Chamberlain's policy of appeasement was discredited. Before the entry of the United States into the war he met President Roosevelt at sea and the Atlantic Charter was framed. He twice addressed the United States Congress. He attended a series of international conferences—Casablanca; Quebec; Cairo; Yalta; Teheran; Potsdam. After the Labour Party victory in 1945 he became leader of the opposition. Conservative victory in 1951 brought him back as Prime Minister. He is the author of several histories, biographies and memoirs: *Arms and the Covenant*, 1938; *Step by Step*, 1939; *Into the Battle*, 1942; *The Unrelenting Struggle*, 1942. Much of Churchill's income was from authorship. His book *The World Crisis* earned him $100,000.

His writing is like his oratory. Mastery of the spoken and written word was not easy. Indeed, Churchill had to correct a lisp and a stutter which naturally interfered with his early parliamentary career. He developed a baritone delivery which was agreeable to hear and capable of conveying the cut and thrust, attack and defense, of his ideas. A word like *Nazi* on his tongue carried all the overtones of disgust, fear, hate and defiance.

During his career he delivered more than 10,000 speeches and during this time he developed a characteristic manner of delivery. Vincent Shean described it thus: "In delivering these speeches he depends very little upon gesture for emphasis. One of his favorite positions on the floor of the House seems to be one foot forward and one foot back, with his thumbs stuck into the armholes of his waistcoat, and those scanty pencilled notes lying before him. . . . In the greatest, gravest hour, Mr. Churchill, too, became very simple."[3]

Phyllis Moir was Winston Churchill's secretary. She has left us a record of the preparation of his speeches. "I was genuinely sorry

---

[3] Vincent Shean, "We Shall Never Surrender," *Book-of-the-Month-Club News*, April, 1941, p. 4.

when such dictation ended and I had to go off and transcribe my notes. As soon as I had finished them I took the typewritten pages in to Mr. Churchill for revision. Fountain pen in hand, he would go over the manuscript two, three, sometimes as many as six times, deleting whatever seemed redundant or superfluous, adding a word or a phrase here and there in his delicate, flowing handwriting. Then I would take it away and make a clean copy. Generally the process had to be repeated at least once, sometimes three or four, until the manuscript seemed to him as near perfect as possible.

"Whenever Mr. Churchill has time he memorizes every word, every joke, every gesture of a speech. I understand that when he was younger he even used to rehearse before a mirror; but long experience has made that, at least, unnecessary. He likes his speeches typed on small pieces of note paper with every line of each paragraph indented so that the first word catches his eye more easily.

"As one might guess from all this, Mr. Churchill is not a good extemporaneous speaker. For many years before entering the House of Commons he would learn by heart and have typed out in full two or three and sometimes as many as six speeches, to be ready for any turn the debate might take. Nevertheless, Mr. Churchill has taught himself by years of patient practice to create the impression of spontaneity when he speaks. He is always in close touch with his audience and can rise magnificently to a difficult situation.[4]

The name of Winston Churchill is written as indelibly on the pages of British history as are the names of those great orators of the eighteenth century Burke, Pitt, Fox and Sheridan and those of the nineteenth century Disraeli and Gladstone. When England was threatened with invasion by Hitler, Churchill turned to the speeches of William Pitt, whose England was threatened by an invasion by Napoleon.

THE SETTING

After Pearl Harbor, President Roosevelt and Winston Churchill lost little time in getting together. Japan had driven the two nations into each other's arms. The first meeting between the President and the Prime Minister, held at sea before America entered the war, laid the foundation for cooperation of the English-speaking peoples in the world problems certain to arise after the war. The second meeting, held in Washington during the Christmas holidays, was necessitated by Japan's attacking Pearl Harbor and driving the United States into

---

[4] Phyllis Moir, *I Was Winston Churchill's Private Secretary* (New York: Wilfred Funk, Inc., 1941), p. 158.

the war against the Axis powers. The problems now facing us were war problems stretching to every corner of the globe. An American army was fighting with its back to the wall in a far off setting. Great Britain had just survived the air blitz. But would there be an invasion? Only two weeks after the United States had entered the war it was facing a possible defeat as serious as the fall of France—the loss of the entire Far East and Malaya and the Philippines. In this situation President Roosevelt and Winston Churchill met to map their campaign. While in Washington Prime Minister Churchill was invited to speak before Congress. He received an ovation.

1. *The general end of the speech seems to be to impress the audience with the fact that at last the two great nations are together. Notice how the speaker handles the amenities of the situation: he acknowledges the invitation. He wins the good will of the audience by being pleased with the invitation; he is the one being honored. Note the beginning of the "you and I" device which is continued throughout the speech. The first four paragraphs of the speech are aimed at securing the good will of the audience.*

1. Members of the Senate and of the House of Representatives of the United States, I feel gratefully honored that you should have thus invited me to enter the United States Senate chamber and address the Representatives of both branches of Congress.

2. *Quickly, the speaker gets to the important common bond existing between him and his audience. There is a mention of his life and work, which would serve as personal proof. Note how the speaker builds up his authority. Through the centuries the blood relationships between the two countries have been emphasized. Here the Prime Minister reminds us that he is half American. What a splendid common bond!*

2. The fact that my American forebears have for so many generations played their part in the life of the United States and that here I am, an Englishman, welcomed in your midst makes this experience one of the most moving and thrilling in my life, which is already long and has not been entirely uneventful.

3. *Here is emotional proof. There is appeal to affection. This tender reference to his mother is a wish common to all men. It is one of the universals in the speech. Note the figure of speech "veil of years." This poetic quality is omnipresent in Churchill's speeches. Note the humor: a clever twist of the situation. Only the quick-witted see such openings in a speech situation.*

3. I wish indeed that my mother, whose memory I cherish across the veil of years, could have been here to see me. By the way, I cannot help reflecting that if my father had been American and my mother British, instead of the other way around, I might have got here on my own.

4. In that case, this would not have been the first time you would have heard my voice. In that case I would not have needed any invitation, but if I had it is hardly likely that it would have been unanimous. So, perhaps, things are better as they are. I may confess, however, that I do not feel quite like a fish out of water in a legislative assembly where English is spoken.

5. I am a child of the House of Commons. I was brought up in my father's house to believe in democracy; trust the people, that was his message. I used to see him cheered at meetings and in the streets by crowds of working men way back in those aristocratic Victorian days when Disraeli said "The world was for the few and for the very few." Therefore, I have been in full harmony with the tides which have flowed on both sides of the Atlantic against privileges and monopoly and I have steered confidently towards the Gettysburg ideal of government of the people, by the people, for the people.

6. I owe my advancement entirely to the House of Commons, whose servant I am. In my country, as in yours, public men are proud to be the servants of the State and would be ashamed to be its masters. On any day, if they thought the people wanted it, the House of Commons, could, by a simple vote, remove me from my office. But I am not worrying about it at all.

7. As a matter of fact, I am sure they will approve very highly of my journey here, for which I obtained the King's permission, in order to meet the President of the United States, and to

4. *A sly reference to his own turbulent career is contained in the words "It is hardly likely that it would have been unanimous." This sentence takes it for granted that his audience knows a great deal about him. It is an astute reference to the experience of the audience. In this paragraph the tie of the common language is stressed.*

5. *Here the speaker identifies himself with democracy. Again, the personal proof, the authority of the speaker is built up. Testimony as a type of material is used. Churchill knows that America fought Tory rule. "The Gettysburg ideal" is an interesting way to put it. Read these paragraphs over again and note the skill with which Churchill stresses the common bonds.*

6. *Churchill has coined another apothegm to put alongside the Gettysburg ideal, "Public men are proud to be the servants of the State and would be ashamed to be its masters."*

7. *The speaker again stresses his self-confidence. He is "not worrying about it at all." Note how the previous paragraph prepares for this one. This one seems to be a logical outgrowth of the preceding. He not only has personal assurance but he has*

DOWNS-JONES LIBRARY
HUSTON-TILLOTSON COLLEGE

the assurance of the British Empire. Personal proof. Note how mapping seems to be exactly the correct word.

This paragraph seems to end the introduction, in which the speaker has identified himself with the audience and the occasion. He has given his credentials. He now has the right to speak. He has created the mood to receive what he is going to say.

8.   *The experienced speaker marks off his speech, "First of all . . ." The first point he wants to make is that the United States has taken the war in its stride. This compliments the nation and the audience. He tells the audience what they want to hear. Here is the veteran complimenting the recruit. Churchill in the body of his speech takes up the past, the present and the future. Indirectly, he states that he understands the United States. He further gains the confidence of the audience by understanding them. Note the use of the magic three—"excited, disturbed, self-centered" . . . "novel, startling and painful . . ." There are many other examples of this rhetorical device.*

9.   *Note the transitional phrase after all. Note the use of words "attacked and set upon." It sounds like the combination we so often hear in English—"last will and testament." These combinations of foreign words and Anglo-Saxon words are common in the language. Here we have the speaker driving the audience into an either-or situation. There is no compromise. There is an antithesis. There is an appeal to self-preservation. The speaker makes much use of compound words: Here we have the word well-grounded.*

10.   *One is impressed with Churchill's historical perspective. He sees the present in terms of the past and future, i.e. "these memorable days." Like Edmund Burke, Churchill thinks in images. His imagination is no little part of his power, "mask of an inflexible purpose." Note the repetition of the thought which opened this part of the speech. The phrase Olympian fortitude is masterful: Scan it.*

arrange with him for all that mapping of our military plans and for all those intimate meetings of the high officers of both countries, which are indispensable for the successful prosecution of the war.

8.   I should like to say, first of all, how much I have been impressed and encouraged by the breadth of view and sense of proportion which I have found in all quarters over here to which I have had access. Anyone who did not understand the size and solidarity of the foundation of the United States might easily have expected to find an excited, disturbed, self-centered atmosphere, with all minds fixed upon the novel, startling and painful episodes of sudden war as it hit America.

9.   After all, the United States has been attacked and set upon by three most powerfully armed dictator States, the greatest military power in Europe, the greatest military power in Asia—Japan, Germany and Italy have all declared and are making war upon you, and the quarrel is opened, which can only end in their overthrow or yours.

10.   But, here in Washington in these memorable days, I have found an Olympian fortitude which, far from being based upon complacency, is only the mask of an inflexible purpose and the proof of a sure, well-grounded confidence in the final outcome.

11.   We in Britain had the same feeling in our darkest days. We, too, were sure that in the end all would be well. You do not, I am certain, underrate the severity of the ordeal to which you and we have still to be subjected. The forces ranged against us are enormous. They are bitter. They are ruthless. The wicked men and their factions, who have launched their peoples on the path of war and conquest, know that they will be called to terrible account if they cannot beat down by force of arms the peoples they have assailed.

11.   *The speaker now brings Britain and America together in this section. The next five paragraphs stress the common problems for Americans and Britains. Note the punch of the short sentences in this paragraph. "They are bitter. They are ruthless . . . They will stop at nothing." Note the directness—"you and we."*

12.   They will stop at nothing. They have a vast accumulation of war weapons of all kinds. They have highly trained and disciplined armies, navies and air services. They have plans and designs which have long been contrived and matured. They will stop at nothing that violence or treachery can suggest. It is quite true that on our side our resources in man power and materials are far greater than theirs. But only a portion of your resources are as yet mobilized and developed, and we both of us have much to learn in the cruel art of war.

12.   *Swiftly defined style as "proper words in proper places." The word* cruel *is surely in its right place here. Note the repetition of the binding sentence "They will stop at nothing." Coherence is served by the use of repetition.*

13.   We have, therefore, without doubt, a time of tribulation before us. In this same time some ground will be lost which it will be hard and costly to regain. Many disappointments and unpleasant surprises await us. Many of them will afflict us before the full marshaling of our latent and total power can be accomplished.

13.   *Note the frankness of the speaker. Much of Churchill's strength is his "cards above the table" policy. Note the use of the word* afflict. *Throughout his speeches one finds words that are reminiscent of the Bible:* wicked, tribulation, salvation, curse.

14.   For the best part of twenty years the youth of Britain and America have been taught that war was evil,

14.   *This paragraph is developed by contrast and comparison, a splendid rhetorical device. Here is the philosopher try-*

ing to show why we are unprepared. Each sentence is matched by a sentence on the other side. Note the magic three: "time, courage and untiring exertion can correct." Such phrases promote oratorical rhythm.

which is true, and that it would never come again, which has been proved false. For the best part of twenty years the youth of Germany, of Japan and Italy have been taught that aggressive war is the noblest duty of the citizen and that it should be begun as soon as the necessary weapons and organization have been made. We have performed the duties and tasks of peace. They have plotted and planned for war. This naturally has placed us, in Britain, and now places you, in the United States, at a disadvantage which only time, courage and untiring exertion can correct.

15.   *Note the element of conflict, which is a factor of interestingness. Here begins a recital of the things to be thankful for. This paragraph stresses the fact that Germany missed her chance. Note the compound word "easy-going."*

15.   We have indeed to be thankful that so much time has been granted to us. If Germany had tried to invade the British Isles after the French collapse in June, 1940, and if Japan had declared war on the British Empire and the United States at about the same date, no one can say what disasters and agonies might not have been our lot. But now at the end of December, 1941, our transformation from easy-going peace to total war efficiency has made very great progress.

16.   *Note the appeal to the sense of power. Again contrast and comparison are used. The speaker knows his audience.*

16.   The broad flow of munitions in Great Britain has already begun. Immense strides have been made in the conversion of American industry to military purposes, and now that the United States is at war, it is possible for orders to be given every day which in a year or eighteen months hence will produce results in war power beyond anything which has been seen or foreseen in the dictator States.

17.   *Note the long sentence. The meaning is perfectly apparent as it unfolds. The*

17.   Provided that every effort is made, that nothing is kept back, that the whole man power, brain power, virility, valor and civic virtue of the English-speaking world, with all its galaxy of loyal, friendly or associated communities and States, provided that it is bent unremittingly to the simple but supreme task, I think it would be reasonable to hope that the end of 1942 will see us quite definitely in a better position than we are now. And that the year 1943 will enable us to assume the initiative upon an ample scale. Some people may be startled or momentarily depressed when, like your President, I speak of a long and a hard war.

inverted sentence is characteristic of Churchill's style. Note the alliteration "virility, valor and civic virtue." The audience is always in Churchill's consciousness, i.e. "like your President." The note of hope is struck. Hope helps morale. Note the energy of the words "long and hard war."

18. Our peoples would rather know the truth, somber though it be. And after all, when we are doing the noblest work in the world, not only defending our hearths and homes but the cause of freedom in every land, the question of whether deliverance comes in 1942 or 1943 or 1944 falls into its proper place in the grand proportions in human history.

18. *Churchill has based his whole philosophy of government on this principle of telling the people the truth and then asking them for support. Walter Lippmann thinks that this is Churchill's strongest principle of government. Note the phrase "the grand proportions of human history." Churchill not only knows history but has written it.*

19. Sure I am that this day now we are the masters of our fate, that the task which has been set us is not above our strength, that its pangs and toils are not beyond our endurance. As long as we have faith in our cause and unconquerable will-power, salvation will not be denied us.

19. Sure *gains in power because of its position in the sentence. "Masters of our fate" may be a remembered phrase from Henley's poem. Here is another compound word—"will-power." The religious note is struck here, and provides for the quotation in the next paragraph. Religion is a common bond between America and Britain.*

20. In the words of the Psalmist: "He shall not be afraid of evil tidings, his heart is fixed, trusting in the Lord."

20. *This is from Psalms 112:7. Read the rest of the psalm. Churchill has undoubtedly chosen the best verse for the quotation, although the entire psalm is pertinent.*

21. Not all the tidings will be evil. On the contrary, mighty strokes of war have already been dealt against the enemy—the glorious defense of their

21. *The thought of this section of the speech, that we have hope for the future, is stressed in this paragraph. Note the key-word* tidings, *which is a favorite Churchill*

word. It is also Biblical. The power of Churchill's imagination is apparent in this paragraph. How strong is this image. "Wounds have been inflicted upon the Nazi tyranny and system . . ."

native soil by the Russian armies and people. Wounds have been inflicted upon the Nazi tyranny and system which have bitten deep and will fester and inflame not only in the Nazi body but in the Nazi mind.

22. *I'll never forget the scorn which Churchill poured into this epithet boastful. The paragraph deals quickly with Mussolini, as if he did not deserve more attention. The political philosophy of separating the leader from the people is back of these remarks. Don't these places mentioned here stir your imagination? Again note the compound word ill-equipped.*

22. The boastful Mussolini has crumpled already. He is now but a lackey and a serf, the merest utensil of his master's will. He has inflicted great suffering and wrong upon his own industrious people. He has been stripped of all his African empire, Abyssinia has been liberated. Our armies of the East, which were so weak and ill-equipped at the moment of French desertion, now control all the regions from Teheran to Bengazi and from Aleppo and Cyprus to the sources of the Nile.

23. *Libya at the time of speaking was one of Churchill's trump cards. He makes the most of it here. His sense of the audience again impels him to show how the audience has played a part in current victories. The phrase "very considerable" is a favorite one. It also occurs in paragraphs 34 and 37.*

23. For many months we devoted ourselves to preparing to take the offensive in Libya. The very considerable battle which has been proceeding there for the last six weeks in the desert has been most fiercely fought on both sides. Owing to the difficulties of supply upon the desert flank we were never able to bring numerically equal forces to bear upon the enemy. Therefore we had to rely upon a superiority in the numbers and qualities of tanks and aircraft, British and American.

24. *Note use of repetition for emphasis —"For the first time." Note the graphic character of "the sharp edge of those tools." The word Hun is loaded with connotations. The speaker in this paragraph gives inside information. He knows more than the audience. He instructs. General Auchinleck is the symbol of the Libyan army. He is mentioned again in paragraph 30.*

24. For the first time, aided by these —for the first time we have fought the enemy with equal weapons. For the first time we have made the Hun feel the sharp edge of those tools with which he has enslaved Europe. The armed forces of the enemy in Cyrenaica amounted to about 150,000 men, of whom a third were Germans. General Auchinleck set out to destroy totally that armed force, and I have every reason to believe that his aim will be fully accomplished.

25. I am so glad to be able to place before you, members of the Senate and of the House of Representatives, at this moment when you are entering the war, the proof that, with proper weapons and proper organization, we are able to beat the life out of the savage Nazi. What Hitlerism is suffering in Libya is only a sample and a foretaste of what we have got to give him and his accomplices wherever this war should lead us in every quarter of the globe.

26. There are good tidings also from blue water. The lifeline of supplies which joins our two nations across the ocean, without which all would fail— that lifeline is flowing steadily and freely in spite of all that the enemy can do. It is a fact that the British Empire, which many thought eighteen months ago was broken and ruined, is now incomparably stronger and is growing stronger with every month.

27. Lastly, if you will forgive me for saying it, to me the best tidings of all, the United States, united as never before, has drawn the sword for freedom and cast away the scabbard.

28. All these tremendous steps have led the subjugated peoples of Europe to lift up their heads again in hope. They

25. *Addressing the members of his audience shows that he is always conscious that he is addressing them. There is hope here. Say over the words "We are able to beat the life out of the savage Nazi" to yourself and feel the power, the determination in these words. The use of the word "accomplices" implies the idea of gangsters. Suppose Churchill had said "lead us in the world" instead of "every quarter of the globe," what effect would have been lost?*

26. *Note the use of the keyword tidings which helps bind this section of the address together. Note the descriptive phrase "blue water" instead of "ocean." A writer of textbooks would seize upon this illustration to show the use of the picture phrase instead of the unimaginative one. Note the figure of munitions flowing which was used also in paragraph 16. Again, the speaker uses contrast and comparison. Many in the present audience predicted the fall of the British Empire 18 months ago.*

27. *Note that the experienced speaker in this section makes a final point and states it, "Lastly . . ." The speaker is careful to carry his audience with him as he makes his points. The keyword tidings is used again. In paragraph 26 good tidings was used; here the superlative is used. Note again the graphic way in which the speaker states the entry of the United States. Artists intensify, clarify and interpret. Here the speaker gives expression to a thought all Americans have been thinking, "united as never before."*

28. *In the following paragraphs Churchill dwells upon the effects of the entrance of the United States into the*

struggle. The theme of hope *runs through the address. Don't miss this note. Churchill does not hesitate to point out the evil omens but he also stresses the elements of hope in the case. Note the power of the words in this paragraph,* shameful, brutal, corrupt, fiercely, filthy *and* suborned. *Suborned is the only word in the entire address which is not in everyday speech. It is defined as "to procure privately or unlawfully, as a person by bribery to commit some crime; incite secretly; instigate." How beautifully the word fits in here. The epithet "filthy quislings" is masterful.*

have put aside forever the shameful temptation of resigning themselves to the conqueror's will. Hope has returned to the hearts of scores of millions of men and women, and with that hope there burns a flame of anger against the brutal, corrupt invader. And still more fiercely burn the fires of hatred and contempt for the filthy quislings whom he has suborned.

29. *Let us put this paragraph in units as they were spoken, and note the oratorical rhythm:*
In a dozen ancient States
Now prostrate under the Nazi yoke
The masses of the people
All classes and creeds
Await the hour of liberation
When they, too, will once again
Be able to play their part
And strike their blows like men.
Note the metaphor, "That hour will strike . . ."

29. In a dozen famous ancient States, now prostrate under the Nazi yoke, the masses of the people—all classes and creeds—await the hour of liberation when they, too, will once again be able to play their part and strike their blows like men. That hour will strike and its solemn peal will proclaim that night is past and that the dawn has come.

30. *The introduction of conversation into this paragraph introduces the dramatic element. The debater here is justifying, explaining. He realizes that there is opposition. He is always conscious of the opposition. Such opposition is part of the democratic process. The speaker thinks in terms of alternatives. Note the connotative force of the word* theatres. *How weak would* places *have been in comparison.*

30. The onslaught upon us, so long and so secretly planned by Japan, has presented both our countries with grievous problems for which we could not fully be prepared. If people ask me, as they have a right to ask me in England, "Why is it that you have not got an ample equipment of modern aircraft and army weapons of all kinds in Malaya and in the East Indies?" I can only point to the victory General Auchinleck has gained in the Libyan campaign. Had we diverted and dispersed our gradually growing resources between Libya and Malaya, we should have been found wanting in both theatres.

31. *Again, note that the speaker is addressing a particular audience. What*

31. If the United States has been found at a disadvantage at various points in the Pacific Ocean, we know well that that is to no small extent because of the aid which you have been giving to us in munitions for the defense of the British Isles, and for the Libyan campaign, and above all, because of your help in the Battle of the Atlantic, upon which all depends and which has in consequence been successfully and prosperously maintained.

the speaker says is determined partly by the audience. The strategy of the conflict is revealed in this paragraph. He is still talking about the effect of the entrance of the United States into the struggle. The speaker drives home the point that the battle of the Atlantic is being won.

32.   Of course, it would have been much better, I freely admit, if we had had enough resources of all kinds to be at full strength at all threatened points, but considering how slowly and reluctantly we brought ourselves to large-scale preparations, and how long these preparations take, we had no right to expect to be in such a fortunate position.

32.   Churchill does not claim everything and admit nothing. He knows the power of admission. He knows that his type of government rests upon the consent of the governed. He trusts the people. Churchill is no miracle worker. His approach to the solution is rational.

33.   The choice of how to dispose of our hitherto limited resources had to be made by Britain in time of war and by the United States in time of peace. And I believe that history will pronounce that upon the whole, and it is upon the whole that these matters must be judged, that the choice made was right.

33.   The perspective of history is again appealed to. The speaker is addressing reasoning people. He is using reasons as a type of material. The phrase "on the whole" summarizes Churchill's total outlook.

34.   Now that we are together, now that we are linked in a righteous comradeship of arms, now that our two considerable nations, each in perfect unity, have joined all their life energies in a common resolve, a new scene opens upon which a steady light will glow and brighten.

34.   This paragraph ends and summarizes this section of the address. Churchill is fond of the figure of speech of a light glowing. One finds it in many of his speeches. The introduction of the phrase "we are together" should be noticed. It is used again in paragraph 41.

35.   Many people have been astonished that Japan should, in a single day, have plunged into war against the United States and the British Empire. We all wonder why, if this dark design,

35.   The next five paragraphs deal with the entrance of Japan into the war. The speaker dwells upon the common attitude of distrust toward the Japanese. It is suggested by such words as "dark design," "laborious and intricate preparations," "secret minds." The historian Churchill knows the turning point of the war: it was 18 months ago. The Saturday Evening Post of January 31, 1942 puts it this way: "England standing alone, was then at the zero point of her strength; Germany, on the other hand, was at the top of hers in terms of both material power and morale. No democracy could have done worse than to boggle that opportunity."

with its laborious and intricate preparations, had been so long filling their secret minds, they did not choose our moment of weakness eighteen months ago.

36. *The overtone of all these paragraphs dealing with Japan is the thought that it was an act of desperation. Such phrases as "plunged into war," "irrational act," "to reconcile Japanese action with prudence or even with sanity." The words are one with the thought. The speaker gains the confidence of his audience by his evaluation of the situation, by his caution.*

36. Viewed quite dispassionately, in spite of the losses we have suffered and the further punishment we shall have to take, it certainly appears an irrational act. It is, of course, only prudent to assume that they have made very careful calculations, and think they see their way through.

37. *Note the transitional phrase "Nevertheless, there may be another explanation. . . ." Note the alliteration "secret societies of subalterns." The speaker has knowledge of the Japanese form of government. Such a phrase as dazzled and dizzy is memorable. The speaker suggests a conflict within Japan. Note the sarcasm in the last sentence of this paragraph.*

37. Nevertheless, there may be another explanation. We know that for many years past the policy of Japan has been dominated by secret societies of subalterns and junior officers of the army and navy who have enforced their will upon successive Japanese cabinets and parliaments by the assassination of any Japanese statesman who opposed or who did not sufficiently further their aggressive policies. It may be that these societies, dazzled and dizzy with their own schemes of aggression and the prospect of early victory, have forced their country against its better judgment into war. They have certainly embarked upon a very considerable undertaking.

38. *Note the specific reference. Suppose he had said, "After the outrages they have committed upon us, they must know that the stakes for which they have decided to play are mortal." But the mentioning of each place brings up memories. The speaker stirs up meaning in the minds of his audience. He awakens and canalizes*

38. After the outrages they have committed upon us at Pearl Harbor, in the Pacific Islands, in the Philippines, in Malaya and the Dutch East Indies they must know that the stakes for which they have decided to play are mortal. When we look at the resources of the United

States and the British Empire, compared to those of Japan, when we remember those of China, which have so long valiantly withstood invasion and tyranny, and when also we observe the Russian menace which hangs over Japan, it becomes still more difficult to reconcile Japanese action with prudence or even with sanity.

their experience. The use of contrast and comparison is used again. Churchill knows the relations of Russia and Japan, so his phrase "Russian menace" is full of meaning.

39. What kind of a people do they think we are? Is it possible that they do not realize that we shall never cease to persevere against them until they have been taught a lesson which they and the world will never forget?

39. *This opening sentence of this paragraph was repeated time and again in newspaper editorials. How powerful is the question! Here is the speaker promising reprisals, threatening to get even. This motive is strong in man. Churchill's style gains in energy by the use of these rhetorical questions. This paragraph concludes his treatment of Japan.*

40. Members of the Senate and members of the House of Representatives, I will turn for one moment more from the turmoil and convulsions for the present to the broader spaces of the future.

40. *The experienced speaker again tells the audience what he is going to do. He does not leave them to guess what he is going to say next. He turns from the present to the future. The time pattern is used.*

41. Here we are together facing a group of mighty foes who seek our ruin. Here we are together defending all that to free men is dear.

41. *The speaker identifies himself with his audience completely. The common bond is stressed again. The theme of freedom is repeated.*

42. Twice in a single generation the catastrophe of world war has fallen upon us. Twice in our life time has the long arm of fate reached out across the oceans to bring the United States into the forefront of the battle. If we had kept together after the last war, if we had taken common measures for our safety, this renewal of the curse need never have fallen upon us.

42. *Twice is emphasized by its place in the sentence. The speaker repeats his sentence form and secures a climax in his mentioning of the United States. The theme of this section is introduced, that of sticking together for a world peace. Note the figure of speech "the long arm of fate." The Biblical character of the phrase "renewal of the curse" should be noted.*

43. Do we not owe it to ourselves, to our children, to tormented mankind, to make sure that these catastrophes do

43. *Note the persuasiveness of the question. How much better this is than if it had been stated as a declarative sentence.*

The mentioning of pestilences reminds one of Roosevelt's quarantining speech. The figure of disease is carried on into the next paragraph. Churchill's power of imagination cannot be stressed too much. He thinks in terms of images. Here is a veiled attack on isolationism. Churchill's phrase "catastrophes do not engulf us" reminds one of Shakespeare's "sea of trouble."

44. *Coherence is secured by the carrying on of the figure of speech, pestilence. In paragraph 17 there was a mention of* civic virtue. *Here is a mention of* duty. *Morality is one of the aims of the war. Prudence was mentioned by Churchill in paragraph 38.*

45. *Back of this paragraph is Churchill's insistence in the 1930's that Germany was a menace. Read his book* While England Slept. *His audience knows his predictions. Note the graphic character of "shedding a drop of blood." Also, this is a phrase from everyday life.*

46. *Here is a suggestion as to the peace of the future. Here, perhaps, is a suggestion as to the cause of the war which he seeks to remove. Here is a bid to the thoughtful people of Germany. Note the phrase "victor or vanquished." It is better than "victor or defeated."*

47. *One feels the tragedy in these short sentences. The theme of being together is repeated.*

48. *The religious note creeps into these closing paragraphs. Man would like to feel that he is part of "one increasing purpose." Note the Biblical phrases "blind soul," "faithful servants."*

not engulf us for the third time? It has been proved that pestilences may break out in the Old World which carry their destructive ravages into the New World from which, once they are afoot, the New World cannot escape.

44. Duty and prudence alike command, first, that the germ centers of hatred and revenge should be constantly and vigilantly curbed and treated in good time and that an adequate organization should be set up to make sure that the pestilence can be controlled at its earliest beginning before it spreads and rages throughout the entire earth.

45. Five or six years ago it would have been easy without shedding a drop of blood for the United States and Great Britain to have insisted on the fulfillment of the disarmament clauses of the treaties which Germany signed after the Great War.

46. And that also would have been the opportunity for assuring to the Germans those materials, those raw materials, which we declared in the Atlantic Charter should not be denied to any nation, victor or vanquished.

47. The chance has passed. It is gone. Prodigious hammer strokes have been needed to bring us together today.

48. If you will allow me to use other language I will say that he must indeed have a blind soul who cannot see that some great purpose and design is being worked out here below, of which we have the honor to be the faithful servants.

49. It is not given to us to peer into the mysteries of the future. Still I avow my hope and faith, sure and inviolate, that in the days to come the British and American people will for their own safety and for the good of all walk together in majesty, in justice and in peace.

49. *This is a fitting closing paragraph. Say the final sentence over and capture the rhythm. Note the use of the prepositions to round out the last part of the paragraph. In paragraph 41 the word* together *was used; it is used again in the closing words of the speech. It is the keyword of the entire speech. Note the alternation of heavy and light syllables in the closing phrases.*

JAPAN IS FIRST U.S. FOE[1]

MADAME CHIANG KAI-SHEK

Delivered to a Joint Session of the Congress of the United States of America, Washington, D.C., February 18, 1943.

IN HIS ARTICLE on Mme. Chiang Kai-shek in *Harper's Magazine* of July, 1966, Clayton Fritchey states that Mme. Chiang does not charge directly for her speeches but that over the years they have brought in about $100 million per talk in the way of foreign aid for Taiwan.

Mme. Chiang Kai-shek was one of the famous Soong sisters. Her father was a most interesting man. He was born in the village of Weichan on Hainan Island, off the south coast of Kangtung Province in 1866. As a boy of 14, he found himself in America on board a cutter of the United States Coast Guard. Befriended by Americans in Wilmington, N.C., he became a Christian and a missionary of the Methodist church. He took the name of Charles Jones Soong to honor one of his chief benefactors. On his return to China, in addition to his missionary work, he grew interested in a Methodist publishing house and gradually became an industrialist. He kept his interest in Christian work. He was a leader in organizing the YMCA and in nearly everything that looked toward the conversion of his people and the Christianization of the nation.

Dr. Sun Yat-sen was a Christian and Charles Jones Soong joined with him in the Revolution of 1912.

Charles Jones Soong wanted his children to be educated in America. In 1908, at the age of ten, Mme. Chiang Kai-shek, then Mayling

---

[1] *Vital Speeches*, Vol. IX, No. 10.

Soong, went to Macon, Georgia with an older sister to attend Wesleyan College, which boasted that it was the oldest chartered women's college in the world and the first to confer a degree upon a woman. Since Mayling was not ready for even sub-freshman classes at Wesleyan, she was tutored during the next two years by a member of the faculty. She was admitted in the fall of 1912 as a bona fide student. In 1913 Mayling went to Wellesley and entered the freshman class. She majored in English literature with a minor in philosophy, and studied languages, elocution, science and the Bible. She was a member of Tau Zeta Epsilon, a local sorority; and at her graduation she was designated as a Durant Scholar, the highest academic distinction at Wellesley. Mayling graduated from Wellesley in 1917. During her nine years in America she had used the time to acquire a culture and self-possession unusual for one of her years. She had been all over the United States and her use of the English language, including the Georgia accent, was nearly perfect. This was to prove a great asset when she was to return as her country's publicist a few decades later.

Her sister Chingling had married Sun Yat-sen. When Mayling was visiting her sister, not long after her return from America, in the Sun home in Shanghai, she met the young soldier Chiang Kai-shek. It was an encounter to be expected sooner or later, in view of the Soong family's part in the Revolution. Mayling married Chiang Kai-shek in 1927.

China was in continual turmoil. In addition to fighting the Communists Chiang had to reckon with the Japanese, who kept nibbling away at the Chinese mainland. In 1936 the Japanese took Manchukuo, with the dethroned Manchu Dynast Henry Pu Yi as emperor. Encroachment followed upon encroachment, with no apparent resistance. In July, 1937 the military rulers of Tokyo, realizing that Chiang's temporizing policy was but preparation for the day when he could drive them from Chinese territory and crush their imperial aspirations, began a full-scale undeclared war. Chiang was immediately able to unite all Chinese forces against the aggressors. After the Japanese attack on Pearl Harbor on December 7, 1941 brought the United States, Britain and their allies into the conflict in the Orient, China became one of the Allies, and Generalissimo Chiang Kai-shek the supreme commander of the Allied land and air forces in the Chinese theatre of the war.

In 1942 Wendell Willkie met the Chiangs at Chungking, the Chinese capital, when he was on his One World mission. He declared, "Someone from this section with brains and persuasiveness and moral force must help educate us about China and India and their people. Madame would be the perfect ambassador. Her great ability—and I know she will excuse me for speaking so personally—her great devo-

tion to China, are well known in the United States. She would find
herself not only beloved, but immensely effective. We would listen
to her as to no one else. With wit and charm, a generous and understanding heart, a gracious and beautiful manner and appearance, and
a burning conviction, she is just what we need as a visitor."[2] Mme.
Chiang accepted the challenge.

One day in 1942 President Roosevelt announced that Madame
Chiang Kai-shek had arrived in America for treatment and that she
would be a guest of the White House later.

Mme. Chiang took America by charm. Everywhere she spoke large
crowds greeted her. She spoke in faultless English with lingering
traces of the soft accent of Georgia, and her vocabulary and knowledge of American history pleased her audiences. China's First Lady
spoke to the United States Senate and the House of Representatives;
she and Queen Wilhelmina of the Netherlands are the only women
non-members who have ever addressed the Congress.

That Mme. Chiang is a welcome guest in Washington today is
shown by the many courtesies showered upon her. Clayton Fritchey
points out that the Chairman of the Armed Services Committee,
Richard Russell, took her on a tour of her old school, Wesleyan College in Georgia, that she and her entourage had been welcomed by
the Secretary of State, that she had had a pleasant talk with the
President, that she had had tea with the First Lady and that she was
feted at a lunch by the Chairman of the House Armed Services Committee, L. Mendel Rivers.

Mme. Chiang holds many honorary degrees from such institutions
as Goucher, Wellesley, the University of Michigan and the University
of Hawaii. She is the author of many books, such as *Peace and War,*
1939; *China Shall Rise Again,* 1939; *This Is Our China,* 1940; *We
Chinese Women,* 1941; *Little Sister Su,* 1943; *Album of Reproduction
of Paintings,* 1952; *The Sure Victory,* 1955; *Madame Chiang Kai-shek's
Selected Speeches,* 1959.

THE SETTING

Historians will devote space to the appearance of Mme. Chiang Kai-
shek in the United States during the spring of 1943. Nowhere in recorded history has the power of the spoken word been demonstrated
more clearly than in her appearance on the public platform and
before the Senate and House of Representatives. Indeed, America
went out of its way to be kind to this distinguished woman, for the
American people felt they had had a hand in her rise to fame.

---

[2] Wendell Willkie, *One World* (New York: Simon and Schuster, Inc., 1943), p.
58.

At the beginning of the Chinese war, five and a half years before, Mme. Chiang Kai-shek drove to the Shanghai front. Her car rolled into a ditch and Mme. Chiang was flung out, causing an injury to her back. Late in 1942 she was flown secretly to the United States by the American army and for several months was under medical treatment in a New York hospital. On her recovery she took the case of China to the American people.

Mme. Chiang Kai-shek proved by her appearance in America the statement once made by Generalissimo Chiang Kai-shek that his wife's presence in Washington would be worth ten divisions to him. In the speech given before Congress, which is reproduced here, Mme. Chiang challenged the military opinion that Hitler was Enemy No. 1. In the opinion of China, Japan occupied that position and Mme. Chiang was persuasive as she drove home the point in such words as these: "Let us not forget that Japan in her occupied areas today has greater resources at her command than Germany or that the longer Japan is left in undisputed possession of these resources the stronger she must become. Each passing day takes more toll in lives of both Americans and Chinese."

Such a powerful plea did not go unheeded. In the debate on the extension of the lend-lease program several Congressmen uttered the warning that if more aid did not go to China, she might be forced out of the war for lack of supplies. And the President stated that the United States would rush additional aid to China as fast as it was possible. The flawless eloquence of Mme. Chiang had awakened the United States to the danger in the Far East.

1. Mr. Speaker and Members of the Congress of the United States: At any time, it would be a privilege for me to address Congress, more especially this present august body which will have so much to do in shaping the destiny of the world. In speaking to Congress I am literally speaking to the American people. The Seventy-seventh Congress, as their representatives, fulfilled the obligations and responsibilities of its trust by declaring war on the aggressors.

1. *Come back to this opening sentence after you have read the speech. In the phrase "shaping the destiny of the world" we have the key to the speech. Consider the good will created by this sincere appreciation of the audience. Her understanding of the American system of government reveals the American background of the speaker; she knows the group to whom she is speaking. The third sentence reviews the past and prepares the way for the central idea of the speech proper.*

2. That part of the duty of the people's representatives was discharged in

2. *Here is a restatement of the thought of paragraph 1 and a statement of the*

theme of the address. Note the alliteration, "sacrifices and sufferings." The ear of the speaker is trained to English sounds.

1941. The task now confronting you is to help win the war and to create and uphold a lasting peace which will justify the sacrifices and sufferings of the victims of aggression.

3. *From paragraph 3 to 13 is a digression which is especially pleasing to the audience. The speaker plants the thought in the mind of the audience that is to be the theme of her remarks, "Before enlarging on this subject . . ." The audience knows what is in store. The speaker knows what she is doing, where she is going. Note the alliteration here, "bled and borne the burden." In this paragraph the speaker further marks off the province of her speaking. What she is not going to talk about is important, for the audience will not be led to think that she is going to talk on a theme that would be natural under the circumstances. The speaker follows the technique of first telling her audience what she is going to do and then identifies herself with her audience by saying, "our united effort."*

3. Before enlarging on this subject, I should like to tell you a little about my long and vividly interesting trip to your country from my own land, which has bled and borne unflinchingly the burden of war for more than five and a half years. I shall not dwell, however, upon the part China has played in our united effort to free mankind from brutality and violence. I shall try to convey to you, however imperfectly, the impressions gained during the trip.

4. *Good will is obtained by praising the American soldier. The paragraph has unity. The speaker tells of the American soldier in out-of-the-way stations. Note the use of hyphenated words. The style is enhanced by such combinations as "dreary drabness," and "day after colorless day." How much more tactful it is to talk about the American soldier than the Chinese soldier. The speaker appeals to the self-interest of her audience.*

4. First of all, I want to assure you that the American people have every right to be proud of their fighting men in so many parts of the world. I am particularly thinking of those of your boys in the far-flung, out-of-the-way stations and areas where life is attended by dreary drabness, this because their duty is not one of spectacular performance and they are not buoyed up by the excitement of battle. They are called upon, day after colorless day, to perform routine duties such as safeguarding defenses and preparing for possible enemy action.

5. *Note the personal proof. Again the ability of the speaker to create atmosphere by the choice of words is exemplified by "humble and humdrum." The war is kept in focus.*

5. It has been said, and I find it true from personal experience, that it is easier to risk one's life on the battlefield than it is to perform customary humble and humdrum duties which, however, are just as necessary to winning the war.

6.   Some of your troops are stationed in isolated spots, quite out of reach of ordinary communications. Some of your boys have had to fly hundreds of hours over the sea from an improvised airfield in quests, often disappointingly fruitless, of enemy submarines. They, and others, have to stand the monotony of waiting, just waiting. But, as I told them, true patriotism lies in possessing the morale and physical stamina to perform faithfully and conscientiously the daily tasks so that in the sum total the weakest link is the strongest.

6.   *Directness is secured by "Some of your troops"; "Some of your boys." The power of repetition in speaking is seen in such a phrase as "waiting, just waiting." The humdrum of military life is echoed in the word "monotony." There is a clever turn of the idiom "the weakest link is the strongest."*

7.   Your soldiers have shown conclusively that they are able stoically to endure homesickness, the glaring dryness and scorching heat of the tropics, and keep themselves fit and in excellent fighting trim. They are among the unsung heroes of this war, and everything possible to lighten their tedium and buoy up their morale should be done. That sacred duty is yours.

· 7.   *The sympathy of the speaker is evident in this first sentence. The ability of the speaker to understand the hardships is apparent. Note the vividness of the phrases "glaring dryness and scorching heat" and "fighting trim." The word "tedium" again echoes the thought of monotony and humdrum.*

8.   The American Army is better fed than any army in the world. This does not mean, however, that they can live indefinitely on canned food without having the effects tell on them. These admittedly are but minor hardships of war, especially when we pause to consider that in many parts of the world starvation prevails. But peculiarly enough oftentimes it is not the major problems of existence which irk a man's soul; it is rather the pin pricks, especially those incidental to a life of deadly sameness, with tempers frayed out and nervous systems torn to shreds.

8.   *Again the speaker refers to the "pin pricks." The total effect of these five paragraphs is inescapable. The monotony of the existence of the soldier in far-away places is the first point that the speaker makes when speaking of the American soldier. Is it not peculiarly a woman's observation? Does it not reveal the kindness, the sympathy and the motherliness of the speaker?*

9.   The second impression of my trip is that America is not only the cauldron

9.   *The speaker has thought through her material. The second observation on*

her trip to America is being undertaken. The figure "not only the cauldron of democracy but the incubator of democracy," was repeated many times on the radio and in the press. The speaker gives an illustration of what she means. The use of the idiom "the butter knife" makes it seem as if the one speaking were a native American.

of democracy but the incubator of democratic principles. At some of the places I visited, I met the crews of your air bases. There I found first generation Germans, Italians, Frenchmen, Poles, Czechoslovakians and other nationals. Some of them had accents so thick, that if such a thing were possible, one could not cut them with a butter knife.

10. *Note the repetition of "all" and its cumulative effect. Man is a philosopher and he delights in conclusions. Here is a profound conclusion. The phrase "identity of ideals" is memorable.*

10. But there they were, all Americans, all devoted to the same ideals, all working for the same cause and united by the same high purpose. No suspicion or rivalry existed between them. This increased my belief and faith that devotion to common principles eliminates differences in race and that identity of ideals is the strongest possible solvent of racial dissimilarities.

11. *The conclusion of her observations about her trip is reassuring; it is not fault-finding; it is inspiring. A speech should instruct, interest and inspire.*

11. I have reached your country, therefore, with no misgivings, but with my belief that the American people are building and carrying out a true pattern of the nation conceived by your forebears, strengthened and confirmed.

12. *Note the transition devices from paragraph 11. Synonyms are used: forebears and ancestors. This thought prepares the way for the next paragraph. Note the unusual word "thews." The word "opportunity" ties together paragraphs 12 and 13.*

12. You, as representatives of the American people, have before you the glorious opportunity of carrying on the pioneer work of your ancestors, beyond the frontiers of physical and geographical limitations. Their brawn and thews braved undauntedly almost unbelievable hardships to open up a new continent. The modern world lauds them for their vigor and intensity of purpose, and for their accomplishment.

13. *Note the speaker's directness. There is recognition of the audience, "You have . . ." and much use of personal pro-*

13. You have today before you the immeasurably greater opportunity to implement these same ideals and to help bring about the liberation of man's spirit in every part of the world. In order to accomplish this purpose, we of the United Nations must now so prosecute the war that victory will be ours decisively and with all good speed.

14. Sun-tse, the well-known Chinese strategist, said: "In order to win, know thyself and thy enemy." We have also the saying: "It takes little effort to watch the other fellow carry the load."

15. In spite of these teachings from a wise old past, which are shared by every nation, there has been a tendency to belittle the strength of our opponents.

16. When Japan thrust total war on China in 1937, military experts of every nation did not give China even a ghost of a chance. But, when Japan failed to bring China cringing to her knees as she vaunted, the world took solace in this phenomenon by declaring that they had overestimated Japan's military might.

17. Nevertheless, when the greedy flames of war inexorably spread in the Pacific following the perfidious attack on Pearl Harbor, Malaya and lands in and around the China Sea, and one after another of these places fell, the pendulum swung to the other extreme. Doubts and fears lifted their ugly heads and the world began to think that the Japanese were Nietzschean supermen, superior in intellect and physical prowess, a belief which the Gobineaus and the Houston Chamberlains and their apt pupils, the Nazi racists, had propounded about the Nordics.

nouns in the address. She hastens to identify herself and other allied nations with the common task. Here is an echo of the thought of paragraph 1.

14. The speaker introduces the next thought, that of knowing the enemy. The speaker does not develop the saying "It takes little effort to watch the other fellow carry the load." Perhaps it would not be tactful to do so.

15. The next nine paragraphs deal with the thought of estimating Japan's strength correctly. The theme of this portion of the address is expressed in, "there has been a tendency to belittle the strength of our opponents."

16. The four attitudes toward Japan and her military power are here summarized. Two of them are in this paragraph; the other two are in the next two paragraphs. Note how much ground the speaker covers in this and the next paragraph. Note the colloquial "ghost of a chance."

17. The speaker talks the language of the West. The reading background of the speaker is evident in her reference to theories of racial superiority. Here is exemplified an intelligent and educated speaker's vocabulary—"inexorably," "perfidious," "propounded."

18. *The speaker seems here to give the message which is nearest her heart. All that she says before this is in preparation for this thought. Note how she phrases this thought in terms understandable to the West, "the sword of Damocles." The speaker skillfully ties up what she wants with what the audience wants.*

18. Again, now the prevailing opinion seems to consider the defeat of the Japanese as of relative unimportance and that Hitler is our first concern. This is not borne out by actual facts, nor is it to the interests of the United Nations as a whole to allow Japan to continue, not only as a vital potential threat but as a waiting sword of Damocles, ready to descend at a moment's notice.

19. *Those who heard Madame Chiang Kai-shek will never forget her delivery of the following four paragraphs. Here are four reasons to support her contention expressed in paragraph 18. There are no excess words in these four paragraphs; they illustrate the principle of energy in style. The speaker does not say, "You must not forget . . ." But she says, "Let us . . ."*

19. Let us not forget that Japan in her occupied areas today has greater resources at her command than Germany.

20. *Note the repetition of the "Let us not forget . . ." Note the appeal to self-preservation, "Each passing day takes more toll in lives of both Americans and Chinese." The speaker does not weaken her case by pleading for the Chinese alone.*

20. Let us not forget that the longer Japan is left in undisputed possession of these resources, the stronger she must become. Each passing day takes more toll in lives of both Americans and Chinese.

21. *"Intransigent" means uncompromising, irreconcilable. Throughout the address note the vocabulary influenced by the classics.*

21. Let us not forget that the Japanese are an intransigent people.

22. *The speaker pours her heart out in this plea. The effect of the word "alone" is heartbreaking; note its position in the sentence.*

22. Let us not forget that during the first four and a half years of total aggression China has borne Japan's sadistic fury unaided and alone.

23. *This paragraph completes the treatment of the relation of the United States to Japan. The speaker compliments the audience on their victories. The long road ahead is reviewed. Confidence in victory is expressed. The other Allies are brought in. The speech, which was undoubtedly rebroadcast, would thus appeal to the other Allies. But the speaker will not*

23. The victories won by the United States Navy at Midway and the Coral Sea are doubtless steps in the right direction—they are merely steps in the right direction—for the magnificent fight that was waged at Guadalcanal during the past six months attests to the fact that the defeat of the forces of evil, though

long and arduous, will finally come to pass. For have we not on the side of righteousness and justice stanch Allies in Great Britain, Russia and other brave and indomitable peoples? Meanwhile the peril of the Japanese Juggernaut remains. Japanese military might must be decimated as a fighting force before its threat to civilization is removed.

let go of the theme that the Japanese remain a serious threat. The word Juggernaut is a word of the East; look it up in the dictionary.

24. When the Seventy-seventh Congress declared war against Japan, Germany and Italy, Congress, for the moment, had done its work. It now remains for you, the present representatives of the American people, to point the way to win the war, to help construct a world in which all peoples may henceforth live in harmony and peace.

24. The final thought of the address is introduced in this paragraph, that of the peace to come. We have here an echo of the thought expressed in the opening paragraphs. Thus the speaker ties her speech together. She makes it coherent. In saying that Congress must "point the way to win the war" there is a repetition of the thought of beating Japan while she is capable of being beaten. Then the final thought of the address is introduced, "to help construct a world in which all peoples may henceforth live in harmony and peace."

25. May I not hope that it is the resolve of Congress to devote itself to the creation of the post-war world? To dedicate itself to the preparation for the brighter future that a stricken world so eagerly awaits?

25. Here is a personal plea. We are reminded by this address that the best public speaking is personal. Note the use of the question. The question is persuasive. The question is inherent in good public speaking. The question is born out of the audience relationship.

26. We of this generation who are privileged to help make a better world for ourselves and for posterity should remember that, while we must not be visionary, we must have vision so that peace should not be punitive in spirit and should not be provincial or nationalistic or even continental in concept, but universal in scope and humanitarian in action, for modern science has so annihilated distance that what affects one people must of necessity affect all other peoples.

26. This paragraph was widely quoted. Its Christian spirit moved her vast audience. In the phrase "while we must not be visionary, we must have vision," the neat distinction between these words is possible only to one who knows English intimately. The speaker gives logical reasons, "for modern science has so annihilated distance that what affects one people must of necessity affect all other peoples."

27. The term "hands and feet" is often used in China to signify the rela-

27. The Oriental tone gives flavor to the address. The Biblical "nearer than hands and feet" comes to mind. This is a strong appeal for international brotherhood. Note the use of personal pronouns in these paragraphs: I, You, We, Our.

tionship between brothers. Since international interdependence is now so universally recognized, can we not also say that all nations should become members of one corporate body?

28. *The relations of China and the United States are especially treated. The speaker knows that America has had traditional friendship for China. The friendship of these two peoples can help bring order in the new world, the theme of these paragraphs. The words "arrogant or predatory" echo the word "intransigent."*

28. The hundred and sixty years of traditional friendship between our two great peoples, China and America, which has never been marred by misunderstandings, is unsurpassed in the annals of the world. I can also assure you that China is eager and ready to cooperate with you and other peoples to lay a true and lasting foundation for a sane and progressive world society which would make it impossible for any arrogant or predatory neighbor to plunge future generations into another orgy of blood.

29. *The devotion of China to her ideals is admirable; this is expressed, "Nor will she demean herself and all she holds dear to the practice of the market place." The speaker is uttering the truth that China is a country of principles.*

29. In the past China has not computed the cost to her manpower in her fight against aggression, although she well realized that manpower is the real wealth of a nation and it takes generations to grow it. She has been soberly conscious of her responsibilities and has not concerned herself with privileges and gains which she might have obtained through compromise of principles. Nor will she demean herself and all she holds dear to the practice of the market place.

30. *The nobility of these words is moving: "We in China, like you, want a better world, not for ourselves alone, but for all mankind, and we must have it." The idealism of the speaker is evident. The speaker lifts the audience to new determination.*

30. We in China, like you, want a better world, not for ourselves alone, but for all mankind, and we must have it. It is not enough, however, to proclaim our ideals or even to be convinced that we have them. In order to preserve, uphold and maintain them, there are times when we should throw all we cherish into our effort to fulfill these ideals even at the risk of failure.

31.   The teachings drawn from our late leader, Dr. Sun Yat-sen, have given our people the fortitude to carry on. From five and a half years of experience we in China are convinced that it is the better part of wisdom not to accept failure ignominiously, but to risk it gloriously. We shall have faith, that, at the writing of peace, America and our gallant Allies will not be obtunded by the mirage of contingent reasons of expediency.

31.   *Here is an appeal to the forefathers. The speaker knows that Dr. Sun Yat-sen is also highly regarded in the United States. This splendid phrase is rhythmic, "It is the better part of wisdom not to accept failure ignominiously, but to risk it gloriously." The use of "obtunded" is one of the few evidences of a foreigner speaking English. What a magnificent thought, "We shall have faith, that, at the writing of peace, America and our gallant Allies will not be obtunded by the mirage of contingent reasons of expediency." "Obtunded" is not in everyday use; it is a dictionary word. Note the other Latin words.*

32.   Man's mettle is tested both in adversity and in success. Twice is this true of the soul of a nation.

32.   *The speaker closes with a truth that is universal. Note the word order used for effect.*

❦❦❦❦❦

THE POWER
TO SEE IT THROUGH[1]

HARRY EMERSON FOSDICK

HARRY EMERSON FOSDICK (1878–   ) has written a fascinating autobiography entitled *The Living of These Days*. He was ordained in the Baptist ministry in 1903. He became pastor of the First Baptist Church in Montclair, New Jersey, where he served from 1904 to 1915. He was instructor in homiletics at Union Theological Seminary from 1908 to 1915. Of this teaching post he said, "You can not teach an art simply by talking about it. Years afterward, along with Henry Sloane Coffin and others, I played a small part in helping to make the teaching of homiletics at the seminary an affair of practical drill. We brought groups of students into the chapel, heard them preach, and then fell upon them with approval where they deserved it and with rigorous criticism of their faults. That kind of training would have saved me a protracted struggle in my first pastorate, but in those old days theologues had little or nothing of such discipline. What saved me was my earlier training in public speaking so that, however little I had to say, I could somehow manage to say it."[2] Fosdick was professor of practical theology at Union from 1915 to 1948. He is now pastor emeritus of Riverside Church.

Fosdick graduated from Colgate University in 1900, where he was elected to Phi Beta Kappa and joined Delta Upsilon fraternity. He

---

[1] Reprinted by permission of the publishers, Harper & Bros., New York.

[2] Harry Emerson Fosdick, *The Living of These Days* (New York: Harper & Bros., 1956), p. 83.

graduated from Union Theological Seminary in 1904. While at Colgate he took an active part in debate and intercollegiate oratory. His
college oration on "Roosevelt's Rough Riders" was long used as a
declamation piece in secondary schools. He began his interest in
speech activities in high school. Of this experience he says, "In high
school I began to speak in public, but I was a shy, embarrassed youngster on my feet. Elected vice-president of the debating society when
the president-elect was absent, I was petrified with stage fright, and
taking the chair, could not even say, 'Thank you.' Those, however, were
the days of public speaking and debate, and like it or not, we were
supposed to be able to stand up and talk. That debating society forced
me into public speaking, and before I was through with it, stage
fright, while always present, was not the whole of the experience.
Once in a while, I got something across and liked it."[3]

He is known for his Modernist stand in the controversies of the
1920's, when he was the preacher of the Fifth Avenue Presbyterian
Church. When he resigned from this pulpit he was invited by John D.
Rockefeller, Jr. to consider the Park Avenue Baptist pulpit. He declined because he did not want to be pastor of a wealthy, aristocratic
church. Out of the negotiations it was decided to build Riverside
Church for him.

Fosdick as a preacher was technique conscious. In these days when
there is not only talk about, but evidence of the decline of the power
of the pulpit, it is not an accident that Fosdick's church was always
crowded. Indeed, strangers were advised to secure tickets early in the
week to insure admittance on Sunday mornings. Loren Reid, when a
student at Grinnell College, tells of running to get a seat in chapel
to hear Fosdick preach.[4] On the technique of preaching his most
valuable article is "What Is the Matter with Preaching?" which appeared in *Harper's Magazine*, July, 1928. "The Christian Ministry,"
which appeared in *The Atlantic Monthly*, January, 1929, is also of
interest. Statements by Fosdick on his theory of preaching are contained in two books, *If I Had Only One Sermon to Prepare*, compiled
by Joseph Fort Newton, and *American Preachers of To-Day*, written
by Edgar DeWitt Jones.

At the outset, the fundamental tenet of Fosdick's rhetorical theory
is that of success. Successful preaching does not countenance empty
pews. Rhetorical instruments which draw people are employed;
others are discarded. The stress on success is seen in the following
quotation: "There is nothing people are so interested in as them-

---

[3] *Ibid.*, p. 41.

[4] Loren Reid, *First Principles of Public Speaking*, 2nd Ed. (Columbia, Mo.:
Artcraft Press, 1962), p. 217.

selves, their own problems, and the way to solve them. That fact is basic. No preaching that neglects it can raise a ripple on a congregation. It is the primary starting point of all successful public speaking, and for once the requirements of practical success and ideal helpfulness coincide." Note how the sermon "The Power to See It Through" is based on this starting point.

Preaching and writing went hand in hand for Fosdick. He authored, among other books: *The Second Mile, Assurance of Immortality, The Manhood of the Master, The Meaning of Prayer, The Meaning of Faith, The Meaning of Service, Christianity and Progress, Twelve Tests of Character, The Modern Use of the Bible*, and *On Being a Real Person*. His books were often on the best seller lists. His *The Modern Use of the Bible* was his series of lectures given under the auspices of the Lyman Beecher Lectures on Preaching. Edgar DeWitt Jones, in his *The Royalty of the Pulpit*, calls Fosdick one of the Titans of the pulpit. Fosdick has been called the Henry Ward Beecher of our day. His published sermons, seven volumes in all, besides other books, outsell those of any other contemporary American preacher.

In a letter to the author Dr. Fosdick emphasized how important he thought the study of public speaking is. "It is encouraging to know that there is a revival of interest in public speaking on our college campuses. In recent years there has been a distinct decline in the interest of students in public speaking as a fine art, and I am sure this is greatly to be regretted.

"Despite the importance of the printed word I think the influence of public speech is likely to increase rather than decrease, particularly in view now presented through the radio and television for influencing public opinion through the spoken word.

"I never can be sufficiently grateful for the fact that in my undergraduate days public speaking was regarded as one of the most important enterprises on the campus, and we were rigorously disciplined and drilled in it."

1. *Dr. Fosdick is a master of the word, the phrase and the sentence. The opening sentence ends with the important Demas. This sentence gives the outline of the paragraph, "three times." This paragraph could well be used as a model in a text on paragraph writing. Demas is to be the symbol of one who did not have the "power to see it through." The second sentence suggests one of the themes of the sermon—"a*

1. There is one character in the New Testament, mentioned only three times, concerning whom one suspects that many Christians have not even heard. His name was Demas and, alas, some of us are much more like him than like the great New Testament figures we know so well. First, in Paul's letter to Philemon, we read, "Demas, Luke, my fellow-

workers." So Demas, along with Luke, and named first at that, was standing by Paul in his Roman imprisonment, a devoted and promising disciple. Second, in Paul's letter to the Colossians, we read, "Luke, the beloved physician, and Demas." Reading that, one wonders why Demas and Luke, who were praised together at the first, were separated in this passage as though Luke indeed retained Paul's confidence as "the beloved physician" but Demas had become merely "Demas." Third, in the Second letter to Timothy, incorporating, we suppose, one of the last messages Paul ever wrote, we read, "Demas forsook me, having loved this present age." Three points on a curve, that enable us to plot its graph! For here is the story of a man who made a fine beginning and a poor ending: Demas, my fellow-worker; Demas; Demas forsook me.

2. One's imagination plays about this condensed biography, especially the relationships between Demas and Luke. Intimate companions of Paul in the Roman circle, they must have known each other very well. Now, Luke is the only narrator of Jesus' life whose gospel records the parable about the man who started to build a tower and was not able to finish. Matthew did not remember that, nor Mark, nor John; only Luke recalled it. One wonders if he remembered it because of Demas. Demas was slipping, let us say. Through Paul's little group in the Roman prison anxious apprehension ran that Demas was not holding out, and one imagines Luke pleading with his friend. The Master himself, he might have said, warned his first disciples about the peril which is besetting

fine beginning." The third sentence repeats the title and the main theme of the sermon. Dr. Fosdick is a master of repetition in all its variations. The principle of embodying a truth in a personality is employed: Demas is to be the antithesis of what the preacher is to proclaim. The title is used as the refrain of the sermon: a device often employed by Dr. Fosdick. The remainder of the paragraph gives the three instances when Demas lacked the power to see it through. Demas is repeated eleven times in this opening paragraph. Demas and Luke are contrasted. Contrast is an elemental rhetorical device. The dramatic disintegration of the character of Demas is portrayed in this paragraph. The climax of the paragraph comes in the third mention of Demas. Dr. Fosdick speaks in a figure the twentieth century can understand, "plotting a curve." The final sentence is a recapitulation of the entire paragraph. If a listener left the church after the opening paragraph, he would have the gist of the entire sermon. This is a good example of Dr. Fosdick's preaching psychology. Any future reference to Demas will bring back this careful delineation.

2. *The transition words "Luke and Demas" keep the listener on the mental track. "Demas" is the keyword of the sermon. "Staying power" is the key phrase. The preacher knows his Bible and sees beneath the surface the significance of Luke's being the only one who records the story about the man who started the tower and did not finish it. Note the dramatic power of introducing conversation, "Which of you, desiring to build a tower," etc. This is an overtone to Dr. Fosdick's preaching. His preaching is symbolic. This quotation might well be the text. By putting it here, he makes the text take on a vitality which it would not have if he had introduced it earlier. The refrain is employed at the conclusion of the second paragraph.*

you. For once he said, "Which of you, desiring to build a tower, doth not first sit down and count the cost, whether he hath herewith to complete it? Lest haply, when he hath laid a foundation, and is not able to finish, all that behold begin to mock him, saying, This man began to build, and was not able to finish." So one thinks of Luke pleading with his friend, and at least Luke, alone among the evangelists, put the parable into his gospel. He had seen its truth too vividly illustrated in the life of a friend ever to forget it. Demas, my fellow-worker; Demas; Demas forsook me.

3. *Starting power and staying power are contrasted. The next three paragraphs are concerned with this contrast. The analogy of the ship is used several times in the sermon, showing the pictorial ability of the preacher. In paragraph 7 one sees an echo of this analogy, "romantic launchings." In this paragraph one finds the use of four members in succession—a rhetorical device much employed by Dr. Fosdick, "fine impulses, generous responses, idealistic loyalties, and eager loves." See paragraphs 21 and 27. The repetition of Demas keeps alive the central idea.*

3. As one considers this familiar experience of a fine beginning and a poor ending, it is obvious, for one thing, that the qualities which make a good start possible are not identical with the qualities that see life through to the end. Starting power and staying power are not the same thing in any realm. A ship can make a grand getaway at the launching only to make a poor stand later against the fury of the waves and winds when the northeasters are unleashed. So one sees in Demas a character—how familiar!—capable of fine impulses, generous responses, idealistic loyalties, and eager loves; only he lacked staying power.

4. *The preacher's ability to phrase is seen in "festival of fresh beginnings." Note the alliteration. In speaking of a good beginning, Dr. Fosdick is treating the antithesis of his theme, which is staying power, or a good ending. We may consider all the material up to paragraph 9 as an introduction. At the beginning of a new year the congregation would expect the preacher to speak on a good start; therefore, Dr. Fosdick uses psychology by disposing of this phase of the subject first. He terms*

4. One thinks of this not simply because of the New Year season, which is naturally a festival of fresh beginnings, but because our generation, above every other generation in history, has stressed the gospel of a good start. How we have emphasized the importance of childhood and of the influences that play on childhood! To give a child a good start, we have said, is the most essential benedic-

tion that can be bestowed upon a human life. So we have thought and accordingly have labored. Now, that gospel of a good start is profoundly important and it tells the truth; only, not the whole truth. For many of us here had a good start. We have no complaints about that. In family and church, in school and early Christian training, we had a fine beginning. But for all that, some of us are Demas and all of us know we could have been. Over what thin ice have we skated! How easily we could have broken through! How many of us here have already fallen far from a faith that once was strong and a character that once was clean. We know Demas. The mirror shows him to us. Introspection reveals the process of his downfall. Nearly two thousand years ago he lived and died, his very name barely preserved, as though by accident, and yet how vivid he is in our imaginations! Demas, my fellow-worker; Demas; Demas forsook me, having loved this present age.

5. Another general truth concerns our thought: namely, that however beautiful one's start, nothing matters much in human life without a good ending. Of course one does not mean that we may demand an outwardly successful and fortunate conclusion, as in old sentimental novels where everything had to come out all right. But without a *good* end, without morale and staying power and steady character to see a man through to a worthy conclusion what else in human life can be much worth while? Jesus could have spoiled everything in the Garden of Gethsemane and, had he done that, all for nothing would have gone his unremembered Sermon on the

preaching "animated conversation." Note the personal pronouns you, I and we. The one who makes a poor ending is identified with Demas. Never again will the congregation think of Demas without being reminded of this sermon. Familiar analogies are used: "Over what thin ice have we skated!" Note the exclamatory sentences and the short sentences. The desired, oral style is apparent. The refrain is repeated.

5. *Note the use of definition. What is a good end? "Staying power" is repeated. Again Dr. Fosdick employs a Biblical illustration. Jesus in the Garden is the best illustration he could have found. It is familiar to his audience. "Could have spoiled everything" is in the vernacular. Watch the use of the word "indispensable." When Dr. Fosdick gets the word he wants, he does not hunt for synonyms. Again, he uses the familiar analogy of chopping a tree. The climax of this paragraph is powerful.*

Mount and his unselfish months of ministry. The career of Jesus was like splitting a log. Every previous blow of the ax is indispensable but it is the last blow that splits it. So we know there was a Christ, and the rich meanings of his ministry have come to us because he had staying power to go through to the end, where he could say, "It is finished."

6. *In this paragraph note the use of well-chosen adjectives: "lamentable," "tragedy" and "disheveled." The oral style is illustrated in the use of rhetorical questions. The theme phrase "staying power" is used. One can cut this sermon at any point and it bleeds with the central idea. Coherence is achieved not only by the thought but by the use of keywords and key phrases. "All their flags flying when they came into port" is another instance of the analogy of ships, familiar to people who live at a great port. This paragraph seems to be built out of the preacher's experience. He speaks with authority. It is like the synopsis of a life which he has witnessed. Note the metaphor "shining metal." The major theme, Demas, forms the climactic sentence of this paragraph.*

6. What would you consider the most lamentable tragedy in human life? To face suffering, to be cruelly handicapped? Surely not! For we have seen some terribly handicapped people who had moral staying power so that they came through to a great conclusion, all their flags flying when they came into port. But there is a tragedy so appalling that when one has seen it in the circle of one's friends the very reminiscence of it makes one's blood run cold—to be so fortunately born, to have so glorious a boyhood, to rise to such responsible position, to be so loved, so trusted, and then to crack as though all the time the shining metal had had a flaw in it, to betray one's trust, deceive one's friends, blow out one's brains! You see, whether it be in dramatic fashion like that or in homelier wise, where a fine beginning lapses by slow degrees into a disheveled ending, Demas is the tragedy.

7. *"Marriage" is one of the great common denominators of life. It touches the experience of most of his hearers. "Romantic launchings" reverts to the figure of the ship. In the previous paragraph and in this, consider the declamatory sentences. Another minor theme, "loyalty," is introduced. The word "tragic" is associated with a poor ending. In the final sentence "a good beginning" and "an unhappy end" are contrasted. This paragraph seems to close the introductory part of the sermon,*

7. In this regard life is like marriage. How beautifully love begins! With what romantic launchings can it get its start! But we elders, who watch the young folks at their lovemaking and their weddings, habitually ask a deeper question. They have qualities that can start a home; have they the qualities that can keep one—the deep fidelity, the long-term loyalty, the steady and abiding love

that can keep a home? For in marriage, as in all life, a good beginning only makes more tragic an unhappy end.

8. On this first Sunday of the New Year, therefore, let us talk together not about starting power—there is no soul here that has not more than once made a fine beginning—but about staying power. I celebrate the qualities of faith and character that enable a man to see life through.

9. For one thing, staying power is always associated with a certain central integrity of conscience. Whatever else life may give or may deny, one thing is absolutely indispensable to a man—that he should not break faith with himself, that he should not inwardly be a failure. Such quality of conscience, making it indispensable that a man live on high terms with himself, whatever happens, is of the essence of staying power, and it is the glory of great artists that so commonly in their art they have exhibited it. Elsner was a teacher of music in Warsaw to whom came, one day, a young man for music lessons, and at the end of the first term one finds this in Elsner's record: "Lessons in musical composition: Chopin, Fryderyk, third year student— amazing capabilities, musical genius." That was a fine start. But to finish that career was costly. It cost hard work— one would take that for granted. It cost discouraged hours—one would expect

if it can be called that. Dr. Fosdick does not use the traditional, textbook introduction.

8. *Note the paragraph of transition. Dr. Fosdick never leaves his congregation in doubt as to where he is in the development of his theme. The minor theme of a good beginning which the congregation might expect on the first Sunday of the year is now temporarily put aside for the development of the unusual topic "staying power." Note the Walt Whitman style, "I celebrate the qualities of faith and character that enable a man to see life through." This sentence pattern is repeated in paragraphs 25 and 26. The preacher is about to explore two words, "faith and character." He permits no lost motions in his preaching. The first two points taken up in regard to staying power have to do with character, the third has to do with faith.*

9. *Note the use of "For one thing," and in the 13th paragraph "In the second place" and in the 21st "Finally." These are definite landmarks in the development of the theme which the listener cannot escape. "Staying power" is repeated. The preacher is telling the congregation how they may obtain "staying power." He not only tells about it but he shows the congregation how to get it. The congregation, being cultured, is interested in music. This interest is reflected in the illustration of Chopin. The conclusion, the 21st paragraph, employs music again. The words "indispensable" and "absolutely indispensable" are repeated many times. The preacher's insight into the spiritual life is very evident here, "live on high terms with himself." Note the use of alliteration—"career cost conscience." The conclusion is an echo of this thought. The weaving and interweaving of ideas help make Dr. Fosdick's preaching very effective. "So Chopin became Chopin." This emphasis is suited to oral presentation. This use of the maxim is suited to public speaking, for it gives the audience something easy to remember.*

that. Once Chopin was so disheartened he talked of turning to interior decorating instead of music. But, deeper yet, Chopin's career cost conscience. He would not, for popularity's sake, write music that violated his own interior standards. One thing was absolutely indispensable, no matter what happened: he must not break faith musically with himself. So Chopin became "Chopin." As another put it, "the artist's conscience is a fearful thing."

10.   *The transition sentence discusses Paul's experience in Rome. Paul is held up as the ideal. "Having loved this present age" is a new theme which will be used more and more as the sermon progresses. It is the reason why Demas slipped. The comparison of Roman civilization with our own makes the sermon pertinent. Note the alliteration, "Paul's poor prison house" and the echo, "no Chopin in his character." The preacher's imagination is evident in "Christ had never dug so deep as that into Demas." "To be loyal to the royal" is a sentence that pleases the ear. The use of assonance can be used by the speaker as well as the poet. This phrase comes from Tennyson. Again, note the concluding sentence of this paragraph.*

10.   Now, as we see Paul and Demas in Rome, it is obvious Paul had "that." He would have liked outward good fortune and success could he have had them on honorable terms—of course he would! But whether fortune or misfortune befell, one thing was absolutely indispensable—he must not break faith with himself and the Christ within him. Not simply as a matter of duty but as a matter of happiness, that was indispensable. Demas, however, was of another sort. He soon found something else that was indispensable. "Demas forsook me," wrote Paul, "having loved this present age." So that was it! Roman civilization was brilliant like our own. It had ugly aspects, but for agile minds and grasping hands there were prizes to be gained. All around Paul's poor prison house was Rome. So Demas, no Chopin in his character, wrote his music down. He did not have an artist's conscience, Christ had never dug so deep as that into Demas. To be loyal to the royal in himself was not absolutely indispensable. He loved this present age.

11.   *We have a good example of the preacher's direct style, "You see . . . Listen!" In thought, too, the preacher is*

11.   You see, I am not really talking about Demas now, but about us. One would not minimize the sacrifices that

such a conscience as we are speaking of often costs in a world like this, but the great souls who have most possessed such conscience have commonly thought of it not as a burden of duty but as a gospel of liberty. Listen! No man ever needs to be a failure. Trouble, outward breakdown of hopes, may come, but a man who cares most that he should not be a failure can capitalize trouble. "All sunshine," say the Arabs, "makes Sahara." Men may give the hemlock to Socrates, nail Jesus to the cross, behead Paul outside the gates of Rome. Livingstone may die in the heart of Africa, his work unfinished, and Lincoln may be shot by a crazy man. All such souls have known an inner liberty. Whatever happened, they did not need to *be* failures. That was within their control. Still they could be loyal to the royal in themselves and come to their last port with their flags a flying.

direct, "I am talking about us." Echo of the cost of conscience should be noted. Here is help for man in trouble. Again, note the use of the maxim: an audience can remember this. The succeeding illustrations follow each other in rapid succession, each forming a complete picture. The audience can understand these concise, familiar illustrations. Dr. Fosdick uses illustrations with which his congregation is familiar. A less skillful speaker would go into greater detail. The preacher is careful to point out how his hearers can avoid being failures. The repetition of "loyal to the royal" with the slight difference in phrasing is pleasing and is a characteristic of good composition. The ear is pleased with the old and the new. The image of the ship should be noted. This is one of the minor repetitive themes.

12. That is the final difference between people. Paul faced many kinds of failure but he himself was no failure. If, however, the old legend is correct, Demas went back to Thessalonica and became a priest of idols in a pagan temple. He himself was a failure.

12. Dr. Fosdick is careful to use internal summaries. The point must be driven home. Nothing must be left to chance. Those who have not listened must be made to see the point. The contrast between Paul and Demas is drawn again. Note the picture painted of Demas. The imagination pictures Demas tending the idols of the pagan temple. The distinction between facing failure and being a failure is personified.

13. In the second place, staying power is always associated with the experience of being captured by a cause, laid hold on by something greater than oneself to which one gives one's loyalty —an art, a science, a vocation, a social reform, an object of devotion which one conceives to be more important than oneself. This was the common property of those to whom we have turned as

13. The structure of the sermon is bared. "In the second place . . ." Dr. Fosdick uses this device of enumeration with no apology. He wants to be sure that the congregation is following. The alliteration "captured by a cause" shows the care with which the sermon is composed. The minor theme of loyalty is repeated. Note the enumeration of the specific types of causes one can be devoted to. The preacher economizes the attention of his listeners by reverting to the illustrations already em-

ployed. Dr. Fosdick makes his point with the least mental effort on the part of his congregation. He is immediately intelligible. Note the vernacular "They stood the gaff." The major theme, "staying power," is repeated.

illustrations of persistent character—Chopin in music, Socrates in philosophy, Livingstone as a missionary, Lincoln as a statesman with a cause. They all cared for something so much superior to themselves, to which they gave their long-term loyalty, that they stood the gaff, as we say, so far as their individual fortunes were concerned, and followed through to a strong conclusion for their cause's sake. All staying power in character is associated with that.

14. *In paragraph 10 we had the thought of digging deep into Demas. Here, then, is an echo of that thought. Notice the balanced sentences. There is an echo here of the thought in paragraph 2, that of building a tower. The theme of this section is repeated in different words. There is a clever distinction in this paragraph of being possessed by some of the detail but not by the cause itself.*

14.   Christ had never gotten so deep as that into Demas. Demas had laid hold on some of the more comfortable aspects of the Christian gospel, but the Christian gospel had never laid hold on Demas. Demas had possessed himself of this or that detail of Christ's message, but Christ had not possessed himself of Demas. So the man's Christianity was a superstructure easily put up, easily taken down—jerry-building on slim foundations. For the foundation of enduring character is always laid in something greater than oneself which one will serve through life and death.

15.   *The word "fascinating" reveals Dr. Fosdick's enthusiasm for his craft of preaching. While he uses repetition he does it skillfully. Here a new light is thrown on the theme. A new facet of the truth is shown. The idea which he has planted in the mind of his audience is compared with a new aspect of the theme. Again the truth comes from the Bible. Note the development of the theme by definition.*

15.   There is a fascinating contrast between two phrases in the New Testament: the first, Paul's description of a true Christian in the Epistle to the Hebrews as one who has "tasted the . . . powers of the age to come." So, *that* is the difference, as the New Testament sees it. An apostate is a man who loves the *status quo*, this present age; a Christian is a man who has tasted the powers, been laid hold on by the hopes, of the age to come.

16.   *The preacher's knowledge of the thinking process of his audience is appar-*

16.   When someone tries to tell you that the Christian social gospel is a modern innovation not in the New Testament, face him with that. The Christian social gospel is in the very heart of the New Testament—set, to be sure, in mental frameworks appropriate to the first century and different from ours but indubitably there. The primary emphasis in Jesus' teaching on the Kingdom of God and in the first church was so dominant that they tested Christian discipleship by it. A man who loved this present age was an apostate; a man who had tasted the powers of the age to come was a Christian. Whenever we see a New Testament Christian carrying through to the finish, one fact is always apparent: he had set his devotion on a coming Kingdom of God on earth for which he was willing to live or die.

ent. Here is the debater overcoming objections. Note the direct address, the new application, the new turn of the theme of having a cause to live for: the Kingdom of God. Note the repetition in the form of a balanced sentence. The preacher is the teacher; he instructs his audience.

17. The upshot is that one often sees today outside the church men who seem closer of kin to New Testament Christianity than many inside the churches. Sometimes a downright unbelieving scientist who gives himself to his science and for the sake of humanity stands by it, serving it through thick and thin to the end, seems closer to a New Testament Christian than many of us in the churches. At any rate, he has tasted the powers of the age to come.

17. In the next three paragraphs we find three illustrations of men who have found a cause worth living for. In this paragraph attention is called to the scientist. Note the use of the phrase from everyday life, "through thick and thin." The preacher gives a yardstick of measurement, the giving of oneself to humanity. All three of the following paragraphs end in the same way: "At any rate, he has tasted the powers of the age to come."

18. Or here is a man who puts his conscience above narrow nationalism, who not simply on Sunday, as in the Navy, but every day runs the white flag of the gospel to the top of the mast with the Stars and Stripes under it. He will no longer subjugate his conscience before God to the mad paganism of nationalistic policies that even now, by old familiar steps, are leading mankind to another holocaust. Such a man may be, and often

18. Note the transition "Or consider the man. . . ." Again, he is concerned with ships, with which his congregation is familiar. The preacher paints pictures with words. He employs symbolism which the audience is bound to remember. Note the use of "white flag" and "Stars and Stripes." Dr. Fosdick never misses an opportunity to employ the image-provoking word. The prophetic quality of the preacher is evident here. (This sermon was preached in 1935.)

is, very disturbing but he is closer akin to a New Testament Christian than many in our churches. At least he has tasted the powers of the age to come.

19.   *The country is emerging from the depression; therefore, the preacher is speaking of a timely topic. In this paragraph Dr. Fosdick speaks of several of the evils of the day: old-law tenements, sharecroppers, a living wage, maldistribution of income, the weakness of the capitalistic system in seeking to create an economy of scarcity. Such illustrations show the background of the preacher; his grasp of facts; his interest in contemporary social problems. Note the use of the word "tinkering"; it colors the entire sentence.*

19.   Or here is a man who is not beguiled by the present pick-up in business. He knows it is here. Millions of our people are better off than they were, and he, of course, is glad for all improved conditions for anyone. But he knows that not by a thousand miles does that mean that we have solved our economic problem. He is aware that in this, in prosperous days, 1,800,000 people are living in old-law tenements not fit for human occupancy. He knows that in the Southern cotton fields are a million and a half sharecroppers living under a kind of peonage which by comparison makes preferable the lot of many a serf in the medieval age. He knows that in so wealthy a city as Chicago in the heyday of our prosperity an investigation by the organized philanthropies revealed that city charities were giving to families on their poor list a stipend larger than two-thirds of the unskilled laborers investigated could possibly earn for their families when they were fully employed. He knows that it is conservatively estimated that, in 1929, of our American families one-tenth of one per cent at the upper end of the economic scale was getting a combined income equal to that of forty-two per cent at the other end of the scale, a condition in the face of which words like "democracy," "liberty," "equality," lose their meaning. He knows that whereas we have been plowing under cotton, killing off livestock, reducing wheat acreage and all the rest, the fact is that an interesting study recently made revealed that if American families maintained a good standard of health diet it would require 41,000,000 more acres under cultivation, not less. A man who keeps hammering on such facts, who will not let them drop, who keeps saying with Jesus, "Inasmuch as ye did it unto one of these brethren, even these least, ye did it unto me," who insists that we must go deeper, think harder, face changes more profound than the things we are tinkering with now, may be disturbing, but once more he is closer to New Testament Christianity than many of us are. He has tasted the powers of the age to come.

20.   I suspect that this is the outstanding challenge to us in the churches —our attitude not on theological questions but on practical, ethical, social questions. We find it easy to love this present age. We make fine beginnings, especially at New Year's time, but then some comfortable corner of this present age invites us and we nestle down. So our Christian profession lapses, our faith grows formal, and we do not amount to much in the end as Christians. If I should accuse some of you of being Judas Iscariot you would be indignant. You would never deliberately sell anybody out. But Demas—ah, my soul, how many of us have been that!

21.   Finally, staying power is commonly associated with profound resources of interior strength replenished by great faiths. There is a phrase in the Bible on which a colleague of mine once preached a sermon entitled "An Appalling Alternative"—"I had fainted, unless I had believed." That is true of life. We do faint, peter out, go flat, lose our morale unless our interior resources are re-

20.   *This paragraph is an application of what he has been speaking about to the audience. Dr. Fosdick will not let his congregation escape their Christian responsibility. "Fine beginnings" recalls the first part of the sermon. "Comfortable corner" recalls paragraph 14, where Demas is pictured as laying hold of some of the more comfortable aspects of the Christian gospel. Dr. Fosdick is speaking of a condition which he knows exists in his congregation. By going from the greater to the less, the preacher may get some of his hearers to admit that they have acted like Demas. How powerful is the phrase "sell anybody out"!*

21.   *Dr. Fosdick is careful to let his hearers know where he is in the sermon: "Finally." In this point he touches upon faith. His first two points under staying power were concerned with character. Under this third point there are three subdivisions. Note how a text is employed to reinforce the thought. The congregation can remember this. Dr. Fosdick is careful to aim at the memory of his audience. Great truths are carefully packaged. Here is an example of a favorite rhetorical de-*

vice, a string of four synonyms: "do faint, peter out, go flat, lose our morale." The keyword of the section is "faith." The repetition of "staying power and Demas" link up the thought with the main theme.

22.   *Dr. Fosdick does not preach about the power to see it through but shows how it can be gained. He is practical. Note the power, the energy of such a sentence as "That is off our hands if God has it on his." It is idiomatic. In the following sentence Dr. Fosdick uses five phrases to describe a Godless world. Testimony is a valuable type of material. Dr. Fosdick does not use much quotation. The imagination of the preacher is apparent in the phrase "be haunted by a huge, cosmic apprehension."*

23.   *In this paragraph and the next one the same transitional phrase is used, "Deeper yet, a vital faith in God . . ." The listener cannot escape the thought of the preacher. Dr. Fosdick's style is saturated with Biblical language: "a thousand years are as yesterday when it is past and as a watch in the night." The second sentence is born of experience in dealing with troubled folk. The paragraph then goes into an illustration of contrast and comparison: the immediate versus the long-run view. Note colloquial language—"got Demas." The consciousness of the audience is expressed in the "you see." Note the idiomatic "carries on."*

plenished by faith in something. We may be sure that Demas, before he left Paul, had lost some of his first convictions about Christ and the God whom Christ revealed.

22.   Suppose that someone should ask you what your faith in the Christian God really does for you. What would you say? For one thing, I should say that when a man believes in God he does not need to worry about the universe any more. That is off our hands if God has it on his. If I imagined the universe as without any God, aimless, purposeless, an accidental dance of atoms, spiritually meaningless, then I would worry about it. As Carlyle said, a cosmos like that is "one huge, dead, immeasurable Steam-engine, rolling on, in its dead indifference to grind me from limb to limb." But if a man believes in God, that is off his mind. He can concentrate upon the task in hand, get on with his moral business here on earth with some high hopes about its outcome, and not be haunted by a huge, cosmic apprehension.

23.   Deeper yet, a vital faith in God means a faith in an eternal moral purpose in the light of which a thousand years are as yesterday when it is past and as a watch in the night. That gives a man wide horizons, long outlooks, steady hopes, so that when people lose heart over the disappointment of some immediate expectation, such faith still has standing ground and carries on. Of all mad things in history can you think of anything madder, with Nero upon his throne and Paul in his prison, than to have believed that the gospel for which Paul stood would outlast and wear down the empire? That is, of course, what

"got" Demas: the tremendous power of Rome on its eternal hills, with its inveterate and triumphant evils, against the seeming weakness of Christ's gospel. Who in a sober and realistic hour could have supposed that Paul would outwear Nero? But that, you see, is exactly what happened. A man who has faith in God always expects that to happen, though it take a thousand years, So, of course, he carries on.

24.   Deeper yet, a vital faith in God gives a man available resources of interior power. We never produce power. We always appropriate it. That is true from the harnessing of Niagara to eating a dinner or taking a walk in the fresh air. We never create power; we assimilate it. So, a man with a real faith in God senses around his spiritual life a spiritual presence as truly as the physical world is around his body, and as truly from that divine companionship he draws replenished strength. He knows the deep wells of staying power.

25.   I celebrate the resources of a Christian faith to see a man through.

26.   If faith in God means such things, how do men live life through without it? How do they meet the shocks of fate, the ugliness of evil, the shame of man's inhumanity to man, the disheartenment of moral failure, the impact of personal sorrow, and still keep their morale? I celebrate the resources of Christian faith.

27.   Technically I know little or nothing about music. I venture this com-

24.   *This third way of getting staying power forms a climax to the thought. Dr. Fosdick illustrates his uncommon ability to find spiritual power in everyday events. "We never produce power. We always appropriate it." The illustrations are from everyday occurrences. In comparing the presence of the spiritual to the presence of the physical he goes from the known to the unknown. Note the figure of speech "deep wells of staying power."*

25.   *In this sentence set off as a paragraph we have a repetition of paragraph 8, and in the next paragraph it is repeated again. This and the next paragraph form a conclusion to this part of the sermon.*

26.   *Here is the application to man's need of what has been said. The sermon should help man solve his spiritual problems. This paragraph mentions five such problems.*

27.   *Dr. Fosdick ends with an analogy which his cultured audience can appreciate.*

Living is an art like music. This analogy has the vitality to live on in the memory of his congregation; when they recall the analogy or hear music in the future they will be reminded of the theme of this sermon. Note the powerful phrases "noisy cacophony," "unimportant discontinuities." Dr. Fosdick in this sermon has followed the pattern of the symphony. He keeps to his theme until it marches back once more into the sermon, "glorious like an army with banners." Note the use of the rhetorical device "develops, expands, elevates, and glorifies, fine at the beginning, loveliest of all at the last." This sentence has a noticeable rhythm, a sweep which is characteristic of effective oral composition.

ment, however, about the difference between the best of the old music and the ordinary run of the new. The trouble with so much of the new music, as an older man at least sees it, is not its noisy cacophony but something deeper; it never seems to believe in anything enough so that it thinks it worth while to say it over and over again. It picks up a trivial theme and drops it. It never goes through with anything. It lacks sustained convictions. It is fulfilled with unimportant discontinuities. But when one hears a great symphony by Tschaikowsky, let us say, or Beethoven, *there* are convictions so profoundly believed that the music goes through with them to the very end. One says to himself, Surely that theme has been said as beautifully as ever it can be said. Yet that theme returns again and again, elevated and resplendent beyond our dream. A man says to himself, Now, surely, all the possibilities have been exhausted and, lo, at last the theme marches back once more into the music glorious like an army with banners. Whatever may be your judgment about music, great living is like that. Is there anything a man could wish for his friends at New Year's time better than a life like that—great convictions which life develops, expands, elevates, and glorifies, fine at the beginning, loveliest of all at the last? And is there anything that a man could better pray against for himself or his friends than the opposite?—Demas, my fellow-worker; Demas; Demas forsook me.

ᘇᘇᘇᘇ

THIS TONGUE-TIED DEMOCRACY[1]

On Conversation, Chiefly Academic

A. WHITNEY GRISWOLD,
President of Yale University

Delivered at the Opening Convocation of Brown University's 191st Academic Year, Providence, R.I., September 20, 1954.

PRESIDENT A. WHITNEY GRISWOLD (1906–1963) has said that he found happiness to offset the cares of a college presidency in the writing of essays and addresses on sundry topics and occasions, mostly academic. One can readily believe he relished giving this speech at Brown University.

While an undergraduate at Yale he wrote for the *Yale Daily News* and was managing editor and acting chairman of the college humor magazine, *Yale Record*. One can see his sense of humor cropping out in his address, "This Tongue-Tied Democracy." His audience must have enjoyed the fun with him. He was elected to the Pundits, Psi Upsilon fraternity, the Elizabethan Club and Wolf's Head, the senior honorary society. His fellow students named him the "wittiest" and "most original" member of the class.

During the summer months of the year of his graduation, Griswold worked in a brokerage office in New York. On returning to Yale he

---

[1] *Vital Speeches*, Vol. XXI, No. 2. Reprinted by permission of Yale University Press.

taught freshman English for a year. He then spent a summer in Germany; on his return to Yale he changed his major from English to history. He received his Ph.D. in 1933 and was also appointed an instructor in history that year. He rapidly climbed the academic ladder and in 1947 was made a full professor. As a lecturer he was extremely popular among the students. He spoke with a blazing passion that suddenly broke into a colloquial epigram and a grin.

When Yale was looking for a president to succeed Charles Seymour they undoubtedly remembered that Griswold in 1934 was one of the founders of the Yale Political Union, a student forum on public affairs. They also no doubt remembered that he was active in trying to bring Yale alumni into closer association with the university. A council was formed to study major constituent parts and activities of the university and to make recommendations for their improvement and develop plans for their support. No doubt they also remembered that during World War II he was director of the Foreign Area and Language Curriculum of the Army Specialized Training Program, in addition to being director of the Civil Affairs Training School held at Yale for the Army.

The election of Griswold as President Seymour's successor was made public by the Yale Corporation on February 12, 1950. Between this time and July 1 when he took over as president, Griswold visited other universities in the United States and abroad to see how the various universities could share fields of learning.

This historian has been a frequent contributor to a number of publications, among them *Yale Review, Virginia Quarterly Review, Atlantic Monthly, New England Quarterly, Annals of the American Academy, American Journal of Sociology, Foreign Affairs, Asia, Harper's, The American Political Science Review* and *Life*.

He is the author of several books: *The Far Eastern Policy of the United States,* 1938; *Farming and Democracy,* 1948; *Essays on Education,* 1954; *Liberal Education and the Democratic Ideal,* 1959; *In the University Tradition,* 1957.

His originality is shown in such a book as *Farming and Democracy*. The preface states, "This is a book about an idea—that farming as a family enterprise is the 'backbone of democracy.'" Published in 1948, it was the result of a study of 150 years of farming and the democratic processes in Great Britain, France and the United States, a study begun in 1943 on a Guggenheim Fellowship.

President Griswold's thinking about education is revealed in his address on "The Aims of Yale." These aims could be held for all institutions of higher learning.

He said, "In the light of our own ideals and first principles it seems to me we should be able to agree on the following seven aims:

"1. To strengthen and support liberal education as the *fons et origo* of higher education.

"2. To strive for a balance between the arts and sciences in which each becomes instructive and useful to the other, as an object lesson to the country that such a thing is possible.

"3. To have the best of two worlds, the college world with its emphasis upon the communication of knowledge and the university world with its emphasis upon discovery.

"4. To preserve the residential principle in the fullness of its strength as the most powerful ally of formal education.

"5. To maintain the highest possible ratio of teachers to students in order that education, which is fundamentally a two-way process, may continue to flourish as such at Yale and never descend to mass production.

"6. To maintain for our Faculty the greatest possible opportunities for original research side by side with the most favorable possible conditions of teaching.

"7. To support an extracurricular life for students and faculty in which both may find inspiration as well as recreation from their labors."[2]

In these days when students shun extracurricular activities because they are afraid their grades will suffer, the seventh aim is of great interest.

1.   Conversation in this country has fallen upon evil days. The great creative art whereby man translates feeling into reason and shares with his fellow man those innermost thoughts and ideals of which civilization is made is beset by forces which threaten its demise. It is forsaken by a technology that is so busy tending its time-saving devices that it has no time for anything else. It is drowned out in singing commercials by the world's most productive economy that has so little to say for itself it has to hum it. It is hushed and shushed in dimly lighted parlors by television audiences who used to read, argue, and even

1.   *The title is short and to the point. It is a figure of speech. The subtitle contains the keyword* conversation, *which is used more than 40 times in the address. The introduction is philosophical. In it, the speaker tells you that his speech is to be about forces that threaten the demise of* conversation. *Would you expect a college president to speak on such a subject at a college convocation? Would you think he could find enough to say about it? Is it not a good example of invention, of developing a theme, turning the idea this way and that? The subject* conversation *is close to the daily lives of his listeners. Where did president Griswold get the idea for this address? One wonders if it did not occur to him while reading Lucien Price's* Dialogues of Alfred North Whitehead (*Boston:*

---

[2] Alfred Whitney Griswold, *In the University Tradition* (New Haven: Yale University Press, 1957), p. 86.

*Little, Brown & Co., 1954), for there are
many references on the value of conversation in this book. Notice the effectiveness
of the sentence structure of the opening
paragraph:*

It is forsaken . . .
It is drowned . . .
It is hushed . . .
It is shouted . . .
It is subdued . . .
It starves . . .
It languishes . . .

*"Fallen upon evil days" is an example of
a phrase from literature which has passed
into everyday speech. Notice the figure of
speech "like so many family physicians."
The speaker uses many sound images that
please the ear: "hum," "hushed," "shushed,"
"shouted down," "soft-voiced." He is dealing with sound as well as sense. He also
uses sight images such as "dimly lighted
parlors by television audiences," "play
bridge."*

play bridge, an old-fashioned card game
requiring speech. It is shouted down by
devil's advocates, thrown into disorder
by points of order. It is subdued by soft-
voiced censors who, in the name of public relations, counsel discretion and the
avoidance of controversy like so many
family physicians breaking the news
gently and advising their patients to cut
down on their calories. It starves for
want of reading and reflection. It languishes in a society that spends so much
time passively listening and being talked
to that it has all but lost the will and the
skill to speak for itself.

More safe I sing with mortal voice, unchanged.
To hoarse or mute, though fall'n on evil
days
On evil days though fall'n, and evil
tongue
　　Milton, *Paradise Lost,* Book VII, Line
　　　　　　　　　　　　　　　　　24

2. *The speaker, aware of the speaking
situation, identifies with the audience—
"how many of us." Notice the historical development of the paragraph: Socrates, New
Testament, Dark Ages, Whitehead.*

*The speaker uses testimony by White-
head to support his assertion. The truth is
personalized through a great figure, Helen
Keller. Conversation, the keyword in the
paragraph, is defined by the function
method, which tells what the word does.
"Conversation is the handmaid of learning,
true religion, and free government." Notice,
also, the prose rhythm of the statement.
There is an echo of demise in the final sentence of this paragraph. The speaker uses
the words "decay," "decadence" and "predicament" to tie this paragraph and the
next two paragraphs together.*

2. I wonder how many of us are
aware of this predicament and interested
in its possible consequences. It was conversation, reaching its orderly and exalted climax in the dialogues of Socrates,
which, in an age without books or their
latter-day substitutes, laid the foundation of the civilization we are dedicated
to defend. It was conversation of which
the New Testament, the greatest teaching ever recorded, was composed. It was
conversation, among small groups of
university scholars still in a bookless
world, that revived learning at the end
of the Dark Ages. "I am a great believer
in conversation," said Whitehead toward
the end of his life. "Outside of the book-
knowledge which is necessary to our
professional training, I think I have got
most of my development from the good

conversation to which I have always had the luck to have access." Conversation is the oldest form of instruction of the human race. It is still an indispensable one. Great books, scientific discoveries, works of art; great perceptions of truth and beauty in any form all require great conversation to complete their meaning: without it they are abracadabra—color to the blind or music to the deaf. Conversation, inventing its own substitute for words, has accomplished the greatest miracle known to pedagogy in piercing the veil that hung between the infant Helen Keller and nothingness and bringing her into mature objective knowledge of the world after a normal subjective experience of it of only nineteen months. Conversation is the handmaid of learning, true religion, and free government. It would be impossible to put too high a price on all we stand to lose by suffering its decay.

3. How then do we account for the symptoms of decadence? Are they the result of a sinister softening-up process such as preceded the dictators of recent history, not to mention Big Brother of 1984? Or are they our own fault? Are we being softened up or are we merely softening? In either case, what can we do about it? Ladies and gentlemen, I think that the present predicament of conversation in America is our own fault, and I take courage from the thought. For what is our own fault lies within our power to correct. I think there are a number of things we can do about it, and I propose to suggest a few that are already going on right here in this University and that ought to be encouraged and capitalized for the benefit of the nation.

3. *This paragraph is developed pretty largely by means of questions. The question technique is indigenous to conversation. The speaker arouses interest by using an indirect reference to Hitler and Orwell. In using the direct address "Ladies and Gentlemen," the speaker wants to make sure he has the full attention of the audience before he makes the statements that will arouse curiosity as to his solution of the problem he presented. By saying that the solution is in the University, he compliments his audience. Is this not a problem-solution speech? The speaker states a problem and offers a solution. This is the transition paragraph. He is going to diagnose and prescribe. The speaker uses alliteration—"sinister softening-up process"—which has a pleasing effect on the ear and impresses the thought on the hearer's memory. The figure of speech softening makes the idea powerful because of the overtones in the word.*

4. *The speaker supports his thesis by means of a specific instance. He anticipates an objection and answers it. By means of questions, he carries on a conversation with his audience. He talks about things the audience is interested in: television and 3-D movies. Throughout these paragraphs, the speaker has identified himself with his audience.*

Attention should be called again to the speaker's use of words that are pleasing to the ear and his use of alliteration: "tools and toys," "industrial tautology," "something slipped over on us by conspiracy." Notice the colloquial flavor of "slipped over."

4. Let me first defend the thesis that the predicament from which we suffer is our own fault and not something slipped over on us by conspiracy. Consider all the tools and toys of our prolific economy—the time-saving, labor-saving devices, the automatic cookers and washers, the almost automatic automobile that will present us with a new industrial tautology when it becomes complete, the 3-D movies and the television sets. Do these distract us from conversation any more than the toil and drudgery they have supplanted? Perhaps not, but that is not the point. The point is that they have given us more leisure than the human race has ever known and in more equal, democratic measure; yet instead of making that leisure the ally of conversation we seem content with it as no less of a distraction than drudgery. Is this the result of machination or conspiracy? I find it hard to believe so.

5. *The speaker states his opinion. This paragraph and the next three paragraphs begin with "I." Maxims of conduct are quick ways of gaining acceptance: "the customer is always right." Notice the development of the paragraph by the use of the three enthymemes beginning with "If." Say these sentences aloud and listen to their rhythm. The speaker closes paragraphs 4, 5 and 6 on the same thought: the trouble is of our own making. He likes the device of using one word as a tie-in with his next paragraph. In paragraphs 5 and 6 the word is scapegoat. In paragraph 4 the speaker uses the word toys. Here is an echo of that word in the phrase "toys, not traitors." Notice the use of vivid images: "fatter, more expensive cars," "bubble gum and comics."*

5. I find it much easier to believe that it is nobody's fault but our own, and I rest my case on a cardinal principle of American business. The principle is, the customer is always right. If he wants fatter, more expensive cars, he shall have them. If he wants bubble gum and comics, he shall have them too. And if he wants to spend his time looking and listening without ever discussing with his friends the meaning of what he sees and hears, that, too, is his prerogative. No, ladies and gentlemen, we look in vain for scapegoats in this quarter. The trouble here is toys, not traitors.

6. *Is the scapegoat "communism?" The first look the speaker has at the decay of conversation is in the parliamentary*

6. I would argue the same of scapegoats in general. Orderly conversation in its parliamentary sphere, the sphere essential to free government, has been much abused and disrupted of late, and the abuses and disruptions have spread like ripples from a stone cast into a pond, stirring up strife all over the country. The effect of this strife has been to inhibit conversation and make a case for the public relations experts; and some critics have found individuals responsible for the phenomenon. I do not agree with them. On the contrary, I think we are responsible for the individuals. I think we are responsible because we, the people, elected and appointed such individuals to represent us, and that is exactly what they are doing. They are representing our fears and suspicions.

7. This, I think, constitutes a real peril to the country, but not of the kind commonly deplored by the critics of such individuals. Bacon told us long ago that believing a rumor was as bad as starting a rumor. He said,

Suspicions amongst thoughts are like bats among birds, they ever fly by twilight. Certainly they are to be repressed, or at least well guarded, for they cloud the mind; they loose (lose) friends; and they check (interfere) with business, whereby business cannot go on currently and constantly. They dispose Kings to tyranny, husbands to jealousy, wise men to irresolution and melancholy. They are defects not in the heart but in the brain. . . . There is nothing makes a man suspect much, more than to know little; and therefore men should remedy suspicion by procuring to know more . . .

Suspicions arouse passions. If we become creatures of passion the individuals who represent us will represent passion. The danger is not that one or another of them may attempt to make himself dictator: I have enough faith in this country to believe that such an attempt would inevi-

sphere. He says that the decay is not due to traitors but to our own fears and suspicions. This paragraph reminds one of Wendell Phillips's remark that we elect scoundrels to Congress to represent us and they do.

The speaker balances his paragraph with long and short sentences. The statement "I do not agree with them" indicates a conflict, which is a source of interest. The simile "spread like ripples from a stone cast into a pond" is very effective because it emphasizes the point by tying it up with an experience that is familiar to the audience. Notice how the word suspicions *leads into the quotation by Bacon in the next paragraph.*

7. *The speaker, in the development of his theme, uses a quotation from a recognized philosopher and essayist, Francis Bacon (1561–1626). A college audience enjoys such erudition. Notice the chain of reasoning: "Suspicions arouse passions. If we become creatures of passion the individuals who represent us will represent passion." When the speaker refutes the idea that a dictator (a creature of passion) could arise in this country, he reaffirms his faith in the audience. When he refers to Pearl Harbor, which has become synonymous with disaster, he is using a symbol the audience understands. Passion is the keyword of this paragraph. How many times is it repeated? Notice the alliteration of "clear eyes and calculate with cool heads." That the speaker is fond of the echo is apparent in repetitions such as "procuring to know more," a phrase from the Bacon quotation. His use of the foreign phrase* coup d'état *appeals to the college audience. The speaker ends the paragraph by reasserting his solution. Does this solution remind you of Shakespeare's lines?*

The fault, dear Brutus, is not in our stars,
But in ourselves . . .
                              Julius Caesar, *Act I, Scene ii*

The speaker uses the rhetorical device of the magic three: "cloud our minds, interfere with our business, and so bring us to disaster."

tably fail, all European analogies to the contrary notwithstanding. The danger is that we ourselves allow passion to blind us to things we should see with clear eyes and calculate with cool heads and so lead us to a Pearl Harbor compounded of hydrogen. In either case—the hypothetical one of a foreign-style *coup d'état* or the imminent danger that passions may cloud our minds, interfere with our business, and so bring us to disaster—the remedy is "procuring to know more" ourselves, not hunting scapegoats to blame for our own shortcomings.

8.   *Here again the speaker uses the phrase "procuring to know more" from the Bacon quotation. This time he uses it as a transition. The speaker has talked about conversation on the national level; now he is going to talk about conversation in the University. He further specifies the institution as "a residential liberal arts college." He develops this paragraph by means of the question technique. All of these thoughts might have been expressed in declarative sentences. However, as questions, they promote a conversational atmosphere, promote persuasion and act as transitions from one phase of the subject to the next. When the speaker uses this technique, he is consulting the opinions of his listeners. They, in turn, are more inclined to agree with him.*

Read again John Henry Newman's "Knowledge Viewed in Relation to Learning" from his Discourses on University Teaching. There is a similarity in the following thought to the theme of the address:

When a multitude of young men, keen, openhearted, sympathetic, and observant, as young men are, come together and freely mix with each other, they are sure to learn one from another, even if there be no one to teach them; the conversation of all is a series of lectures to each, and they gain for themselves new ideas and views, fresh matter of thought, and distinct principles for judging and acting, day by day.

8.   By this path I return to this University and the extraordinary opportunity that is yours who are about to enter it. Can you think of a better place for "procuring to know more" or for conversation to prove itself as a means to that end? Where else save Elysium itself is life so congenial to this combination as it is in a residential liberal arts college? Where else does conversation play so vital a part in the central purpose of the institution? Where else, though hard pressed from without, does it yet survive so stubbornly and hold out so much hope to those who would encourage it? Whitehead is but the most distinguished of educational philosophers, most of whom appear to us in the more familiar context of alumni reunions, to testify to its value in his own education. Our civilization and our sacred liberties can be offered as potential evidence of its value to ours.

9. How then, shall we make the most of it? Shall we have courses in conversation? Perish the thought. Let us have conversation in courses but no courses in conversation. By conversation in courses, moreover, I do not mean whispering at lectures. I mean as much give and take between teacher and student as is possible in this day of soaring enrollments, teacher shortages and financial deficits. Let us not forget that there is a point in relation to these seemingly ineluctable limits beyond which teaching becomes mass-production and the law of diminishing returns sets in. At its best, teaching is a two-way process, an exchange of thought between teacher and student, by which both profit and the thought exchanged becomes ennobled in the transfer. I do not see how we can make very great compromises with this principle without dashing our hopes for conversation and for higher education as well.

9. *The speaker begins this paragraph with a transitional question. There is balance in the sentence "Let us have conversation in courses but no courses in conversation." The speaker defines his use of the phrase "conversation in courses" by first telling what he does not mean and then stating what he does mean. This definition by the negation method is very useful in amplifying an idea. The speaker holds attention by reminding his audience of some of the difficulties in the way of using conversation as a vital part of our teaching method.*

Ineluctable is an unusual word. What does it mean? "Mass-production" and "law of diminishing returns" are economic terms that have crept into our everyday speech.

(Do you agree that classes in conversation have no value? Some universities have them.)

10. This is a hard row to hoe and we must have help with it. To maintain the proper ratio of teachers to students necessary to avoid such compromises will tax our resources to the utmost; it may well overtax them. Where then shall we look for help? Where better than to our own students imbued with Whitehead's respect for conversation as an educational process, with a sense of its value to the world into which they will graduate, and with the heaven-sent opportunities of cultivating and putting it to use afforded them in college? Here is potential relief from the teacher shortage that would cost nothing, that is present in every liberal arts college worthy of the name, and that needs only to be galva-

10. *In thinking about the increased enrollments of students and the teacher shortages, the speaker feels that spontaneous conversation among students is a solution. He presents another phase of the solution of the problem of a "Tongue-tied Democracy." The speaker talks directly to his audience. He wants their cooperation. He supports, with an analogy, his assertion that organized conversation would kill the incentive. Notice the use of the attributes of nurses' aides, "thermometers and bed pans." These are the insignia of the aides. The speaker repeats Whitehead's views on conversation. The speaker's use of words is skillful, "galvanized—not organized." His graphic, vivid style and his humor enliven the address. The idea of "disciples of Socrates" is planted here and will be touched upon again in paragraph 15.*

nized to prove its value. I say galvanized, not organized. Organization would kill it. Self-conscious circles of undergraduate pedagogues would, I predict, become ever-decreasing and concentric in character. Undergraduate assistants to professors on the model of hospital nurses' aides would find ideas harder to handle than thermometers and bed pans and finish by proving that teaching is a profession. But undergraduates who resisted the distractions of their elders and, in their own time and place, gave themselves over to conversation that tested and distilled into wisdom the knowledge derived from lectures and books would do honor to the disciples of Socrates and give our universities and our civilization a new lease on life.

11. *This paragraph is a further explanation of the speaker's thesis. Here the liberal arts and the residential college are defined. He defines the residential college as "a corporate society of teachers and scholars." In linking Brown and Yale, the speaker thus wins the audience's good will. He identifies with the audience; he makes his listeners feel good by complimenting them. He supports his assertion by restatement: the same idea in different words.*

Pay attention to the idiomatic style of the speaker, "scarcely been tapped."

11. To a certain extent this is already happening at Brown and Yale. Yet in relation to capacity the reserves of power have scarcely been tapped. They should be. Here is the strength of the residential liberal arts college waiting to be called upon, the principle of self-education waiting to be demonstrated. Both liberal education and the residential college were founded upon that principle, the liberal arts to train men and women to think for themselves, to learn by themselves, to go on educating themselves for the rest of their lives; the residential college to initiate and foster that process not as a club or hotel but as a corporate society of teachers and scholars. Only part of the process can be accomplished through formal instruction. The other, and not always the lesser part, is accomplished in the social life and intercourse of students outside the classroom.

12. British educators have made much of these principles—the liberal arts and the residential—as they are reflected in the remarkable systems of adult education developed in the Scandinavian countries, especially Denmark, which have served as models to proponents of adult education in Britain since the war. They say, in effect, that they would rather have a group of adult students living together as a residential community for two weeks than they would individually attending night school or taking correspondence courses for two years; and they have carried their convictions into Western Germany. There, for example, one finds in the Collegium Academicum of Heidelberg a conscious (and, so far, apparently successful) attempt to foster the residential principle in a national system of higher education which, like most continental systems, has been almost wholly non-residential. I cite these cases to show that in the judgment of a people whose educational experience goes back nearly eight hundred years and from whose universities our own are lineal descendants, the residential principle is neither a whim nor a luxury but a vital necessity.

12. The speaker supports his thesis that students educate each other in the residential college through conversation. To develop his idea further, he uses literal analogies from England, Denmark and Western Germany. He cites cases. Having great confidence in the principle of a "residential college," the speaker offers proof as to its necessity not only for the undergraduate colleges but for adult education as well.

13. This is in keeping with the character of the American liberal arts college. All any such college needs to do to realize the educational potential I have suggested for it is to live up to that character. With its predominantly residential system of higher education, the United States is favored beyond any other nation in having ready to hand the very means which others emulate and strive to develop with scant resources. Our undergraduate students do not know

13. Compare the openings of paragraph 11 and paragraph 13. The speaker enlarges his focus. He now includes all liberal arts–residential colleges. In comparison with the cases the speaker has just cited, the United States is especially favored. If these other countries can do it, we can do it even better. Notice how the speaker encourages his listeners, how he inspires them and how he cheers them on to their task. He tells them they have power of which they are not aware—they "do not know their own strength." The speaker invites them to join in the enterprise of edu-

cation. He motivates them. They belong. They are a part of the community.

14. *The speaker supports his idea through explanation and definition. Here again he defines by negation and also by the function method. In this paragraph he tells what conversation is not. In the next paragraph he expands on what he does mean by conversation. This is the use of contrast and comparison. The speaker does not let the audience lose sight of the current importance of his theme.*

15. *In this paragraph the speaker tells what the conditions of true conversation are. The ideal of conversation, as Socrates presented it, is treated in this paragraph. There are other references to Socrates throughout the address. In the previous paragraph mention was made of Greek philosophy. The audience is a part of Western civilization, which is in part an outgrowth of the fourth and fifth centuries in Greece.*

The speaker first makes the generalization that conversation after the model of Socrates applies to the liberal arts college,

their own strength. They do not realize the educational benefits they might confer upon all of us and themselves in the bargain by refinement and more extensive practice of the art of conversation.

14. The forms such conversation takes and the rules it should follow are of course important. Like all art it cannot be formless and it must show obedience to certain classic principles. Jargon is not conversation. Plain English, the purer the better, is essential. One of the things that made possible the attainments of Greek philosophy was the extraordinary fluidity of the Greek language, which the philosophers who are still read used in its purity and never in adulteration. Small talk and gossip are not conversation. Neither is indictment, with which I include any and all one-way processes of insinuation, invective, diatribe, denunciation, excoriation, anathema, and so on, notwithstanding their current popularity. Conversation is an exchange of thought that leaves all parties to it a grain the wiser. It implies progress. Though it may begin anywhere, even in the realm of trivial, it should try to get somewhere and carry everyone with it as it goes.

15. The basic principles of conversation were established by Socrates both by example and by precept more than two thousand years ago. One of the most important of these was that conversation should take place among friends, in a congenial atmosphere, with common interests at heart. Best of all would be one common interest, namely wisdom. It is interesting to see how these principles anticipate the nature and purposes of our liberal arts colleges. Wisdom, to Socrates, was "the one true coin for which all things ought to be exchanged, . . . and only in exchange for this, and in company with this, is anything truly bought or sold, whether courage or temperance or justice. And is not all true virtue the companion of wisdom, no matter what fears or pleasures or other similar goods or evils may or may not attend her?" Such were his last words to his disciples just before he drank the hemlock. How close they come to the charters of Brown and Yale. Again, in an earlier dialogue, Socrates declares:

> "Some things I have said of which I am not altogether confident. But that we shall be better and braver and less helpless if we think that we ought to enquire, than we should have been if we indulged in the idle fancy that there was no knowing and no use in seeking to know what we do not know—that is a theme upon which I am ready to fight, in word and deed, to the utmost of my power."

Where could we find a better motto for higher education? These are, it is true, the utterances of a consecrated teacher and philosopher rather than merely a gifted conversationalist. Yet they tell us much about both learning and conversation. If Carlyle could define a university as a collection of books, Socrates might well have defined it as a conversation about wisdom. In any event we may conclude from what he did say that conversation about wisdom is true conversation.

16. To facilitate conversation of this kind, to keep it moving and make it truly productive, Socrates established one practical rule that has served both conversation and learning well ever since. This was his separation of the hypothesis and its consequences into two distinct

and then he makes the specific reference to Yale and Brown. He continues to identify himself with his audience. Again we have the development of the theme by direct quotation and by contrast and comparison.

The speaker introduces the figure of speech "one true coin." It will be used again in paragraphs 18 and 21.

16. *The speaker goes into some detail to explain what Socrates meant by conversation. He gives a formula. He does not leave the audience in doubt as to what he meant. How does this formula differ from a college debate? from a college discussion? The speaker makes his observation relevant to the times. (The address was given at the* *height of the 1954 Congressional campaign.) The audience, thinking along with the speaker, would make applications of his generalizations.*

questions. The hypothesis was first assumed as true. Then the consequences of the hypothesis were deduced, those which agreed with it being accepted as true and those which disagreed rejected as false. The hypothesis was never taken as axiomatic or self-evident and if called into question was debated in its turn. By this method the parties to a conversation were brought onto common ground, unity and relevance were ensured for their discussion, and the whole range of human knowledge was infinitely expanded. What a boon it might be to our troubled world that wastes so much time and temper arguing at cross-purposes if we could apply this rule more generally to the discussion of human affairs today. Criticism would have to be answered on its merits rather than by attacks on the critic. Concealed or unstated promises would be brought out into the open. It might even become possible to discuss our foreign policy without raising our voices and accusing one another of treason. Who knows what enlightened dispensations in the national interest might not result? But I am afraid that for such exalted conversation as this we should either have to bring Socrates back to earth or wait as he did in the conviction that the ideals of men were laid away in heaven.

17. *The speaker capitalizes upon the occasion, the opening convocation, the fall of the year. Students are thinking of football. The amusing dialogue shows the inventive skill of the speaker. The speaker is a historian. He gives Socrates character and dramatizes him against the backdrop of the present. The dramatic form of dialogue holds attention. It catches the audience by surprise. There is a change of pace to literary form. This lends variety to the composition. The speaker, through his dia-*

17. Even supposing we did bring him back to earth and summoned his thought to the matter at hand—the revival of conversation among students in residential colleges of the liberal arts— he might not find the going so easy at first, particularly at this season of the year. I can see him now returning, not from the army of Potidaea or a religious procession at the Piraeus, but, let us say, from a meeting of the Association of Colleges in New England, where he has been demonstrating the impossibility of computing the essential worth of each member institution on four pieces of paper eight and one-half inches long by eleven inches wide. On the train he has encountered graduates of two of the member institutions whose names, with apologies to Owen Johnson and J. P. Marquand, are Dink Stover and Bojo Brown. They engage Socrates in a discussion of education and arrive with the utmost despatch at the following proposition:

Bojo: I don't like this new Ivy League Agreement.

Dink: Neither do I. All this business about spring practice and recruiting players!

Socrates: Players? What is the Ivy League, a group of actors?

Bojo: No, a group of colleges.

Socrates: Ah, and they have just agreed to recruit actors?

Dink: No, they have just agreed not to recruit football players.

Socrates: But why should they wish to recruit football players? I thought colleges were for students. At first I thought you were talking about players in the sense of actors or possibly musicians, who would entertain the students and recreate them after their studies. But why football players?

Dink: You tell him, Bojo.

Bojo: Well, you see, a lot of colleges award football scholarships . . .

Socrates: But what has football got to do with scholarship?

Bojo: Well, I see what you mean, but that's what they call them.

Socrates: That may be what they call them, but what *are* they?

Dink: (interrupting) They're grants of financial assistance . . .

Socrates: Financial assistance? You mean money? You mean young men are paid money to play football in college?

Bojo: In some cases, yes, but not in the Ivy

logue, brings out the difference in the meaning of education. The enthusiasm of the speaker for his subject and its careful composition would be factors in winning the attention of the audience.

It is interesting that, in publishing this speech as an article in the Association of American Colleges' Bulletin, President Griswold omitted this dialogue. He recognized the difference between the demands of the platform and the demands of the written word and realized that the dialogue form was especially suited to the public platform.

Poking fun at our academic weaknesses and our current practices of evaluation is always good for a laugh. The speaker derives humor from the incongruity of Socrates talking to two college students. Of course, it is not Brown or Yale that gives the scholarship; it is Princeton.

Notice the specific references that evoke mental images: Buffalo, Greenwich. The speaker makes use of his knowledge of everyday speech and the conversation of undergraduates.

Dink Stover and Bojo Brown are characters invented by Owen Johnson and J. P. Marquand. The novels referred to are: Owen Johnson, Stover at Yale (New York: Frederick A. Stokes Co., 1912) and J. P. Marquand, H. M. Pulham, Esq. (Boston: Little, Brown & Co., 1941).

Potidaea was a Corinthian colony of Macedonian Chalcidice. Its revolt from the Athenian League (432 B.C.) was one cause of the Peloponnesian War; it was taken by the Athenians (429 B.C.). Piraeus is the harbor of both ancient and modern Athens.

League. Although by the way, Dink, a friend of mine in Greenwich told me the other day . . . Of course I don't believe it, but I thought you ought to know it's going the rounds, that a Princeton man in his office told him that he knew for a fact that a group of your alumni had offered . . .

Dink: I deny that! And anyway, what about that fellow up in Buffalo who was registered in our freshman class and then a group of your alumni grabbed him as he was stepping off the train and . . .

Bojo: Oh, that old chestnut! I . . .

Socrates: Gentlemen, all this talk about football and chestnuts! I thought we were discussing education.

Dink and Bojo, testily, and in unison: WE ARE!

18. *This address was undoubtedly read but it does not interfere with the direct style of the speaker. This is exemplified by the "No, ladies and gentlemen. . . ."*

In this paragraph the speaker develops his theme by taking a look at the difference between liberal arts education and vocational education. He states that Yale and Brown must be careful that they adhere to their original purpose, that of liberal arts. Again the speaker, by the example of vocation, shows what he does not mean by liberal education. The analogy of ancient Greece again serves the speaker by substantiating his point. The speaker is temperate. He does not antagonize the advocates of vocational education. But he tells what he is against, and noone can quarrel with that. Socrates is the symbol of the ideal.

Notice the idiomatic style: "followed suit," "cash in." Is public speaking a vocational subject masquerading as liberal education? Can public speaking be made suitable to liberal education?

18. No, ladies and gentlemen, even with the help of Socrates we should have work to do before the art of conversation in our colleges came into its own. We should have to ensure our students a proper subject of conversation. Fortunately we have this, too, ready to hand in our liberal arts curriculum. This is the educational birthright of undergraduates at Brown and Yale. Its currency has never been devalued: it is still at par with the currency of Socrates' one true coin. With its perceptions of greatness and excellence, its intimations of immortality, it embodies the full meaning the Greeks gave to virtue and Socrates himself gave to wisdom. As a source of great conversation it has never been equalled. I do not decry vocational training. In some form or other it is essential for most of us and has something to offer all of us. What I do decry is vocational training masquerading as liberal education and usurping its place. The demand of society for the immediate and the utilitarian is unremitting. The Sophists

answered it in Socrates' day. Suppose Socrates had followed suit. Education can always cash in on this demand, nor do I criticize the educational institutions that do. I just hope Yale and Brown won't.

19. Is this a pious hope, visionary and impractical in this practical world? I ask you what might have happened if we had started cashing in on the demand when it was first felt. Let us take the timely case of television. It is said to be revolutionizing American life and we are urged to introduce courses in it in our curriculum. There have been several such inventions that were thought by contemporaries to be revolutionary agents of change in American life. The first was the telegraph, whose inventor and his associates, as I recall it, were so awe-struck by their handiwork that their first signaled message was "what hath God wrought!" Next came the telephone, then movies, then radio, and finally TV. Each one of these inventions, speedily put into mass production and consumption, was fraught with no less revolutionary consequences for our society and accompanied by no less apocalyptic prophecies than those which accompany television today.

19. *Notice again the device of using the idea of "cashing in" as the transitional phrase to the next idea. The paragraph mentions several inventions, developing them chronologically. A phrase such as "by no less apocalyptic prophecies" delights the ear of the college audience.*

20. Suppose, in view of this, Yale had added courses in the techniques and uses of each to its liberal arts curriculum. I can imagine an entering freshman with the Course of Study Catalogue in his hand. He finds courses in telegraphy, telephony, cinematography, radiotelegraphy and telephony and—words fail me to describe the science of television. Then come the influence courses, the influence of the telegraph on the tele-

20. *The speaker goes from the general to the specific. He reduces the subject to an absurdity. Again the speaker puts his imagination into play. Notice how graphic he is. The phrase "in hand" evokes a picture for the audience. The final sentence is powerful in enforcing the speaker's point. The conversation between the freshman and the Dean makes the passage dramatic. This is an excellent satire on the college catalogues of many institutions.*

phone, the influence of the telephone on radio, the influence of radio on the movie, and so on. Then the influence of influence courses, e.g. the influence of radio and telephonic techniques on communication and its impact on the American family. The freshman reads on in despair. He is looking for a course in English. He can't find one. He goes to the Dean. "English?" says the Dean. "Oh, we don't bother with that any more. We have developed more effective means of communication."

21-22. This passage has a hard-hitting rhythm. Notice the series of propositions which are conclusions. The return to Socrates' solution in advocated. The main ideas of the address are restated. See the contrast of the utilitarian versus wisdom and virtue, the contemporary versus the everlasting. How different is this from the ideal of the "great books" put forth by Robert M. Hutchins?

This is an application form of conclusion. What can we do about it? The keyword conversation *creeps back into these final paragraphs. The title of the address is repeated in the last sentence. We often speak of an individual as tongue-tied who cannot speak his mind. How neat to apply this to our democracy!*

21. The most important thing about any form of communication is what is communicated. The most important thing about what is communicated is its valuation in the currency of Socrates' coin. The utilitarian skills and techniques of each generation are soon outmoded. The search for wisdom and virtue never is. Not all the technological triumphs of history have satisfied man's need for these, nor displaced or even approached them as the most inspiring and fruitful of all subjects of human conversation.

22. We must manage to present this subject to our undergraduates in such a way as will inspire them to help revive conversation in this tongue-tied democracy that has such good ideas yet cannot speak its own mind.

EDUCATION DETERMINES CIVILIZATION[1]

The Importance of Liberal Education Policies

WENDELL L. WILLKIE,

1940 Republican Presidential Candidate

Delivered at Duke University, Durham, N.C., and broadcast over the Mutual Broadcasting Company Network, January 14, 1943.

HOW TRUE IT is that a student's interest in college foreshadows what he will do in his life. Not only is this true in the life of Lyndon Baines Johnson, but it is true in the life of Wendell Willkie (1892–1944). Both Willkie's parents were lawyers and it was impossible for him to escape a career in law. His father had a fine legal mind and, when Wendell was practicing law in Akron and on Wall Street, he frequently would call his father to discuss some legal point. Willkie's skill in discussion and debate is the result of his training as a debater and discussant at Indiana University. His home on the edge of the campus (he lived with his sister, who was studying for a master's degree) was a proving ground for all students interested in public affairs. He was a member of Beta Theta Pi, and when asked at the

---

[1] *Vital Speeches*, Vol. IX, No. 9.

height of his career to address the Interfraternity Conference he said, "I care greatly about public discussion in America. The democratic process rests upon discussion. There is no other method by which it can function. And it will function satisfactorily and effectively in such a time as this only if the channels of public discussion are kept completely open."

Wendell Willkie completed the requirements for his A.B. degree at Indiana University in three years. He entered in 1910 and finished in 1913. In addition to his undergraduate work he took some law courses, so that he was able to complete the work for his law degree in one year. He had come to the university with four years of English composition and literature, three and a half years of Latin, three years of history and two years of science, including short courses in botany, zoology and physics.

The lifelong drive of advocacy for ideas which he thought important found expression when he accepted a position, on completion of his college course, as a teacher of history in Coffeyville, Kansas. Only twenty-one years old, he was the youngest member of the high school faculty. He had the drive, energy and interest to organize a debate group called "The Senate," patterned after the United States Senate. He took his debate students all over the state of Kansas for competition. He coached the basketball team and founded the YMCA, where there was still more opportunity for fellowship and discussion. Wi' ı some money in his pocket from his year's stint of teaching, he return 1 to Indiana to get his law degree.

Willkie early tied himself to the Democratic party. Woodrow Wilson, who was elected Governor of New Jersey the year that Willkie graduated from high school, was to become his political idol. But disturbed by the New Deal of Franklin D. Roosevelt, he then became a Republican with liberal leanings.

Wendell Willkie was nominated for President by the Republican Party in Philadelphia in 1940. The chants of the galleries "We Want Willkie" still seem to reverberate to those who remember this outburst. His nomination was acclaimed by the press as the most revolutionary action in Republican politics since Lincoln was chosen in 1860. A vivid new personality had swept aside the experienced leadership in the convention of such men as Taft, Dewey and Vandenberg. His nomination connoted aid to the Allies and especially succor to England for the Battle of Britain. It meant support by the Republicans for foreign trade and for the lowering of tariff barriers. It also meant a reinterpretation by the Republican party of the meaning of free enterprise. It was the Republicans' answer to the New Deal.

The 1940 election returns gave Roosevelt 27,343,466, and Willkie 22,304,755 popular votes. The victory in the Electoral College was decisive. Roosevelt won 38 states, and Willkie only 10 states. This gave F.D.R. 449 Presidential electors, and Willkie 82. But he had the satisfaction of carrying Indiana.

But even though he lost the election of 1940, he put a new emphasis on the liberal wing of the Republican Party. Walter Lippman, with perception, wrote: "His part has been to save his country from an irreconcilable partisan division in the face of the most formidable enemies who were ever arrayed against all that America is and means. Historians will say . . . that second only to the Battle of Britain, the sudden rise and nomination of Willkie was the decisive event, perhaps providential, which made it possible to rally the free world when it was almost conquered. Under any other leadership but his the Republican Party would in 1940 have turned its back upon Great Britain, causing all who still resisted Hitler to feel that they were abandoned . . . His rivals for the nomination at Philadelphia, (had) made the Republican the isolationist party (which) would have made it almost impossible thereafter to reinforce our Allies by Lend-Lease and to gain the time we had to have to prepare for war."[2]

Before the coming of Willkie to party councils, the Republican Party had opposed the Man in the White House for the simple purpose of opposing. "Willkie taught his party a technique more serviceable to the American people: oppose when the Administration is wrong but co-operate when it is right."[3]

History will remember Wendell Willkie as the One World advocate. In the summer of 1942 he set forth upon his tour of a war-torn world in forty-nine days. His flight around the world in time of war was an act of outstanding courage. It warned Germany, Italy and Japan that America was devoted to her allies and would fight on to the very end. Willkie was the leader of the Loyal Opposition, and this trip dissipated any thought regarding the unity of the American people in carrying the war to an Allied victory. Willkie was a fighter against isolationism in the Republican Party. Willkie was more an advocate of causes than a politician. He threw his hat into the ring again in 1944 but when he was beaten in the Wisconsin primary by the politicians he quit the race. He supported Dewey in the campaign.

Willkie's interest in ideas is evident in this analyzed address "Education Determines Civilization." He was pleased to participate at other colleges and universities, and gave such addresses as, "The American College" at the College of Wooster, Ohio, January 29, 1940;

---

[2] May Earhart Dillon, *Wendell Willkie, 1892–1944* (Philadelphia: J. B. Lippincott Company, 1952), p. 338.

[3] *Ibid.*, p. 337.

"Choose Leaders with Principles Not Poll Wobblers," at the 147th Commencement of Union College, May 11, 1942; and an address at the University of Indiana on Foundation Day, Bloomington, Indiana, May 4, 1938.

Willkie's concern with ideas, of being a publicist, came out in a conversation with his old friend Sinclair Weeks, a few weeks before his death. He disclosed his weariness of the practice of law. "I can make money," he said, "but that is not what I want. I want something more than just a law business. Life is bigger than that."[4]

It will be remembered that the five canons of rhetoric are invention, arrangement, style, memory and delivery. In order to emphasize the importance of arrangement in the presenting of ideas the following speech by Wendell Willkie is arranged in the form of a brief. Here is a former debater and lawyer dealing with materials that fall easily into the pattern of a logical storehouse of materials. The student may be asked by his instructor to brief a speech. This rhetorical analysis may help him to understand the process of briefing and how to show the logical arrangement of materials. This ability to state ideas in a logical fashion is also shown in the analysis of a paragraph of the speech by Robert M. Hutchins which will be found on p. 113.

INTRODUCTION

I. *I think it can be stated as almost an historical truism that the greatest civilizations of history have been the best educated civilizations.*

A. *When I speak of education in this sense I do not have in mind what so many claim as education, namely, special training to do particular jobs.*

1. *Clearly, in a technological age like ours, a great deal of training is necessary.*

a. *Some of us must learn how to be mechanics, some how to be architects, or chemists.*

b. *Some will have a special aptitude for medicine.*

c. *And a great many will have —or think they have—a mysterious talent which induces them to undertake the practice of law.*

I think it can be stated as almost an historical truism that the greatest civilizations of history have been the best educated civilizations. And when I speak of education in this sense I do not have in mind what so many today claim as education, namely, special training to do particular jobs. Clearly, in a technological age like ours, a great deal of training is necessary. Some of us must learn how to be mechanics, some how to be architects, or chemists. Some will have a special aptitude for medicine. And a great many will have—or think they have—a mysterious talent which induces them to undertake the practice of law.

---

[4] *Ibid.*, p. 339.

But none of these specialties constitutes true education. They are training for skills by which men live. I am thinking, rather, of what we call the liberal arts. I am speaking of education for its own sake: to know the sheer joy of understanding; to speculate, to analyze, to compare, and to imagine.

Look back across the panorama of history. Is it not true that the pinnacles of civilization have been achieved by the cities and states most proficient in the liberal arts and occupations? In their contributions to the enrichment of human life, the Greeks, I believe, tower above us all. Yet this is not because the Greeks were good navigators, which they were; nor because they were great architects, which indeed they were. It was rather because almost all their leaders—and many of their citizens whose names we do not know—enjoyed knowledge and reverenced the arts. The Greek cities conquered the eastern Mediterranean with the sword. But they conquered posterity with their minds.

The onrush of what we call modern civilization has obscured this essential truth of history. People—some of them in very high places—have openly disparaged the liberal arts. You are told that they are of little help to a man in earning his living or in making a contribution to his fellow men. The thing to do, you are told, is to get trained; learn an occupation; make yourself proficient in some trade or profession. Of course this advice is sound, so far as it goes. But the inference, and sometimes the outright decla-

B. *But none of these specialties constitute true education.*
  1. *They are training for skills by which men live.*
  2. *I am thinking, rather, of what we call the liberal arts.*
  3. *I am speaking of education for its own sake: to know the sheer joy of understanding; to speculate, to analyze, to compare, and to imagine.*

II. *Look back across the panorama of history.*
  A. *Is it not true that the pinnacles of civilization have been achieved by the cities and states most proficient in the liberal arts and occupations?*
    1. *In their contributions to the enrichment of human life the Greeks, I believe, tower above us all.*
      a. *Yet, this is not because the Greeks were good navigators, which they were.*
      b. *It was rather because almost all their leaders—and many of their citizens whose names we do not know—enjoyed knowledge and reverenced the arts.*
      c. *The Greek cities conquered the eastern Mediterranean with the sword.*
      d. *But they conquered posterity with their minds.*
  B. *The onrush of what we call modern civilization has obscured this essential truth of history.*
    1. *People—some of them in very high places—have openly disparaged the liberal arts.*
      a. *You are told that they are of little help to a man in earning his living or in making a contribution to his fellow men.*
      b. *The thing to do, you are told, is to get trained; learn an occupation; make yourself proficient in some trade*

*or profession. Of course this
advice is sound, so far as it
goes.*

2. *But the inference and sometimes the outright declaration
that frequently follows it strike
at the very roots of our society.*

   a. *The liberal arts, we are told,
   are luxuries.*

      1. *At best you should fit
      them into your leisure
      time.*

      2. *They are mere decora-
      tions upon the sterner
      pattern of life which
      must be lived in action
      and by the application
      of skills.*

   b. *When such arguments gain
   acceptance that is the end
   of us as a civilized nation.*

ration that frequently follows it, strikes
at the very roots of our society. The
liberal arts, we are told, are luxuries. At
best you should fit them into your leisure
time. They are mere decorations upon
the sterner pattern of life which must be
lived in action and by the application of
skills. When such arguments gain acceptance that is the end of us as a civilized
nation.

DISCUSSION

I. *Today we are engaged in a desperate war, and we need for the
fighting forces almost all the young
men who would, normally, have had
an opportunity to acquire a liberal
education.*

A. *It is right and proper that these
young men should abandon their
education temporarily and go
forth to fight.*

B. *It is right and proper that the
universities of this country should
turn over to the armed forces
whatever facilities can be made
useful.*

C. *The government is moving very
vigorously in this direction and no
patriotic citizen will fail to co-
operate.*

II. *But I must confess that the attitude
in which the conversion of the colleges has been undertaken, together
with certain public declarations, fill
me with alarm.*

Today we are engaged in a desperate
war, and we need for the fighting forces
almost all the young men who would,
normally, have had an opportunity to
acquire a liberal education. It is right
and proper that these young men should
abandon their education temporarily and
go forth to fight. It is right and proper
that the universities of this country
should turn over to the armed forces
whatever facilities can be made useful.
The government is moving very vigorously in this direction and no patriotic
citizen will fail to cooperate.

But I must confess that the attitude in
which the conversion of the colleges has
been undertaken, together with certain
public declarations, fill me with alarm. A
few weeks ago, for instance, an Adminis-

tration spokesman advised all young girls to devote their time to technical training courses in college or to leave college and go to work. Now it is clear that we cannot solve our manpower problem without putting women to work. Yet the fact is that there are millions of women above college age, not needed in their homes or for the care of their children, who are still available. Until these older women are all employed there is no need whatever to drag young women out of the colleges and to deprive them of their one great opportunity for a liberal education. On the contrary, it is a very harmful thing to do. For just now millions of our young men are being deprived of this opportunity, and the per capita percentage of college attendance in the United States is going to fall to a record low for our time. At least, therefore, let us preserve, through the women of America, the continuity of the liberal arts.

In fact, so important are the liberal arts for our future civilization that I feel that education in them should be as much a part of our war planning as the more obviously needed technical training. There will be a certain number of young men in every college who, for one reason or another, are not available for military service. They should be given the facilities whereby they may go on with their education. There will be a certain number who will be returned disabled for active service, but of sound and eager mind. Ways should be provided by which they may continue their

A. *A few weeks ago, for instance, an Administration spokesman advised all young girls to devote their time to technical training courses in college or to leave college and go to work.*
1. *Yet the fact is that there are millions of women above college age not needed in their homes or for the care of their children, who are still available.*
2. *Until these older women are all employed there is no need whatever to drag young women out of the colleges and to deprive them of their one great opportunity for a liberal education.*
3. *On the contrary, it is a very harmful thing to do.*
   a. *For just now millions of our young men are being deprived of this opportunity, and the per capita percentage of college attendance in the United States is going to fall to a record low for our time.*
   b. *At least, therefore, let us preserve through the women of America the continuity of the liberal arts.*
B. *In fact, so important are the liberal arts for our future civilization that I feel that education in them should be as much a part of our war planning as the more obviously needed technical training.*
1. *There will be a certain number of young men in every college who, for one reason or another, are not available for military service.*
   a. *They should be given the facilities whereby they may go on with their education.*
   b. *There will be a certain number who will be returned disabled for active service, but of sound and eager*

mind. Ways should be provided by which they may continue their education.

2. *In addition, there should be some provision in the Manpower program for leaving a nucleus in the colleges of men whose aptitudes qualify them as definitely for our long-range needs as, let us say, other men are obviously qualified for medicine.*

3. *So, the structure of the Liberal Arts Colleges will be preserved during the war and so, minds will be trained and enriched for the humanizing and civilizing of the world to come after.*

C. *Furthermore, the men and women who are devoting their lives to such studies should not be made to feel inferior or apologetic in the face of a P.T. boat commander or the driver of a tank.*

1. *They and all their fellow citizens should know that the preservation of our cultural heritage is not superfluous in a modern civilization; it is not a luxury.*

   a. *That it is in fact what gives meaning to that civilization.*

   b. *It is what we are fighting for.*

2. *And they are serving their country just as surely in fitting themselves to preserve it as are the men who fly the planes or man the ships or fire the guns.*

   a. *For we cannot win a true victory unless there exists in this country a large body of liberally educated citizens.*

   b. *This is a war for freedom—freedom here and freedom elsewhere.*

   1'. *But if we are going to risk our lives for freedom, we must at the*

education. In addition, there should be some provision in the Manpower program for leaving a nucleus in the colleges of men whose aptitudes qualify them as definitely for our long-range needs as, let us say, other men are obviously qualified for medicine. So, the structure of the Liberal Arts Colleges will be preserved during the war and so, minds will be trained and enriched for the humanizing and civilizing of the world to come after.

Furthermore, the men and women who are devoting their lives to such studies should not be made to feel inferior or apologetic in the face of a P.T. boat commander or the driver of a tank. They and all their fellow citizens should know that the preservation of our cultural heritage is not superfluous in a modern civilization; is not a luxury. That it is in fact what gives meaning to that civilization. It is what we are fighting for. And they are serving their country just as surely in fitting themselves to preserve it as are the men who fly the planes or man the ships or fire the guns.

For we cannot win a true victory unless there exists in this country a large body of liberally educated citizens. This is a war for freedom—freedom here and freedom elsewhere. But if we are going to risk our lives for freedom, we must at the same time do all we can to preserve the deep springs from which it flows. Recently we have been prone to think of freedom in purely economic terms. It is true that a man cannot be free unless he has a job and a decent income. But this job and this income are not the sources of his freedom. They only implement it. Freedom is of the mind. Freedom is in that library of yours, around which this campus is built. When you range back and forth through the centuries, when you weigh the utterance of some great thinker or absorb the meaning of some great composition, in painting or music or poetry; when you live these things within yourself and measure yourself against them—only then do you become an initiate in the world of the free. It is in the liberal arts that you acquire the ability to make a truly free and individual choice.

> same time do all we can to preserve the deep springs from which it flows.
>
> 2′. Recently we have been prone to think of freedom in purely economic terms. It is true that a man cannot be free unless he has a job and a decent income.
>
> 3′. But this job and this income are not the sources of his freedom. They only implement it.
>
> 4′. Freedom is of the mind.
>
> 5′. Freedom is in that library of yours, around which this campus is built.
>
> 6′. When you range back and forth through the centuries, when you weigh the utterance of some great thinker or absorb the meaning of some great composition, in painting or music or poetry; when you live these things within yourself and measure yourself against them—only then do you become an initiate in the world of the free.
>
> 7′. It is in the liberal arts that you acquire the ability to make a truly free and individual choice.

Our American higher education for many years has felt the influence of the German university. And it has been a harmful influence. It has encouraged the sacrifice of methods that make for wide intelligence to those that are concerned only with highly specialized knowledge; it has held that the subject is more important than the student; that knowledge

III. Our American higher education for many years has felt the influence of the German university.

A. And it has been a harmful influence.

    1. It has encouraged the sacrifice of methods that made for wide intelligence to those that are concerned only with highly specialized knowledge.

2. *It has held that the subject is more important than the student.*
3. *That knowledge is more important than understanding.*
4. *That science, in itself, can satisfy the soul of man.*
5. *And that intelligent men should not be allowed to concern themselves with politics and the administration of the state. Such matters should be left to trained politicians.*

B. *President Hopkins of Dartmouth has stated these trends more clearly than anyone I know and has pointed out that "It would be a tragic paradox if, as a result of the war, we were to allow our system of higher education to be transformed into the type of education which has made it so easy for a crowd of governmental gangsters like Hitler's outfit to commandeer a whole population."*

1. *The destruction of the tradition of the liberal arts, at this crisis in our history, when freedom is more than ever at stake, would mean just that. It would be a crime, comparable, in my opinion, with the burning of the books by the Nazis.*
   1'. *And it would have approximately the same results.*
   2'. *Burn your books—or, what amounts to the same thing, neglect your books—and you will lose freedom, as surely as if you were to invite Hitler and his henchmen to rule over you.*

IV. *The preservation of our system of liberal education during the war will make an enormous difference in the moral and human tone of our society in the future, of the very atmosphere in which the peace is made, and, since we are not an isolated society, of all civilization after the war.*

is more important than understanding; that science, in itself, can satisfy the soul of man; and that intelligent men should not be allowed to concern themselves with politics and the administration of state. Such matters should be left to trained politicians. President Hopkins of Dartmouth has stated these trends more clearly than anyone I know and has pointed out that "It would be a tragic paradox if, as a result of the war, we were to allow our system of higher education to be transformed into the type of education which has made it so easy for a crowd of governmental gangsters like Hitler's outfit to commandeer a whole population."

The destruction of the tradition of the liberal arts, at this crisis in our history, when freedom is more than ever at stake, would mean just that. It would be a crime, comparable, in my opinion, with the burning of the books by the Nazis. And it would have approximately the same results. Burn your books—or, what amounts to the same thing, neglect your books—and you will lose freedom, as surely as if you were to invite Hitler and his henchmen to rule over you.

The preservation of our system of liberal education during the war will make an enormous difference in the moral and human tone of our society in the future, of the very atmosphere in which the peace is made, and since we are not an isolated society, of all civilization after the war. Let me remind you of Irwin Edman's recent fine statement of the significance of the very word "humanities." "It is not trivial art or playful thought. It is the name for the whole of the tradition of civilized life which from the Greeks down has accented freedom in political life and individuality and creativeness in personal relations, creativeness in art, and originality in the experiment of living which is each individual's opportunity. If the humanities, or the humanistic temper which they promote, are permitted to lapse now, we shall have lost the peace before we have gained it, and the real victory after the war will be to the way of life, inhuman, tyrannical, mechanical, of those whom we shall outwardly have conquered."

In pleading for the humanities I am not preaching any gospel of highbrowism. The relationship between a liberal education and freedom is good sound American doctrine. There are hundreds of colleges in this land of more or less advanced education, and in recent years they have been graduating thousands of students every year. Naturally, all of these graduates are not proficient in the liberal arts. And yet no matter how they may have neglected their college courses, or how over-zealously they may have specialized, they have won some measure of equality with all the great minds and all the challenging personalities of all time. That fact has been immeasurably important in making our American doctrine of equality a real and living doctrine.

A. *Let me remind you of Irwin Edman's recent fine statement of the significance of the very word "humanities."*
   1. *"It is not trivial art or playful thought.*
   2. *"It is the name for the whole of the tradition of civilized life which from the Greeks down has accented freedom in political life and individuality and creativeness in personal relations, creativeness in art, and originality in the experiment of living which is each individual's opportunity.*
B. *"If the humanities, or the humanistic temper which they promote, are permitted to lapse now, we shall have lost the peace before we have gained it, and the real victory after the war will be to the way of life, inhuman, tyrannical, mechanical, of those whom we shall outwardly have conquered."*

V. *In pleading for the humanities I am not preaching any gospel of highbrowism.*
   A. *The relationship between a liberal education and freedom is good sound American doctrine.*
      1. *There are hundreds of colleges in this land of more or less advanced education, and in recent years they have been graduating thousands of students every year.*
         a. *Naturally, all of these graduates are not proficient in the liberal arts.*
         b. *And yet, no matter how they may have neglected their college courses, or how over-zealously they may have specialized, they have won some measure of equality with all the great minds and all the challenging personalities of all time.*

2. *That fact has been immeasurably important in making our American doctrine of equality a real and living doctrine.*

I regret that during the last several decades we have had a tendency to overlook this important American fact.

VI. *And I think we are paying the penalty for our shortsightedness in unexpected ways.*

A. *For instance, there has been a trend recently toward what is called "leadership"—but what is really nothing more than the idolization of individual men.*
   1. *In Italy, Mussolini took the title of Il Duce—the Leader—on the grounds that he was the one man who could fulfill the destiny of the Italian people.*
   2. *Not long after, in Germany, Hitler began calling himself Der Fuehrer.*
   3. *The politics advocated by these men were totalitarian and, therefore, antipathetic to our way of life.*
   4. *Yet the overemphasis on single individuals has gone on, even in countries which are fighting totalitarianism now.*
      a. *Everywhere you turn today, you find people clinging to certain men who have been exalted in the public mind out of all proportion to their talents, however great.*
      1'. *In Russia there is Josef Stalin; in China, Generalissimo Chiang Kai-shek; in Britain, Winston Churchill; in the United States, Franklin Roosevelt.*
      2'. *The stature of these men is in every case out of the ordinary and*

I regret that during the last several decades we have had a tendency to overlook this important American fact. And I think we are paying the penalty for our shortsightedness in unexpected ways.

For instance, there has been a trend recently toward what is called "leadership"—but what is really nothing more than the idolization of individual men. In Italy, Mussolini took the title of Il Duce—the Leader—on the grounds that he was the one man who could fulfill the destiny of the Italian people. Not long after, in Germany, Hitler began calling himself Der Fuehrer. The politics advocated by these men were totalitarian, and therefore, antipathetic to our way of life. Yet the over-emphasis on single individuals has gone on, even in countries which are fighting totalitarianism now. Everywhere you turn today, you find people clinging to certain men who have been exalted in the public mind out of all proportion to their talents, however great. In Russia there is Josef Stalin; in China, Generalissimo Chiang Kai-shek; in Britain, Winston Churchill; in the United States, Franklin Roosevelt. The stature of these men is in every case out of the ordinary and they deserve the high positions they have won. And yet, dare we say that any one of them is indispensable? The moment we say that, our world must change.

they deserve the high positions they have won.

b. And yet, dare we say that any one of them is indispensable? The moment we say that, our world must change.

I do not know all the reasons for this emphasis on single individuals. But I do perceive a connection, here in America, at any rate, between that emphasis and the neglect of the liberal arts. Had we more faith in liberal education, we would have, I believe, more faith in ourselves—more faith in the great leavening process of democracy, which forever pushes new men to the top.

5. *I do not know all the reasons for this emphasis on single individuals.*

a. But I do perceive a connection, here in America, at any rate, between that emphasis and the neglect of the liberal arts.

b. Had we more faith in liberal education, we would have, I believe, more faith in ourselves—more faith in the great leavening process of democracy, which forever pushes new men to the top.

I have had the privilege of meeting most of the great men of our time and of conversing with them intimately. I have talked with and know all the allied leaders I have just mentioned, and many more besides. Yet I can say truthfully that, however impressive their abilities— and I have found them impressive—I saw nothing in them that could not conceivably be duplicated in Akron, Ohio, where I practiced law for many years, or here at Duke University. I think it was William Howard Taft who said that you could find a man fit to sit on the Supreme Court Bench of the United States in any town in America of more than 5,000 population. Possibly Mr. Taft exaggerated. Yet surely the *principle* has been proved time after time in American history. The vast American educational system has set men free—free not alone to serve, but free also to lead. Education is the mother of leadership.

6. *I have had the privilege of meeting most of the great men of our time and of conversing with them intimately. I have talked with and know all the allied leaders I have just mentioned, and many more besides.*

a. Yet I can say truthfully that, however impressive their abilities—and I have found them impressive—I saw nothing in them that could not conceivably be duplicated in Akron, Ohio, where I practiced law for many years, or here at Duke University.

b. I think it was William Howard Taft who said that you could find a man fit to sit on the Supreme Court Bench of the United States in any town in America of more than 5,000 population. Possibly Mr. Taft exaggerated.

   c. *Yet, surely the* principle
      has been proved time after
      time in American history.
   d. *The vast American educa-*
      tional system has set men
      free—free not alone to
      serve, but free also to lead.
   e. *Education is the mother of*
      leadership.

B. *Now I think there is another*
   phenomenon of our time which
   is linked with our failure to grasp
   the real significance of liberal
   education.
   1. *This is an excessive indul-*
      gence in the practice of what
      is known as censorship and
      propaganda.
   2. *Of course, censorship of mili-*
      tary matters is necessary in
      order to conduct a war.
   3. *But this principle is being*
      daily, if not hourly, abused
      and extended to many other
      matters that have no military
      significance whatsoever.
   4. *More and more the doctrine of*
      telling us what we should
      know is being adopted.

   5. *It is of course natural for men*
      who attain high office to seek
      to preserve themselves from
      the ordeal of public criticism
      and to attempt to stimulate
      approval of their policies and
      so to perpetuate themselves in
      power.

   6. *And those who are suppressing*
      free discussion among us and
      our allies have of course a
      rationalization for their policy.
      a. *They say that they must*
         conduct political warfare.
      b. *In the conduct of political*
         warfare, they claim, it is
         damaging to say certain
         things.
      c. *The enemy, they tell us,*
         picks them up, distorts

Now I think there is another phenomenon of our time which is linked with our failure to grasp the real significance of liberal education. This is an excessive indulgence in the practice of what is known as censorship and propaganda. Of course, censorship of military matters is necessary in order to conduct a war. But this principle is being daily, if not hourly, abused and extended to many other matters that have no military significance whatsoever. More and more the doctrine of telling us what we should know is being adopted.

It is of course natural for men who attain high office to seek to preserve themselves from the ordeal of public criticism and to attempt to stimulate approval of their policies and so to perpetuate themselves in power.

And those who are suppressing free discussion among us and our allies have of course a rationalization for their policy. They say that they must conduct political warfare. In the conduct of political warfare, they claim, it is damaging to say certain things. The enemy, they tell us, picks them up, distorts them, uses them against us. All this, of course, is true enough. But what of it? The time has never been when men did not seek to distort the utterances of their enemies for their own advantage. And what has won out in the long battle? Always the truth. Spread the facts, analyze them, debate them, make them available to all the world. *There is no other form of political warfare that can possibly win the great political struggle in which we are engaged. Truth alone can win it.*

Is not this worship of leaders, this willingness to be told what to think, this unquestioning acceptance or unnecessary restrictions on our freedom of speech, is not all this part of the same trend—the trend away from self-reliant judgment, the trend away from the little towns, the trend away from the dignity of the common man, the trend away from liberal education, by which men achieve equality in fact as well as in law? We have seen these impulses take root in other countries, which are now our enemies. We have seen them carried to their dreadful conclusions. We have seen the exaltation of government, the abasement of culture, and the resulting violation of all that civilization cherishes. We have seen the devolution of human aspiration. It is a tragedy as great as men have ever witnessed. And it is our task, a task in which we shall be engaged for the rest of our lives, first to stop it, and then to repair it.

       them, uses them against us.
7. *All this, of course, is true enough.*
  a. *But what of it?*
  b. *The time has never been when men did not seek to distort the utterances of their enemies for their own advantage.*
8. *And what has won out in the long battle?*
  a. *Always the truth.*
  b. *Spread the facts, analyze them, debate them, make them available to all the world.*
  c. There is no other form of political warfare that can possibly win the great political struggle in which we are engaged.
  d. Truth alone can win it.

VII. *Is not this worship of leaders, this willingness to be told what to think, this unquestioning acceptance of unnecessary restrictions on our freedom of speech, is not all this part of the same trend—the trend away from self-reliant judgment, the trend away from the little towns, the trend away from the dignity of the common man, the trend away from liberal educa-tion, by which men achieve equality in fact as well as in law?*
A. *We have seen these impulses take root in other countries, which are now our enemies.*
B. *We have seen them carried to their dreadful conclusions.*
C. *We have seen the exaltation of government, the abasement of culture, and the resulting violation of all that civilization cherishes.*
D. *We have seen the devolution of human aspiration.*
E. *It is a tragedy as great as men have ever witnessed.*
F. *And it is our task, a task in which we shall be engaged for the rest*

of our lives, first to stop it, and then to repair it.

VIII. *There is much discussion now—and quite properly—of the matter of war aims.*

    A. *Yet I have listened to some of these speeches with misgiving.*

        1. *I have shuddered to hear a member of our government planning, when the war is over, to police the education of our late enemies, after the traditional manner of conquerors.*

            a. *To disarm those enemies, yes.*

            b. *To take whatever measures are necessary to prevent rearming, yes.*

            c. *To remove from the necks of the people an enslaving totalitarian rule, certainly.*

        2. *(Refutation) But having done that, education is another matter.*

            a. *It must grow out of and carry on a native culture.*

            b. *To determine the nature and manner of their own education is the right of men everywhere.*

            c. *And alien ideals superimposed by force will only produce resentment and hatred.*

IX. *Too many of the planners, I feel, are trying to look ahead by looking backward. Too many are seeking the future in the past.*

    A. *I find in many of their speeches an attempt to solve everything by their pet economic theories—the same attempt that has nearly ruined us during the last ten or fifteen years.*

    B. *The study and practice of sound economics is indispensable to a successful solution of the peace.*

        1. *And yet even sound economics*

There is much discussion now—and quite properly—of the matter of war aims. Yet I have listened to some of these speeches with misgiving. I have shuddered to hear a member of our government planning, when the war is over, to police the education of our late enemies, after the traditional manner of conquerors. To disarm those enemies, yes. To take whatever measures are necessary to prevent rearming, yes. To remove from the necks of the people an enslaving totalitarian rule, certainly. But having done that, education is another matter. It must grow out of and carry on a native culture. To determine the nature and manner of their own education is the right of men everywhere. And alien ideals superimposed by force will only produce resentment and hatred.

Too many of the planners, I feel, are trying to look ahead by looking backward. Too many are seeking the future in the past. I find in many of their speeches an attempt to solve everything by their pet economic theories—the same attempt that has nearly ruined us during the last ten or fifteen years. The study and practice of sound economics is indispensable to a successful solution of the peace. And yet even sound economics cannot define the aim of the

cannot define the aims of the peace, nor the aim of the war.
C. *To discover that aim we must go deeper.*
  1. *We must establish beyond any doubt the equality of men.*
  2. *And we shall find this equality, not in the different talents which we severally possess, nor in the different incomes which we severally earn,* but in the great franchise of the mind, *the universal franchise, which is bounded neither by color, nor by creed, nor by social status.*
  3. *Open the books, if you wish to be free.*

CONCLUSION

Now, in the midst of war, I give you as war aims the perpetuation of this university, your right to attend it, and the certainty that your children, if they so wish it, can follow in your steps.

peace, nor the aim of the war. To discover that aim we must go deeper. We must establish beyond any doubt the equality of men. And we shall find this equality, not in the different talents which we severally possess, nor in the different incomes which we severally earn, *but in the great franchise of the mind,* the universal franchise, which is bounded neither by color, nor by creed, nor by social status. Open the books, if you wish to be free.

Now, in the midst of war, I give you as war aims the perpetuation of this university, your right to attend it, and the certainty that your children, if they so wish it, can follow in your steps.

WHERE DO WE GO
FROM HERE IN EDUCATION?[1]

American University
Has Developed Power to Destroy:
Ill Equipped to Save the World

ROBERT M. HUTCHINS, LL.D.,

Chancellor, The University of Chicago, Chicago, Ill.

Delivered before the Economic Club of Detroit,
Detroit, Mich., May 12, 1947.

ROBERT MAYNARD HUTCHINS was born in Brooklyn, New York in 1899, the son of William James and Anna Laura (Murch) Hutchins. His father was a Presbyterian minister who became a professor of theology at Oberlin College and later president of Berea College in Kentucky.

When Robert was 16 he entered Oberlin College. His education was interrupted by World War I, when he enlisted in 1917 in the ambulance corps of the United States Army. He served with his unit in Italy and was awarded the Italian Croce di Guerra in 1918.

After the war Hutchins continued his studies at Yale University. He

---

[1] *Vital Speeches*, Vol. XIII, No. 19.

received his bachelor's degree with honors in 1921 and was elected to Phi Beta Kappa. He entered the Yale Law School and combined studying with teaching, at the Lake Placid School in New York (from 1921 to 1923). He served as Secretary of Yale from 1923 to 1927. Having received his LL.B. degree in 1925, he began teaching at the Yale Law School and became a full professor in 1927. In the same year he was appointed acting dean of the law school, and in the following year was appointed dean.

At the age of 30 he became president of the University of Chicago and became one of the most controversial figures in American education. One of the first things he did was to abolish intercollegiate football. Students protested and in addressing them Hutchins said, "I would not give you ten cents for all your football games." When Fritz Chrisler, athletic director of the University of Michigan, was told this he replied, "Neither would I if the game was with the University of Chicago."

Convinced that the last two years of high school duplicated the first two years of college, Hutchins advocated a plan which offered a four-year liberal arts program starting in the usual junior year of high school. The plan went into effect in 1937. The university decided, in 1942, to award the bachelor's degree for this program and to use placement tests instead of the high school credit system as the basis of admission to the university. The University of Chicago became largely a graduate school.

Hutchins introduced a "Great Books" course at the University of Chicago in the early 1930's, and his plan was adopted by Dr. Stringfellow Barr, president of St. John's College, Annapolis, Maryland, at that time.

During World War II the University of Chicago had a large part in the development of the atomic bomb. The $2,000,000,000 government research program there led to the first "controlled" chain reaction experiment at Stagg Field on December 2, 1942.

After the war Hutchins no longer maintained his isolationist position, which he called an "anachronism" in the atomic age. He campaigned for the establishment of a world organization and for the international civilian control of atomic energy.

The Fund for the Republic, established in 1953 by the Ford Foundation, with an outright grant of $15,000,000, is headed by Hutchins. He had been an associate director of the Ford Foundation from 1951 until his appointment to the presidency of the Fund for the Republic in May, 1954.

From this recital of Hutchins' accomplishments one can see that he is highly persuasive. An example of his person-to-person persuasiveness is seen in the following anecdote. One day he received a phone call from Walgreen, the drugstore magnate. Walgreen was indignant when he learned that his daughter was studying communism at the University of Chicago. President Hutchins invited Walgreen out to the university for a visit to discuss the problem. The upshot of the conference was that Walgreen endowed the course for $500,000.

As is evidenced in the address "Where Do We Go From Here in Education?" Hutchins is a critic of education. His main doctrines are found in his books: *No Friendly Voice,* 1936; *The Higher Learning in America,* 1936; *Education for Freedom,* 1943; *The Conflict in Education in a Democratic Society,* 1953; and *The University of Utopia,* 1953.

1. *See how the speaker pegs his opening remarks on the remarks of the chairman. Pay attention to the courtesy of the opening sentences and the method whereby one sentence leads into the ad lib introductory remarks. Names are interesting. Here you have Butler, Ruthven and Lovett. The speaker secures humor by self-depreciation. He does not take himself too seriously. The speaker seizes upon a point of common interests—the universities.*

1. Mr. Chairman, Mr. Lovett, gentlemen: I appreciate Mr. Lovett's remarks very much indeed. From one point of view I do deplore them. I deplore them because of the emphasis on the word "new." I must say that I feel very far from "new." Now that Nicholas Murray Butler is out of the way, I am the senior executive in the American Association of Universities, closely pushed by that young man at Ann Arbor, Mr. Ruthven, who had the misfortune to be elected president of the University of Michigan four months after the University of Chicago had the misfortune to elect me.

2. *Note the style—"gray eminence." Here again is depreciation. Might he have said "doubtful eminence?" Note the use of the climax, a sort of anticlimax. Here is the climax made of three parts. This is a favorite device of the speaker. See paragraphs 68 and 71.*

2. From the gray eminence which I occupy, I survey American education with a detachment, a disinterestedness, and, I may add, a pessimism which nobody, except possibly Mr. Ruthven, in the state of Michigan can approach.

3. *The speaker gets a laugh but leaves a sting behind. This result epitomizes what the speaker has been trying to do. Note the specific reference "85 to 0," not "by a big score." Do not escape the thrust of the word "procure."*

3. I have worked long, and occasionally hard, and have seen very little done. My one solid accomplishment I owe to Michigan—it procured a team which defeated mine 85 to 0. Because of this, I was able to abolish football in Chicago.

4. For this and many other favors, I shall never cease to be grateful to you.

5. Now, in the twenty-five years, and more, that I have been in American education, I have noticed that it has certain permanent and abiding problems. They are caused by various paradoxes or contradictions in our educational system, and in our attitude toward it. It is about these problems, paradoxes and contradictions, that I wish briefly to speak.

6.* The first paradox appears in our national behavior in the support of education. It is often said that American education is the American substitute for a national religion, but many countries have been able to reconcile support of an official religious establishment with disregard of its principles, and American support of education often appears to be of this kind. The devotion seems to be to the symbol, rather than to the activity, and is rhetorical rather than real.

4. *The speaker summarizes his ad lib introductory remarks and prepares for launching into his prepared speech, which he undoubtedly read.*

5. *The speaker gives proof of his right to speak: "Twenty-five years." He is giving the results of his observation. This is to be a problem-solution speech. The speaker tells the audience what he is going to do in the speech. The speaker introduces the key-word paradox. If there be those who do not understand this word, the speaker tells them what it means, contradictions. See paragraphs 23, 47 and 66. The speaker cites four paradoxes.*

6.* *Note the number of times the word education—the thing the speaker is talking about—is mentioned. I counted 76 times. Pick up the speech at any point and you'll find the speaker is talking about education. Note the thoughtful analogy. Note the rhythm of the speaker:*
> *The devotion seems to be to the symbol rather than to the activity*
> *and is rhetorical rather*
> *than real.*
The repetition of the s and r sounds is pleasing to the ear.

---

* The organization of the material under the first paradox looks something like this:
I. The first paradox appears in our national behavior in the support of education, for
A. The devotion seems to be the symbol, for
  1. Teachers (350,000) have been driven from the profession.
  2. The expenditures on the schools will be the first cut in a depression and the last restored.
B. England is putting into effect the provisions of the Education Act of 1944, for
  1. The British really mean what we say about education.
  2. An intelligent nation is more likely to succeed.
C. Our expenditures for education are for ulterior purposes, for
  1. The G.I. legislation originated in the forebodings of the economist.
  2. The genesis of the NYA during the depression was the same.

7. *Note the scorn of the speaker. He is graphic all the time. Fourth of July orations are pompous and empty. One of the four types of material is facts. He does not say "a lot of teachers," but "350,000." And note the verb "driven." See how the speaker musters supporting data to maintain his first contention, his first paradox.*

7. Popular education is a splendid subject for a Fourth of July address; yet, 350,000 teachers have been driven from the profession by the pitiful salaries now offered.

8. *The speaker is hard-hitting. He uses facts and historical examples to prove his point. Would anyone in the audience doubt his supporting material? Is he not telling them what they already know?*

8. In some parts of this country, a teacher may count herself fortunate if she receives $500 a year, and we can be certain, I think, that if there is another depression the experience of the last one will be repeated. The expenditures on the schools will be the first cut and the last restored.

9. *The personal authority and the prestige of the speaker are used as proof. Here is a man who knows what he is talking about. To support his contention he employs contrast and comparison: what they are doing in England. Note the sentence made up of three parts. To drive home his point he paints a dark picture of England. Note the repetition of "a country." This gives style to public speaking.*

9. I have come to Detroit directly from the plane that brought me home from a month in England. There is a country in which there is a shortage of all goods; a country whose empire, if not dissolving, is at least changing its shape; a country which has neither man-power, building materials, books, nor paper.

D. In the past there was no particular reason why Americans should take education seriously, for
1. This country was impregnable to enemies from without and apparently indestructible.
2. Now, however, when the Russians have the atomic bomb one false step in foreign policy can mean the end, not only of our institutions, but also of civilization.
E. The United States Scientific and Cultural organizations are operating on an annual budget which is about 25 per cent of the amount which the United States Government spent every year during the war at the University of Chicago alone for the production of new weapons.
(The teacher may wish to require the student to outline other portions of the address.)

10. What is it doing?

10. *In the preparation of his manuscript the speaker uses many one-sentence paragraphs. See paragraphs 20, 26, 32 and 52. This technique helps in the effective reading of a manuscript.*

11. It is putting into effect the provisions of the Education Act of 1944, the main result of which is an extension of the period of compulsory education from 14 to 15 years of age. I do not say that this is a wise decision, or that a mere increase in the school-leaving age produces necessarily sound educational results. I do say that this action which, under the circumstances, is so courageous as to be almost reckless, shows that the British really mean what we say about education.

11. *Note the personal style of the speaker: the "I," "you," "we." Again note how exact the speaker is. There is an echo of his first paradox here: "the British really mean what we say about education." The speaker keeps his audience on the mental track.*

12. They mean that education is important; it is more important than food, tobacco, or even beer; more important than capital equipment, military equipment or houses. They mean that man does not live by bread alone, and that an intelligent nation is more likely to succeed economically and militarily than one which has great material resources but does not know what to do with them.

12. *Note the use here of the three elements of the sentence. Note also the use of the climaxes of three—"food, tobacco, or even beer," "capital equipment, military equipment, or houses." The speaker likes to repeat his sentence forms—"They mean. . . . They mean. . . ."*

13. It is true that our own country is now committed, in the GI Bill of Rights, to the greatest educational expenditure in the history of the race. The appropriations for educational purposes under the GI Bill of Rights will run between ten and fourteen billion dollars. This legislation originated, not in the desire to educate veterans, but in the forebodings of the economist that there would be six to eight million unemployed within six months after the war.

13. *The speaker anticipates the objections raised by his audience. He knows what they are thinking. He introduces refutation into his speech. The speaker develops his themes by means of illustrations. In debating parlance he turns the tables. He proves his point by material which opponents of his contention might use to prove their own point. The audience cannot but agree.*

14. *The speaker does not hesitate to speak unpalatable truths. He uses an historical example to substantiate his point.*

14. The genesis of the National Youth Administration during the depression was the same. It did not result from the conviction that young people must be educated even if the stock market falls, but from a desire to keep young people off the labor market.

15. *The speaker challenges attention by his forthrightness. He does not let his audience enjoy the pleasantness of the thought of educating so many millions. He makes the audience face unpleasant possibilities. Such speaking may disturb an audience but it holds attention.*

15. I applaud the expenditure and the consequences of the National Youth Administration, and the GI Bill of Rights, although I must say it will be a little unfortunate if the young men now studying under the GI Bill of Rights come to the end of their grants and the end of their studies in a period of unemployment.

16. *The speaker comes back to his first contention. He ties up his illustrations with his theme. This paragraph is in the nature of an internal summary. The speaker wants to carry his audience with him. He does not want them to miss the point. The speaker is excusing the American people for their attitude and is getting ready to introduce another turn in his thinking. If in the past there was no urgency to take education seriously, there is today.*

16. I am concerned here, not with what such measures accomplish, but with what they reveal of the American attitude toward education. They do not require any revision of my thesis that the American people, whatever their professions, do not take education very seriously. And, in the past there has been no particular reason why they should.

17. *The irony, the sarcasm, the wit of the speaker reaches a high point in this paragraph. There is no pandering to the audience here. Our sins are hurled at us—"mass stupidity of the people and its government." What does the speaker say about being "detached?" Pay attention to the choice of adjectives in this paragraph: hysterical, mass, blundering, nice, old southern, worse.*

17. This country was impregnable to enemies from without, and apparently indestructible. It could not be destroyed even by the hysterical waste and mass stupidity of the people and its government. Foreign policy, for example, could be the blundering ground of nice old southern lawyers, and education could be regarded as a means of keeping children off the street; the schools kept young people out of worse places until we were willing to have them go to work.

18. Now, when the Russians have the atomic bomb—which I am happy to say was not solely the product of the University of Chicago—and the Russians certainly will have it within five years; Langmuir's prediction is about a year and a half—when the Russians have the atomic bomb, the position of the United States automatically undergoes a dramatic change. The position of the United States, then, is very little beyond that of Czecho-Slovakia before the war—one false step in foreign policy can mean the end, not only of our institutions, but also of civilization. In a war in which both sides have atomic bombs, the cities of both sides will be destroyed.

18. *Note the transition word* Now. *The speaker could put much meaning into this by inflection. The importance of the atomic bomb is underscored by his disclaiming full responsibility for its manufacture. Opinion is one of the four types of material. Note the use of the literal analogy: the United States is compared to Czecho-Slovakia.*

19. And, we cannot place our hope on those agreements for the control of atomic energy, which are just around the corner in the sense in which Mr. Hoover remarked, in 1932, that prosperity was just around the corner. These agreements are absolutely imperative; but they will simply guarantee, if they are effective, that the next war will end with atomic bombs instead of beginning with them. And, if these agreements are ineffective, they will simply increase the element of surprise which the atomic bomb has added to the arsenal of the aggressor. And, if it becomes possible, as it theoretically is, to manufacture atomic bombs out of helium and hydrogen, all plans for control based on the control of uranium must fail.

19. *Pay attention to the transition words of the speaker. See paragraphs 5, 23 and 49. Here* and *is used. See how the speaker refers to the experience of his audience. Anyone who lived through the depression would remember Hoover's prediction with a wry smile. Note the series of conditional enthymemes. The speaker shakes his audience out of any apathy they may feel regarding the atomic bomb by a terrible prediction.*

20. We have now reached the point where we cannot have war and civilization, too!

20. *Here we have the disjunctive enthymeme—it is a case of either or.*

21. Last week in Paris, I met with a staff of the United States Scientific and

21. *The audience cannot escape the thought that it is sitting on the front seat.*

Cultural Organization. There is a group operating, by the way, on an annual budget which is about 25 per cent of the amount which the United States Government spent every year during the war at the University of Chicago alone for the production of new weapons. And this group is dedicated to the proposition that, since war begins in the minds of men, and since education is supposed to have some effect on the human mind, the way to prevent war is to do something about education.

They are listening to a man who is in the know. A speaker reveals himself to an audience in the course of his speech. Again the rhetorical device of contrast and comparison is employed. The speaker permits the audience to draw its own conclusion, i.e. that more money is spent on weapons than on the prevention of war. See how the speaker returns to his theme, and how this paragraph bears out the point that Americans do not believe in education.

22. I put it to you that this proposition is sound; that education, as the British have decided, is the most urgent business before us, and that we must show, by our actions rather than by our speeches, that we regard it in this light.

22. *Here is the concluding paragraph on the first paradox. The speaker uses an echo of his remark in paragraph 11 about the British. Such cross references help knit the speech together. Read over this first section (paragraphs 6 to 23) and notice that every word, phrase and sentence contributes to the total impression that Americans do not take education very seriously. The speaker devotes 17 paragraphs to point 1, 26 paragraphs to point 2, 18 paragraphs to point 3 and 8 paragraphs to point four. The speaker develops his theme psychologically. He is governed by the ability of his audience to listen. He terminates quickly.*

23. Now, while we are about it, we might attack another paradox in American education, which is that a system, nominally democratic, operates in an oligarchial way. An oligarchy, I need not remind you, was a form of government based on wealth.

23. *The speaker gets away from the mechanical "the second paradox." But in order that the audience may know where he is in the development of his points he does, in paragraph 47, refer to the "third paradox." He does not say "fourth paradox" but says, in paragraph 66, "The final paradox. . . ."*

The speaker retains his keyword—paradox. The speaker does not let the word oligarchial *pass without definition. He knows the truth of the remark, "Never underestimate the intelligence of the audience but do not overestimate their information."*

24. American education is founded on the belief that democracy is served if

24. *The speaker takes this paragraph and the next to set up assumptions which*

its schools, colleges, and universities charge low fees, or none; and if, at the same time, there is no discrimination among students in terms of their intellectual ability.

25. We have democratic education, then, if we do not charge for it, and if we make clear that every citizen is entitled, as a matter of right, to as much free education as every other citizen.

26. This assumption is false in all its parts.

27. Actually, the important cost of education is not fees. It is the cost of the pupil's subsistence if he lives away from home, and the loss of his earning power. In this country, however, scholarships given by private foundations rarely cover more than fees.

28. The educational institutions, managed by local and state governments, feel they have performed their full duty if they charge low fees, or none. The books of the University of Chicago will show an expenditure on student aid of more than $600,000 a year, but the figure is meaningless, for almost every cent of this money is paid back to the University in the form of fees by the students who receive it.

29. Universal education in America has, therefore, meant that all those who could afford to continue in school have been able to, and those who have not had the money, have not.

he will tear apart. Most of us unthinkingly accept these beliefs. The speaker shows his reasoning power in analyzing the falsity of them.

25. *This paragraph restates what paragraph 24 set forth. The speaker uses the conditional syllogism:*
If we do not charge for education, we have democratic education.
We do not charge for education,
Therefore, we have democratic education.
(If we affirm the antecedent, we must affirm the consequent.)

26. *But the speaker examines the truth of the assumption, and declares it false. Here is the debater who states what his opponents say and then denies it.*

27. *We have development by definition. The speaker tells what education is not and then proceeds to tell what it is. He shows he has thought through his theme by including earning power. He draws upon his own experience.*

28. *Here is development by example. The audience is instructed. Informing is a way of holding attention. The speaker uses facts. The speaker uses tax-supported institutions and private institutions to support his paradox.*

29. *The speaker draws his conclusion, which reinforces his second contention: that American education operates in an oligarchial way, i.e. education depends upon the pocketbook and not upon brains.*

30. *The speaker emphasizes his paradox by repetition and shows what results flow from that paradox. Note the effect of the verb* trivializes. *The speaker quarrels with modern education because it deals in trifles. So there is much thought behind this word. The verb* overwhelmed *is masterful. Swift said, "Style is proper words in proper places."*

30. Hence the paradox, that in a country which provides free education for all, the length of a young person's education varies directly with his capacity to pay; and since, at these age levels, at least, and probably at all age levels, there is no relation between intellectual ability and capacity to pay, the educational system has been overwhelmed with students who are not qualified for the work they are supposed to be doing, and whose presence inevitably dilutes and trivializes the whole program.

31. *The speaker generalizes from statistical studies. Notice how Hutchins hammers his point. Note his concern with what is democratic as opposed to oligarchial. The speaker is not afraid to end his sentence with a preposition. Why is* impoverished *better than* poor?

31. Every study that has been made in this country shows that there are more good high school graduates out of college than in. The reason is that the ones who go to college are the ones who have the money to go, and it would be undemocratic to say they were not bright enough to go. And, those who are bright enough to go, cannot go unless they have the money to go, because we have no adequate system of financial aid to those who are bright, but impoverished.

32. *The speaker emphasizes his point by placing it in a separate paragraph. The excellent device of contrast and comparison is used. He appeals to the desire to be the equal of others or better.*

32. Here I think it is safe to say that we fall behind every country in the Western world.

33. *The speaker weaves in a previous reference. He develops his thesis by examples.*

33. Until the National Youth Administration and the GI Bill of Rights, nothing was ever done by anybody to recognize the cost of living as an element in the cost of education.

34. *The speaker uses his home state as an example. He knows most about it. Note the use of facts. He does not deal in generalities. Note the everyday English of the speaker. He does not say "subsistence" but "to live on." And he repeats, "if his family could do without his earnings."*

34. Before the war, we used to boast that a student could go to the University of Illinois for $75 a year. He could. That is, he could, if in addition, he could command not less than $750 a year to live on, and if his family could do without his earnings.

35. By contrast, every European country has long since made provision that those who show themselves qualified through a rigorous system of competition to receive aid in their education shall receive aid which enables them to live as well as to study.

35. This evidence bolsters his contention in paragraph 32. The previous two paragraphs show that in the U.S.A. we do fall behind. Note the use of generalization. Would the audience accept this without further proof? Would it have been better if he had cited an example of "every European country?"

36. As a self-supporting student, who tried to live first and study afterwards, I can testify that the combination is possible only because the American university demands so little study.

36. The speaker knows what is going through the minds of his audience, and he spikes it. He uses himself as an example of one who "worked" his way through college. But is it clear whether the speaker means college or university? (He went to Oberlin and Yale.)

37. If we had in this country real intellectual competition in our universities, it would at once become apparent that it is not possible for a boy to work eight hours a day in a factory, as I did, and get an education at the same time. Under those circumstances it must be clear that I did not get an education; I simply graduated from college, which is quite a different thing.

37. Further personal proof is given. Such proof coming from such a speaker carries great weight. The speaker elaborates on the problem. He scores a favorite American delusion, that it is possible and desirable for a boy to work his way through college.

38. What we need is an adequate system of financial aid for those who deserve it, a national system of competitive scholarships—scholarships which are large enough to enable the student to study as well as live.

38. Here is the solution to this part of the address. This will take care of the bright students who can benefit from a university education.

39. We also need a system by which those students, who are not qualified for university work, may be effectually excluded from the university. The basic task of education for citizenship should be performed outside the universities. The universities should be devoted to advanced study, professional training, research, and the education of leaders. Therefore, the university must be limited, if it proposes to succeed in any of

39. But what will happen to those who fail the competitive examinations? This and the following paragraphs take up the solution for those who cannot benefit from a university education. Note the structure of the speech. The speaker has thought through the problem. You have, in this paragraph, the speaker's conception of a university: a four-fold program. Note that he repeats the four functions. Is "leadership" a vague term?

these tasks, to those who have demonstrated their qualifications for advanced study, professional training, research, or leadership.

40. *The speaker again is very definite as to his solution. This is the product of much deliberation and much conference with educational leaders. The speaker is as clear as crystal.*

40. The notion that any American, merely because he is one, has the privilege of proceeding to the highest university degree must be abandoned. A six-year elementary school, a three- or four-year high school, a three- or four-year college, locally organized, would give us a system which would take care of the fundamentals of education, and would relieve the university of the necessity of doing so. Students graduating from this system would come to the end of it between the ages of 18 and 20, and only those who had demonstrated their qualifications to go on should be permitted to do so—at least at the cost of the taxpayer.

41. *The speaker introduces some sarcasm toward the Bachelor's degree.*

41. In order to induce the others not to go on, I should be perfectly prepared to have them receive the Bachelor's degree at the age of 18 or 20.

42. *Further depreciation of the A.B. degree is contained in this reference to Barrett Wendell. It undoubtedly raised a laugh.*

42. I have, in fact, a good deal of sympathy for the proposal of Barrett Wendell of Harvard, that every American citizen should receive the Bachelor's degree at birth.

43. *The speaker reiterates his contention and supports it by appealing to the founding fathers. He attempts to link up his concept with one which his audience may already have accepted.*

43. With a six-year elementary school, a three- or four-year high school, and a three- or four-year college, from which only carefully selected graduates should be permitted to proceed to the university, we might have a truly democratic system of education, democratic in the purest Jeffersonian sense.

44. Jefferson's proposals for the University of Virginia contemplated a rigorous selection of students, the like of which has never been seen in this hemisphere.

44. The speaker elaborates for the sake of those who did not know of Jefferson's plan. He never leaves his audience in the dark. He takes time to explain.

45. There is nothing undemocratic about saying that those who are to receive education at public expense should show they are qualified for it. On the contrary, it is most undemocratic to say that anybody can go as far as he likes in education, when what it actually means he can actually have all the education he can pay for.

45. Fearful that his audience might think his plan undemocratic, the speaker uses refutation. Here is another paragraph by way of summary. He says in effect, "What I am proposing is democratic; what we have now is undemocratic."

46. The creation of local colleges as the culmination of the six-four-four, or six-three-three system of education would give us a chance to develop institutions devoted to liberal education, free from the domination of the university, and would give us a chance to develop universities free from the domination of collegiate interests.

46. Here is the plan:
1. six-four-four college for all.
2. liberal arts for those who can afford it.
3. universities for those who pass competitive examinations supported by taxation.
The speaker shows the advantages of this system. It is no wonder that Dr. Hutchins is listened to with respect, for he has thought through the problems confronting our college and university setup and has arrived at what he feels is a satisfactory solution.

47. We should then have an intelligently organized educational system, democratically operated, and equipped to play its part in the New World that is struggling to be born; but, when all this is done, we shall be left confronting a third paradox, namely, the paradox presented by what the people expect of education.

47. This paragraph forms a peroration for the second paradox. The third paradox is introduced.

48. Our country, in which the rapidity of technical change is more dramatically presented than anywhere else in the world, has an educational program which largely ignores the rapidity and inevitability of such change.

48. In this third section of the address the speaker inveighs against vocational training, social climbing and financial success. This paragraph dwells upon the paradox of a static educational program in a rapidly changing world.

49. *The speaker amplifies what he means by technical change. He blasts a common assumption. He is getting ready to bring forward his theory of the Great Books which set forth everlasting principles.*

49. Now, vocational training assumes that the machinery on which the boy is trained will be in use when he goes to work. Actually, the machines and the methods are likely to be so different that his training will be a positive handicap to him.

50. *An example from army experience is used to prove his point against vocational training. The futility of expecting social position from education is emphasized by quoting Gilbert and Sullivan. Every speaker tries to get the audience to remember, in one way or another, what he says. Here the speaker associates his idea with what is already accepted.*

50. As our experience in war time shows, the place to train hands for industry is in industry. The aircraft companies produced better mechanics in a few weeks than the schools could produce in years. And, it must be obvious that education on a democratic basis cannot supply social standing, as Gilbert and Sullivan pointed out, when "Everybody is somebody and nobody is anybody."

51. *A skilled speaker uses transition words which carry the audience along with him. Note the cumulative effect of the word* moreover. *Here is another of the false expectations. Education cannot and should not be expected to yield vocational training, social success or financial power. Evidently the speaker's concept of education and the prevailing concept of it are in conflict.*

51. Moreover, those who seek education for financial success are doomed to disappointment. Direct training for the purpose of producing financial success, like a course in how to make money, is obviously a fraud, and the number of occupations, I regret to tell you, in which what are known as college conditions are more of a help than a hindrance is certainly limited. Yet, the belief that education can in some way contribute to vocational and social success, has done more than most things to disrupt American education.

52. *The audience is no doubt asking, "What can education do?" The speaker hastens to answer this paramount question.*

52. What education can do, and about all it can do, is to produce a trained mind.

53. *The speaker reinforces his contention that getting a trained mind is hard work by quoting from Aristotle. Here is a hint of his knowledge of the Great Books. A little further on there is to be another reference to one of the great Greeks. Note*

53. Now, getting a trained mind is hard work. As Aristotle remarked, "Learning is accompanied by pain." Those who are seeking something which education cannot supply are not likely to be enthusiastic about the pain which what it can supply must cause; and, since our false sense of democracy requires us to admit them to education anyway, then something must be done with them when they get into it, and it must, of course, be something which is not painful. Therefore, it must be something which interests them.

54. The vocationalism of our schools results, in part, from the difficulty of interesting many boys and girls in what are known as academic subjects, and the whole apparatus of football, fraternities, and fun, is a means by which education is made palatable to those who have no business to be in it.

55. The fact is that the best practical education is the most theoretical one. This is, probably, the first time in human history in which change on every front is so rapid that what one generation has learned of practical affairs, in politics, business, and technology, is of little use to the next, just as to what the father has learned of the facts of life is almost useless to his son. It is principles—everlastingly principles—which are of practical value today; not data, not methods, not facts, not helpful hints, but principles are what the rising generation requires if it is to find its way through the mazes of tomorrow. No man among us can tell what tomorrow will be like; all we know with certainty is that it will be different from today.

56. We can also see that it is principles which the adults of May 12, 1947, must understand if they are to be ready for May 13. The notion that education is something concerned with preparation

the logic of these next few paragraphs. The quarrel that this speaker has with our false sense of democracy appears again.

54. *The logical result of trying to interest students is vocational education. Note the alliteration* football, fraternities, and fun. *The speaker does not mince words.*

55. *The speaker seems to utter a paradox of his own. Here is a good example of the epigram. Notice the repetition of the word* rapid. *See how the speaker uses the familiar "the father has learned of the facts of life is almost useless to his son." There is always a sense of speaking to the audience. Note how the speaker defines his concept of principles by negations—four of them. There is style in the phrase "mazes of tomorrow." The rhythm of the concluding sentence of this paragraph is worth noting.*

56. *In this particular section the keyword is* principles. *Principles are set in opposition to "helpful hints to housewives and bonds salesmen." The speaker keeps to his attack on vocational and social success. The final part of this paragraph leads*

into an attack on adult education as it is now conceived; this, in turn, gives the speaker an opportunity to dwell upon adult education as it should be.

for a vocational and social success, that it is composed of helpful hints to housewives and bonds salesmen, has permeated the education of adults in the United States.

57. *Instead of saying that adult education today is concerned with vocational interests, the speaker is vivid by stating that it is "aimed at making third rate bookkeepers into second rate bookkeepers." Dr. Hutchins's speeches would make good hunting grounds for the student of public speaking in learning how to be vivid. The speaker gets a laugh by means of ridicule. The simile "like the measles" is masterful; and note how he scores a point by driving the analogy home.*

57. Adult education, in general, is aimed at making third rate bookkeepers into second rate bookkeepers by giving them classes at night, and in the general population, this process has not aroused much enthusiasm because we have thought of education as something for children, anyway; we have thought of it as something like the measles—having had education once, one need not—in fact, one cannot—have it again.

58. *The speaker gives a new twist to his theme. He is now talking about comprehension. This paragraph is the result of much thought. An echo of the Great Books theme is contained here, "a learned Greek."*

58. Apart from mathematics, metaphysics, logic, astronomy, and similar theoretical studies, it is clear that comprehension comes only with experience. A learned Greek remarked that young men should not listen to lectures on moral philosophy, and he was right. Moral philosophy, history, political economics, and literature, can convey their full meaning only in maturity.

59. *The speaker is talking to adults. He has a mission. He wants to get them interested in furthering their education. He is preparing them for their part in his program.*

To make his point even more clear the speaker draws upon a classic example. He uses an example known to his audience, drawn from his own experience. One learns much about the speaker by reading his speech. (He worked his way through college and taught in a preparatory school.)

59. Take *Macbeth,* for example. When I taught *Macbeth* to boys in preparatory school, it was a blood and thunder story—a very good blood and thunder story, one well worth reading, but a blood and thunder story still. *Macbeth* can mean what it meant to Shakespeare only when the reader has had sufficient experience, vicarious or otherwise, of marriage and ambition to understand the issues and their implications.

60. *The opening sentence of this paragraph makes the audience sit up and pay attention. The speaker still feels that his*

60. It happens that the kind of things we need most to understand today are those which only adults can fully grasp. A boy may be a brilliant mathematician, or a musician—and I have known several astronomers who contributed to the international journals at the age of 13—but, I never knew a child of that age who had much that was useful to say about the ends of human life, the purpose of organized society, and the means of reconciling freedom and order. But, it is subjects like these about which we are most confused, and about which we must obtain some clarification if our civilization is to survive.

61. The survival of civilization, if the Russians are to have the atomic bomb in five years, depends on those who are adults today. We cannot wait for the rising generation to rise. Even if we succeeded in giving them a perfect education, it would be too late.

62. Therefore, it is imperative that we enter upon a program of mass adult education such as we have never contemplated before. The beginnings of this program are already under way. They can be seen here in Detroit, in the efforts which your library and universities are making to force the consideration of fundamental issues through the study of the Great Books of the Western World. At the rate at which this program is now expanding, I expect to see fifteen million people in it within five years.

63. I do not suffer from the illusion that, if fifteen million Americans are studying the Great Books of the Western World within five years, we shall avert the next war. Education alone cannot avert war; it may increase the chances of averting it. Nor do I deny that, if by reading the Great Books, or otherwise,

audience may not take him at his word, so he illustrates once more. Note the use of the magic three: "ends of human life, the purpose of organized society, and the means of reconciling freedom and order." These are the problems that only adults can understand. The speaker reaches the climax of his speech—the survival of civilization.

61. *The speaker drives home the point that it is up to the adults. The urgency of the time element is in the phrase "if the Russians are to have the atomic bomb in five years."*

62. *The speaker wants his audience to do something about this problem. He is definite. He refers to Detroit. The vision of the speaker comes out in this paragraph. It is bold and holds attention. The speaker answers a question which every audience asks: "What has that got to do with us?"*

63. *Again the speaker is conscious of the objections of his listeners. He meets two possible objections. He no doubt gets a laugh from his witty, "I do not expect the American audience to have enough faith in the immortality of the soul to regard this as more dubious consolation." And he follows this with a sentence that is an anticlimax. Note the vividness of the picture* *"suitable alternatives to liquor, the movies and—if I may say so in Detroit—running around the country in second-hand cars, and catching glimpses of the countryside between the billboards."*

the hearts of the Americans are changed, and the hearts of the Russians remain unchanged, we shall merely have the satisfaction of being blown up with changed hearts rather than unchanged ones. I do not expect the American audience to have enough faith in the immortality of the soul to regard this as more dubious consolation. But, if we do not avert war by this kind of education, we can at least provide ourselves, in the time that is left to us, with some suitable alternative to liquor, the movies and—if I may say so in Detroit—running around the country in second-hand cars, and catching glimpses of the countryside between the billboards.

64. *Again the speaker offers personal proof. He implies more than he says. He lets the audience fill in what he means by "all." The speaker seeks to justify the study of the Great Books. This is one good reason for their study.*

For a further explanation of the Great Books idea see the education page of The New York Times *for Sunday, August 24, 1947.*

64. At the age of 48 I can testify that all forms of recreation eventually lose their charm. I mean all!!! Partly as a result of the universal recognition of the great truth that eventually all forms of recreation lose their charm—partly in recognition of this great truth, the Great Books discussion classes have now begun to sweep the country from New York to Seattle.

65. *In thinking through the question of the Great Books the speaker comes back to his thesis that American education is faulty. Here is an echo of the thesis that American education is concerned with vocations rather than principles. Here is another reason for the study of Great Books, not only by adults but by oncoming generations.*

65. Another explanation of their success is that the people are beginning to realize the shortcomings of their own education. They see now that the books they never read in school or college, the issues they never discussed, the ideas they never heard of, are the books, discussion and issues that are directly relevant here and now. It may be that this generation of parents will see to it that the shortcomings of their children are overcome so that the American of the future may not have to get all his education after he becomes an adult.

66. The final paradox of American education which I wish to mention will become apparent when you look at what the world requires, and what American education has to offer.

67. American education excels in every technological activity, every applied sphere, and it excels as well, in pure science. The British, French, or German physician or engineer who had a chance to study in the United States would be a fool to decline the opportunity; but, he should be educated first and not count on the possibility of getting an education afterward. In every technological, applied, scientific field, the United States is, without question, pre-eminent today.

68. We know, therefore, one thing with certainty about the American university—it can produce weapons of war. Any time that you would like to have weapons of war produced, the American universities will undertake to supply them, and they will be bigger, better, and more deadly than ever.

69. On the other hand, another great segment of the American university, the modern medical school, has done almost as much to lengthen life as the schools of engineering and physics have done to shorten it.

70. In short, wherever the material conditions of existence are in question, the American university can deliver the goods. If you want better bombs, better poison gases, better medicine, better crops, better automobiles, you will find the American university able—and usually willing—to help you.

66. *The conclusion of the treatment of the third paradox leads directly into the fourth. Can you think of any other paradoxes of American education?*

67. *Rhetorically you have the sentence built on the magic three "every technological activity, every applied sphere, and it excels as well, in pure science." To make his point the speaker takes up the foreign student in American universities. He shows that such a student would not get an education, in the sense that he is using the term, in the U.S.A.*

68. *The speaker is frightening in his insistence that the American university can produce weapons of war, "bigger, better, and more deadly than ever."*

69. *The speaker knows that through the minds of his audience there has been running an objection. He takes it up.*

70. *The speaker takes four paragraphs to develop the idea that American education can produce the goods. But the advances are in material things.*

71. *This paragraph is the payoff. This is where the speaker releases his dynamite. Look back at paragraph 2. Note that the speaker said, "I may add, a pessimism which nobody, except possibly Mr. Ruthven, in the state of Michigan can approach." Here is pessimism indeed! Note how the speaker piles up his "becauses." This paragraph is enough to make the audience cry out. Here is the word* trivial *again. The speaker believes that American education is trivial. Note the three* again: *"the trivial, frivolous, and immediately impractical." Note the balanced sentence that concludes the paragraph.*

71. Where the American university cannot help you is where you need help most. Because of the paradoxes I have listed, because of our indifference to the real purposes of education, and because our pre-occupation with the trivial, frivolous, and immediately impractical, the American university is gradually losing its power to save the world. It has developed the power to destroy it; it is ill equipped to save it.

72. *Another epigram opens this paragraph. It is a truism. Note the logic of this paragraph. Each sentence grows out of the preceding one. The verb* mirrors *is suggestive. The rhythm of the final sentence is beautiful. This sentence truly has the oral style.*

72. What is honored in a country will be cultivated there. A means of cultivating it is the educational system. The American educational system mirrors the chaos of the modern world. While science and technology, which deal only with goods in the material order, are flourishing as never before, liberal education, philosophy and theology, through which we might learn to guide our lives, are undergoing a slow but inevitable decay.

73. *Note how the speaker dramatizes the various solutions. He introduces conversation into the speech. The speaker tells the audience what he wants: "a sound character and a trained intelligence." What a masterful phrase is "a transitory phenomenon lost in the confusion of a darkening world." The speaker emphasizes the "spiritual world" as opposite to the "material world" of American education.*

73. It is not enough to say, then, "Let us have lots of education," or even "Let us have lots of expensive education." We must have universal education —let it cost what it may—of the right kind, and that is the kind through which we may hope to raise ourselves by our bootstraps into a different spiritual world; that is the kind which places a sound character and a trained intelligence above all other aims, and which gives the citizen a scale of values by which he can learn to live. Only by such a scale of values, rationally established and firmly held, can a democratic individual hope to be more than a transitory phenomenon lost in the confusion of a darkening world.

74. In a democratic country there is a sense in which there is never anything wrong with education. A democratic country gets the kind of education it wants. I have no doubt that, if the people of the United States understand the urgency of education today, and understand the kind of education they must have, they can get it. I hope they will make the effort to get it before it is too late.

74. *The speaker is a philosopher. Note the directness of the sentence "A democratic country gets the kind of education it wants." There is hope in the third sentence. The prophet takes his seat after pointing the way. Would it have helped if he had said, "I hope we will make the effort to get it before it is too late"? Yet, the speaker warned that he viewed the scene with detachment. This is an application-type conclusion. The speaker wants action.*

THE ART OF CONTEMPLATION[1]

Wise Choices Are the Distinguishing Mark of an Educated Man

VIRGIL M. HANCHER,

President, State University of Iowa

*Delivered at the Commencement, State University of Iowa,
Iowa City, Iowa, June 5, 1948.*

VIRGIL M. HANCHER (1896–1965) was president of the State University of Iowa from 1940 to 1965. In line with his belief that what our cultural life needs today is more general practitioners, he has remodeled the university's curriculum, cutting down the number of vocational courses in favor of a broad liberal arts program. The university has a Rockefeller-financed theatre and a Carnegie-financed art building. He is responsible for building a communication center. Its work in creative writing is well known. The university allows its students to earn their degrees by substituting for a traditional thesis an original novel, a painting, a performance in a play or performance or writing of a musical composition. President Hancher once remarked, "It is my personal opinion that creative effort has a proper place in a balanced fine arts program." Apropos of this concern for the creative arts, it is interesting that *The Atlantic* for September, 1966 devotes

---

[1] *Vital Speeches,* Vol. XIV, No. 19.

three pages to poetry written by people at Iowa State. In introducing these young poets the editor said, "Few campus writing programs in America rival the Writers Workshop at the University of Iowa, where Paul Engle has for many years presided over a rich seedbed of prize winning poets and novelists. *The Atlantic* has selected from among the current crop of Iowa poets three young men whose work gives special promise of distinction."

During his college years he was an intercollegiate orator and debater. He was initiated into Delta Sigma Rho. On his faculty was A. Craig Baird, who founded international debating. Once, when President Hancher was visiting England, the Oxford University debate team met him at his plane to show their respect for Professor Baird. President Hancher and his committee one year invited Professor Baird to give the commencement address. Such instances show President Hancher's attitude toward public speaking activities.

As a student at Iowa he was first in his class in scholarship and was the senior class president. He was graduated with an A.B. degree in 1918. After serving with the U.S. Naval Reserve Forces in 1918–1919 he returned to the university for a year of law study. Having been awarded a Rhodes Scholarship, he studied law at Worcester College at Oxford University. He was granted a B.A. degree in jurisprudence from Oxford University in 1922.

Having returned to his law studies in Iowa in 1922, Hancher became a member of the Iowa Law Review staff and was awarded the J.D. degree in 1924. He was elected to the Order of Coif. He was admitted to the Iowa bar in 1924 and to the Illinois bar in 1925. His article "Oxford and American Legal Education, a Contrast" was published in the August, 1930 issue of the *Journal of the American Bar Association*.

He began practicing law in Chicago with the firm of Butler, Lamb, Foster and Pope in September, 1924. Except for several months in 1926 when he was associated with his firm's Washington office, he practiced law continuously in Chicago until 1940, by which time he was a partner in the law firm of Pope and Ballard. His specialty was corporation law and its related subjects.

Meanwhile, Hancher had continued his interest in his alma mater. He served for several years as a member of the alumni association's board of directors and from 1938 to 1939 was president of the Association. He was elected president of the university on September 10, 1940 and assumed his duties the following November. Upon his inauguration on May 24, 1941 he became the university's thirteenth regular president.

Thus, President Hancher brought his sixteen years of previous experience as a successful Chicago lawyer to the State University of

Iowa. He gave his alma mater an efficient business administration. Until 1951 he taught a course in constitutional law. In January, 1956 President Dwight D. Eisenhower appointed him to an eight-year term on a committee which prepared a history of the Supreme Court, as a memorial to the late Justice Oliver Wendell Holmes.

This address, "The Art of Contemplation," was included by A. Craig Baird in the 1948–1949 edition of *Representative American Speeches* published by the H. W. Wilson Company. Of this speech Professor Baird, who had the opportunity to observe his president, said:

"President Virgil M. Hancher gave this charge to the candidates at the Commencement exercises at the State University of Iowa, Iowa City, Iowa, on Saturday, June 5, 1948.

"At each of the University convocations, held in February, June and August, since his appointment at Iowa in 1940, the President has delivered such final remarks to outgoing classes. This one is typical in its brevity, its direct appeal to the graduating audience, and especially its identification of high educational purpose and endeavor with wisdom, perspective, and motive.

"The structural completeness of the speech is based upon a problem-solution pattern. The vocabulary is strikingly effective in its oral quality, repetition of keywords, figurative phrases, diction appropriate to the academic audience, contrast and comparison, analogies, epigrams, direct address, Biblical allusion, restrained humor, and sentence variety and rhythm.

"President Hancher, although he occasionally uses a manuscript, is primarily an extempore speaker, at home before both university and community audiences. His method of composition is to jot down central ideas, and then write and rewrite the discourse. On the platform he uses few or no 'speaker notes,' his voice is excellent, his manner conciliatory yet forceful. He is an excellent example of one who demonstrates three sources of credibility in orators, as suggested by Aristotle: 'There are three things apart from demonstrative proofs which inspire belief, viz. sagacity, character, and good will.'"

---

1. Contemplation *is the keyword, the echo word of the address. Note that the speaker uses it in his title. Ask any student what President Hancher was speaking about and he no doubt would reply "contemplation." Count the number of times the word* contemplation *is repeated. What a masterful phrase is "staccato tempo": the sound and rhythm echo the sense. It is*

1. The staccato tempo of modern life has made difficult the art of contemplation. The days pass, they gather into weeks and months, arteries grow old and reactions slow down without the acquisition of that wisdom which comes only from the distillation of experience. Cynicism may also be the distillation of ex-

perience; but it is a bitter brew. The wise man, no less than the cynic, will not be taken in by life; but neither will he let the weaknesses and frailties of men blind him to their aspirations. Wisdom knows that men's eyes can be, and are, sometimes turned toward the stars, even though at other times they may be turned toward the gutter.

repeated in paragraphs 8 and 15. In the second sentence note the graphic character of "arteries grow old and reactions slow down." The speaker has a vivid style. Notice the development of the paragraph by comparison and contrast: wise man vs. cynic; and by figure of speech: "distillation of experience" is repeated several times. Count them. The idiom "taken in" is full of vitality. Note the poetic character of the symbols "stars" and "gutter"—they suggest more than they express. In the final paragraphs (look at them now) the thoughts planted in this paragraph are repeated. The personal proof of the speaker shines through his words.

2. "Instinct, Intelligence, Wisdom" are the categories named by Whitehead, and they arrange themselves in an order of progression. If life is to have meaning, if the things we do are not illusion, if there is reality in our efforts and our undertakings, the freedom of choice and of action, which we appear to possess, is more than appearance. It is a real freedom, and the choices which we make are real choices.

2. The theme of the address (of 16 paragraphs and about 1350 words) is that through contemplation we may acquire wisdom. See how testimony is used as a form of support for the central idea. The speaker is addressing college graduates; he lets them think along with him. See the enthymemes. The speaker is arguing against life being ruled by blind chance. Note the repetition of the words "wisdom" and "wise." Note the directness of the oral style—you, we, I. The first subordinate idea (that man has freedom of choice) is introduced.

3. To come to such a decision is in itself an act of faith. It assumes that the universe is not driven by blind, mechanistic forces which we can neither resist nor understand—and, indeed, of which we are a part without our knowledge. Our ultimate view of the universe is always an act of faith, rather than of reason, because our ultimate view of the universe rests upon a first postulate which cannot be proved.

3. The speaker is a lawyer; he uses the vocabulary of logic, i.e. "postulate." He also uses the vocabulary of religion: "faith," "psalm," "God." Paragraphs 3, 4, 5, 6 and 7 deal with faith. Note how the speaker addresses himself to a human need: belief in the meaning of life. To appreciate fully what the speaker has in mind in the second sentence see the September, 1948 Atlantic Monthly for the article, "Man Against Darkness: Has Religion Lost Its Power?" by W. T. Stace. Note the repetition of the phrase "ultimate view of the universe."

4. The ancients said that there could be no dispute in matters of taste. "De gustibus non est disputandum." Men differ in matters of taste, but there are no absolutes. Perhaps the same might be said of postulates, although this will be

4. The speaker uses an analogy to further his argument; he borrows it from the realm of art. He uses a Latin phrase to address an educated audience. The lawyer states the case of the opposition. Note the balanced sentence and the phrases set against each other: "religious orthodox" and

"dialectical materialist." The philosopher is talking: "absolutes" and "postulates." Note what vocabulary the speaker uses to carry his argument.

5.   The speaker has thought through his theme, "What are the implications?" What will the audience think? Note the development of the paragraph by exclusion: "It is not this, but this." Note the use of the commonly used expression "one man's meat will be another man's poison," which comes from Love's Cure, *Act II, Sc. 2, Beaumont and Fletcher.*

6.   Observe in this section the number of times postulate *is repeated. The speaker is conscious of addressing an audience. The speaker is in earnest: "What I desire." In paragraph 9 note the stronger word* crave. *In this section the speaker is talking about faith. You cannot escape it. The speaker penetrates his audience. When the speaker gets the word he wants he does not search for a synonym, i.e.* witness. *The speaker is talking about the most important matter in the life of all of us, i.e. the mainspring of action.*

7.   The transition word here is hypothesis. *This is a paragraph of summarization and transition. Note the short sentences. It is as if the speaker had the audience by the lapel. He just won't let go. He drives home his point. The next seven paragraphs develop the idea of self-mastery. The last two paragraphs develop the conclusion. Note the conversational power of the question.*

8.   Note the repetition of the opening sentence plus the thought of self-knowledge. In paragraphs 8, 9, 10 and 11 this theme is developed. The speaker refers to much of current thinking that is looking back to the old days. (See the book Ideas

disputed and disputed vigorously. For with one postulate you will become a religious orthodox and with another you will become a dialectical materialist.

5.   I do not mean to imply that it is a matter of indifference that you become one or the other, or that you arrive at any one of the infinite number of destinations between the two. Neither do I mean to imply that all postulates are equally valid. What I do mean to imply is that with the infinite variety of men, there will be diversity of outlook, and now, and for a long time to come, one man's meat will be another man's poison.

6.   What I would desire for you is an apprehension of the postulate upon which your faith is founded. Because you do have a faith, or at least a working hypothesis of your relation to the entire scheme of things, on which your life is founded. Whether this hypothesis is formulated or unformulated in your consciousness, it still exists—and your actions, if not your declarations of faith, are witness to it. Indeed your actions may be the true witness.

7.   Your hypothesis may range all the way from a belief that life has purpose to a belief that it is utterly without purpose—that nothing can be done to give it sense or meaning. But your hypothesis exists. Do you know what it is?

8.   The staccato tempo of modern life makes difficult the contemplation necessary for self-knowledge. I make no plea for the good old days. Most of us would not be here if the good old days

had not been changed for the better. Disease or famine would have cut off us or our ancestors, and of those who survived only a fortunate few would have achieved the luxury of an education. The triumphs of science and of scientific method are not to be overlooked. Nevertheless the balance sheet has its debit side.

Have Consequences *by Richard M. Weaver, University of Chicago Press, 1948.) Note such stylistic devices as the alliteration of "bitter brew" and "fortunate few." The speaker uses figures of speech, i.e. "balance sheet." Does it occur to the average college student that a college education is a luxury? Note the use of such words and phrases as "staccato tempo" and "contemplation" that tie the speech together.*

9.   Somewhere along the pathway of progress, the art of contemplation has been lost. The Society of Friends, certain Roman Catholics, an occasional mystic or band of mystics have preserved the art. They retain an anchorage in a sea of ceaseless motion, of disquiet, of drifting. They possess an integrity, a calm and assurance, a wholeness of mind and body that is a kind of holiness. This wholeness, this holiness, I crave for you.

9.   Note the specific reference "The Society of Friends, certain Roman Catholics." The speaker thus makes his meaning clear. Hancher has an active imagination; he thinks in figures of speech: "They retain an anchorage in a sea of ceaseless motion, of disquiet, of drifting." Note the word disquiet. Later on he uses the word quiet with contemplation. The speaker knows the value of words. Note the play on wholeness and holiness. In such ways a speaker sinks his thoughts into the minds of his audience so that they will never forget them. Note how the religious note is again played upon in the word "holiness"! The word crave reveals much of the relation of the speaker to this audience.

10.   It will be difficult to achieve. All the forces of modern life conspire against it. The church which once exercised such great dominion over the bodies and souls of men now competes with a thousand secular rivals. Competition, activity for its own sake, the lust for success and power make difficult the art of self-mastery. We are slaves and not masters. "Things are in the saddle and they ride mankind." The newspaper, the radio, and now television interrupt our days and disturb our nights. Everyone is a little tired, a little distraught, a little below par, a bit inaccurate in judgment.

10.   Here notice the short sentences alternating with the long ones. The paragraph develops the idea that wholeness, holiness, is not easy to achieve. The speaker tells why. There is movement, vitality and energy in these sentences. Note how Emerson is used as testimony. The assertion is supported by a witness. The speaker shows his graphic power: "a little tired, a little distraught, a little below par, a bit inaccurate in judgment." Why did he not say, "a little inaccurate in judgment"? See how the "staccato tempo" of the times is revealed in this sentence.

11.   Yet this need not be so. It is so, because others have willed that it be so, and we have let them have their way.

11.   The speaker develops his theme by contrast and comparison. He pictures the forces of modern life that bring about

*fragmentation of the spirit. Humor is intro-
duced by the quotation from Mark Twain.
The illustration is pertinent. The vocabulary would be understood by the college
student: "schizophrenic," "reprisal." Again
note the figures of speech "remedy" and
"disease." The speaker employs construc-
tive criticism.*

Mark Twain has been quoted as saying
that he once stopped reading the newspapers for seven years and they were the
seven happiest years of his life! This
remedy for our modern distemper seems
a bit drastic, but perhaps nothing less
than a radical remedy will now halt the
disease. Until the radio and the newspapers have learned that men cannot
survive in perpetual crisis, they are in
danger of reprisal. A populace made
schizophrenic by perpetual crisis and in-
accuracy may well construe "the freedom of the press" and the radio to mean
freedom to publish the truth—and nothing less.

12. *Because man has a choice this
need not be so. Note the transition words
of paragraphs 11 and 12, yet and but. Here
is the solution to the problem. Observe the
direct address:* you. *The phrase "quiet and
contemplation" occurs three times in this
paragraph. We have a choice. This is a
public speaking style, not the style of the
essay. The short sentences are relieved by
the long sentences. Count the words of the
sentences. See the repetition of the echo
word. See the contrast of the words* temporal *and* eternal *running through the address.*

*Reference to television in paragraph 10,
and to atoms and fission, speak of today's
concern.*

*Note here how all the keywords of
previous paragraphs are woven together—
postulate, faith, distillation of experience,
wisdom. Note how the style is elevated by
the quotations from the Psalms. The speaker
uses the familiar to drive home his point.*

12. But nothing compels you to give
up your sanity, even though the world
conspire to drive you mad. You can
make it a rule of your life to withdraw
each day into quiet and contemplation—
religious quiet and contempation, if you
will, but quiet and contemplation, in any
event—so that you may put aside the
pressing and temporal things, and look
upon those which come out of the deep
places of human experience. "The
heavens declare the glory of God," said
the Psalmist, "and the firmament show-
eth his handiwork." Modern man cannot
afford to lose the sense of wonder. Perhaps it has been recaptured by some in
the fission of the atom; but, for most of
us, this must remain as great a mystery
as the origin of life or the nature and
destiny of man. Yet against this mystery
we pit our intellect and our wills, however feeble they may be, confident that
the unexamined life is not for us, but
that out of our struggle we shall appre-
hend the postulates of our faith, and
achieve that distillation of experience
which is wisdom.

13. History records the ebb and flow of civilizations, the aspirations and failures of men and nations. Whether it possesses a rhythm or pattern is still a matter for dispute—yet, as one surveys the record, the trend has been upward. There is little evidence that modern man has a better brain than the prophets of Israel or the sages of Greece or Rome, but modern man is the inheritor of ideas and instrumentalities without which our modern civilization could not exist.

13. *Note the lack of illustrations in the speech. This address is for college students who can supply illustrations from their own experience. Note the rhythm of this sentence: "History records the ebb and flow of civilizations, the aspirations and failures of men and nations." Here is a speaker who affirms man's progress. The speaker points out in what particulars modern man is ahead of the ancients. This shows wide reading and much thought.*

Could any idea be more fitting for college graduates than the one the speaker is putting forth? It is a problem-solution speech. The speech attempts to answer the question: "Does life have meaning?"

14. These ideas and instrumentalities have come to us because men have believed that they were free to make choices, and that the choices were real. They have believed that what they did, as individuals and collectively, made a difference in the long history of mankind, even in human destiny itself. They counted it the better part of wisdom to be on the side of the angels.

14. *See the transitions: "these ideas and instrumentalities." This thought is tied up with the idea of choice. The address is compact. The first half of the speech develops the idea that man has faith that he has freedom of choice. The second half of the speech deals with man's freedom to make the right kind of choices. Man has made progress because he has freedom of choice.*

Contrast and comparison are used again, and this time the phrase "counted on the side of the angels" is used. Benjamin Disraeli first used this phrase in 1864. The audience will remember this phrase as a characterization of the kind of life they should lead. This paragraph ends the discussion. The next two paragraphs form the conclusion.

15. You, too, have a choice, and the choice is real. It should be made, not in response to the staccato drum-beat of temporality but in the quiet and contemplation of eternity. You have but one life, and a short one, at your disposal. There is not time to squander it hastily. Only in leisure can you savor it to the full. "Be still and know that I am God," said the voice to the Psalmist long ago. "Be still and know the good" is as modern as tomorrow's television set.

15. *The speaker drives the main point home. He comes back to his thesis: Man does have a choice. In quiet contemplation he should find wisdom. Wisdom should teach him to be on the side of the angels.*

Note the contrast of "staccato drum-beat of temporality" with "quiet and contemplation of eternity." The sound of "drum-beat," a picture word, was introduced this time: sameness with a slight difference, diversity in unity. Note the verbs "squander" and "savor." Again note the masterful quotation from the Psalms and the way the speaker sinks the truth into the listener's memory. See the figure of speech, rather unexpected.

16. *The speaker uses epigrams. Note the reflection of the audience in the sentence. Note the short, driving sentences and questions. Why didn't the speaker open his address with this sentence?—"Wise choices are the distinguishing mark of an educated man." The speaker ends with a question to make his audience think. See the echo of the quotation from Whitehead.*

16. Wise choices are the distinguishing mark of an educated man. You, too, can be on the side of the angels. Can you afford to be anywhere else? With what greater wisdom can you be wise?

THE BANDUNG ADDRESS [1]

CARLOS P. ROMULO,

Member of the Cabinet, Chairman of the Philippine
Delegation to the Asian-African Conference

Delivered to the Asian-African Conference,
Bandung, Indonesia, April 18, 1955.

CARLOS P. ROMULO (1900–   ) is one of the most brilliant
spokesmen of the Far East. He prepared for his career as a spokesman
for democracy in his school and college days. He was captain of the
debating team, both in high school and in college. He was the winner
of a high school oratorical contest on the subject "My Faith in America." In a letter to the author he said, "Public Speaking is an aid to
clear thinking. It has been of great help to me in my career as a member of the foreign service of the Philippines. . . . Freedom of speech
is one of the boons of a democracy. However, it is only when the
citizens make full use of it that it can serve its function of revitalization.
Hence the necessity of being able to think logically and speak clearly.
Dictatorship shuns public speaking. It is only where popular will is
enshrined that speech flourishes."

After he received his B.A. from the University of the Philippines in
1918, the Philippine government sent him to Columbia University in
New York City for further study. His years there, he now says, were
the "happiest in my life." He made many friends and says he found
out that the average American is always for the underdog. He claims

---

[1] *Vital Speeches*, Vol. XXI, No. 16, June 1, 1955, p. 1270.

that because he was boyish looking the debate audiences were always for his side.

He studied for four years under the watchful eyes of his father's friend, William Howard Taft, and then returned to his homeland to teach as an assistant professor of English at the University of the Philippines, later heading the English department.

In September, 1941, before Japan attacked the United States, Romulo set out on an extensive lecture tour of the countries bordering on the Philippines. He lectured at Hongkong, Chungking, down the Burma Road, at Rangoon, Bangkok and Thailand, visited Malaya, Batavia and Bandung, and finally reached French Indochina. Almost everywhere he went he spoke to Rotary Clubs. He was a past President of the Manila Rotary Club. The thesis of his talks was that, when the Japanese came, token resistance would be made and then the Japanese would take over. He told the Bangkok Rotary Club that when the Japanese came—as they surely would—the Thais would make a token resistance of from three to five hours. After he left, the Japanese registered a protest against his speech, and the President of the Rotary Club was called on to make an explanation. But Romulo's prophecy was accurate: actually the resistance in Thailand was of five hours duration. The cry of "Asia for the Asiatics" helped Japan overrun these countries. The pessimism of Romulo was based on the pro-Japanese attitude of the natives, who had suffered under the treatment of their colonial masters. Only the Philippines, because of their long, friendly association with the United States, resisted. His newspaper articles were published in his own Manila newspapers and carried in the United States and elsewhere by the King Feature Syndicate. This series won the 1942 Pulitzer Prize for distinguished correspondence, as well as incurring the hatred of the Japanese. He is the only non-American to receive this coveted prize so far.

Romulo, a major in the Philippine Army Reserves and a close friend of MacArthur since 1928, was called into active service as press aide to the Commander-in-Chief on December 10, 1941. On December 17, the day the Japanese blitz really began, he was given his desk in the Press Relations Section.

Romulo went to Bataan as a public relations man. He was there 14 weeks, following the enemy occupation of Manila. On January 5, 1942 he made his first broadcast over the *Voice of Freedom* from Corregidor, a challenge which the Japanese answered within an hour, and which caused them to put a price upon his head.

One of the best English speaking Filipino orators, in the fall of 1942 he was on leave in the United States for a lecture tour, which was a sensational success. He travelled over 60,000 miles, appeared in about 289 different cities and spoke more than 356 times. This tour was at the insistence of General MacArthur, and created public opinion for the prosecution of the war in the Far East.

The United States knows Romulo as the man who headed his country's delegation to the United Nations Conference at San Francisco in 1945; as the Resident Commissioner of the Philippines to the United States; as President of the Fourth General Assembly of the United Nations; as a member of three Filipino cabinets; and as an Ambassador to the United States.

Not until he was almost 50 was General Romulo (a title won serving under General MacArthur) able to breathe the free air of his own country. Until that time he had fought for Philippine independence under such leaders as Manuel L. Quezon, Sergio Osmeña, Manuel A. Roxas and his own father and grandfather. As he gained in stature among his own people he nonetheless turned down the opportunity to become president of the Philippines in order to serve in the larger arena of the United Nations. His career was climaxed by his dramatic triumph at the historic Bandung meeting, where he was forced to cross swords with Nehru and Chou En-lai.

Now, after the storm, he finds himself President of the University of the Philippines, a post he little imagined himself occupying when he returned from Columbia as an assistant professor of English. He has used his knowledge of English and of America well. In addition to his great ability as a platform speaker, he has found time to write many distinguished books. Among them are: *I Saw the Fall of the Philippines, I Walked with Heroes, Mother America, My Brother Americans, Friend to Friend* and *The Meaning of Bandung*.

Again and again in his writing and speaking he returns to the theme that the only solution to the Asiatic problem is to extend to all the subject populations of the Eastern world the same method that the United States has used in dealing with the Philippines.

THE SETTING

The speech of Carlos P. Romulo on April 18, 1955 made history. It will go down as a classic defense of democracy against communism. India's Jawaharlal Nehru lost his fight to emerge as the Asia-Africa leader and to steer hesitant nations into his world of coexistence and communism. Romulo had long felt that the most effective way to check the advance of communism in Asia was for people of their own kind who knew about communism and understood its divisive and seductive tactics to tell their fellow Asians about it. At Bandung he had the opportunity, but only after unusual parliamentary skill which he had learned in the West was exercised. Let us take the story from the *New York World Telegram and Sun* of April 25, 1955:

> General Romulo came here for fight or frolic, whatever the other side chose. He would play it by ear, he announced on arrival. Right off, on the first day of the Conference, the fight started.
>
> It started on the question of whether opening statements of the delegates should be delivered in person, orally or handed in typewritten. Nehru quickly sensed his side and Chou's would lose the first round if the more adept pro-democracy speakers got an opportunity to address the full sessions. So at the first delegates' meeting, Nehru forcefully demanded no speeches.
>
> "Fine," said General Romulo. "That's a wonderful idea. It will save time and we can get on with the business."
>
> This put Nehru off balance, for General Romulo was matching Chou in amiability and agreeableness. But General Romulo knew what he was doing. The no-speech rule was adopted to Nehru's satisfaction, but General Romulo noted that Pakistan's Mohammed Ali and seven other delegates were not present. When Mr. Ali arrived, General Romulo quickly told him how speeches had been blocked in an outward show of harmony, but suggested Mr. Ali quietly move for reconsideration at the next closed meeting on the ground that he and others had been absent.
>
> This was done, catching Nehru by surprise. The Pandit hit the ceiling. General Romulo mildly insisted it was a valid protest by the absentees. Turkey's Fatin Tustu Zorlu joined and after a word battle with the nervous, fidgety Nehru, the delegates reversed their stand, voting for speeches before the open forum of the first general session.
>
> The free world victory in the opening skirmish may well have been the turning point of the conference. From then on Chou was on the defensive, tossing out peace garlands as he back-pedaled from the burning issue of the conference: whether these former victims of colonialism, now free, were prepared meekly to accept the new tyranny of international communism.

General Romulo had been preparing for this opportunity for many years. He had had speech training. He was the product of American educational philosophy. He believed in democracy.

1. *The salutation identifies the speaker. Emotion is present. An attitude is created. All the Philippines stand for in the Far East gives color to his words. The fight is to be between communism and democracy. This is democracy speaking.*

1. I am proud to bring to this Conference the greetings of the President and people of the Republic of the Philippines.

2–4. *The speaker seeks good will toward himself and his subject. There is a personal touch. The speaker identifies himself with the needs, wants, desires and concerns of his audience. He is one of them. Personal proof is evident. Note the repetition of such*

2. We of the Philippines have a profound sense of the great historic events dramatized by this unique gathering; we were, may I remind you, the first of the new nations to emerge in the great re-

arrangement of the world which began after the end of the Second World War. Our Republic came to being, freely and peacefully, on July 4, 1946. Since that time we have watched with proud solidarity and a feeling of oneness the establishment of the other independent nations of a free Asia, so old and yet so new. We have in these nine years taken our stand firmly behind the struggle of every people to become master of its own fate, to enjoy its own identity, to be responsible for its own acts, to join in the immense task of building a new structure of human well-being and free institutions, the task, indeed, of changing the face of the world. To the peoples of Africa, already setting forth on this same path, we pledge our friendship and all the moral and practical support within our power to give as they join us of Asia in the great universal effort to better man's estate.

phrases as "freely and peacefully," "man's estate," "master of its own fate." What a powerful figure—"one great family," "family reunion," "brothers." It is as if the speaker's life preparation were to get ready to give this important speech. July 4, 1946 is important and full of overtones. The purpose of the speech is to persuade the Asian-African bloc of nations not to adopt communism after rejecting European colonialism. The speech centers on tyranny versus freedom. Note the topic sentence for each paragraph. The importance of the assembly is stressed. The speaker expresses the yearnings of the group. He is their spokesman.

3. We come as members of one great family long separated from each other. In this family reunion we are here to talk of *man's estate*. But I do not think it will serve us well to have come here from our many corners of the earth to shroud the truth about man's estate in platitudes, propaganda, or easy self-deception. The world is too harsh a place for this, our problems too great, too perilous, too complicated to allow us this luxury.

3. *The speaker has sat at the feet of Winston Churchill. Note such phrases as "shroud the truth," "platitudes, propaganda, or self-deception" and "the age of empire is being helped into oblivion." See paragraph 11. "Man's estate" is reminiscent of Francis Bacon's "For the glory of the Creator and the relief of man's estate."*

4. This Conference will justify itself if we share our views frankly and realistically as brothers should. We will serve each other if we examine ourselves, if we state the issues and problems plainly as we see them, if we clarify, as far as we can, our needs, our choices, our

4. *The word "issues" is suggestive of the speaker's debate training. Note the persuasive power of "Let us." Also note the appeal to oneness—"brothers." Throughout the address we have an appeal to the mind.*

goals—and our obstacles. Let us seek a true meeting of minds on those we share in common and where there are differences, let us try at least to understand them.

5. *Study the organization of the address. Each of these three concerns will be discussed; they are the reasons for calling the conference. The speaker does not let the audience forget the importance of the moment. He enlarges the focus of the conference. He then ends his introduction. The argument has been outlined. The speaker has sought the good will of the audience. The speech's purpose has been stated. The speaker gains attention because he is discussing a common problem.*

5. All who are represented here are certainly concerned with the issues of (1) colonialism and political freedom; (2) racial equality; and (3) peaceful economic growth. The history of the world in our time turns on the ways in which these issues are met and resolved, or not met and not resolved. We are part, all of us, of a time of great transformation, for each of us and for all the people on earth. It is a trying, difficult, dangerous time—but with it all a good time to be living in. Never before, surely, have so many people been consciously a part of the history through which they were living.

6. *The speaker uses short paragraphs as transitions, to point the way. Discussion begins with paragraph 7. See paragraph 12.*

6. We in this room are, for our brief moment, a part of this history. How do we see it? How do we understand it?

7. *See the conciliatory character of the speaker toward the United Nations. The audience is aware of the work he has done in the U.N. The speaker uses repetition wisely. He repeats the three problems: freedom, equality, growth-independence. However, he is not afraid to criticize the U.N. Note the figure of speech of the mirror. He is a philosopher. Note how the speaker refutes ideas held by the audience. He adapts his thinking to the thinking of the audience. Throughout the address we have an emphasis on world problems as opposed to national problems, world cooperation rather than nationalism. Communism makes an appeal to nationalism and against colonialism. The speaker bases his appeal on reason. Note the rhythm of the last sentence.*

7. To begin with, the very fact that we have come together here in this manner illustrates the great new fact that these issues of freedom, equality, and growth are no longer merely national problems but *world* problems. Indeed, the United Nations was created as an attempt to grapple with this great new fact. In one sense this Conference suggests that for the peoples of Asia and Africa the United Nations has inadequately met the need for establishing common ground for peoples seeking peaceful change and development. But I think we must also say that if the United Nations has been weak and limited in its progress toward these goals, it is because

the United Nations is still much more a mirror of the world than an effective instrument for changing it. It has been in existence only nine years and through that time always subject to all the pressures and difficulties of national rivalries and power conflicts, large and small. It is a place where man, not quite yet a reasonable animal, is trying very hard to become one.

8.   We do not have to be satisfied with the rate of progress being made. But neither can we be blind to the great changes that have taken place in so short a time. The world is a very different place from what it was a scant fifteen years ago and hence the United Nations is a very different body from the old League of Nations. A primary difference is the presence of the new spokesmen for Asian and African people who never allow the Western representatives to forget that the United Nations Charter pledged the freedom and self-determination of all peoples and that there are peoples in Asia and Africa who take that pledge with literal seriousness, and who will not rest until it is redeemed.

8.   *The speaker has a fine grasp of history. He develops this paragraph by contrast and comparison. The speaker gives his audience hope. He is not concerned with old problems. He brings the audience up to date. He addresses himself to this particular audience and their relation to world problems. The place of the United Nations in the solution of world affairs is central in the speaker's thinking. No one but Romulo could have given this speech. (He was President of the United Nations Security Council in 1949. Look him up in Who's Who in America.)*

9.   The majority of independent nations represented here won their independence only within the last decade. Who would have been bold enough, twenty years ago, to predict that this would be so? Who will be bold enough now to say how soon or how slowly those peoples in Africa strong enough to win it will acquire the right to face their own problems in their own way on their own responsibility? The handwriting of history is spread on the wall; but not everybody reads it the same way or interprets similarly what he reads there. We know

9.   *The speaker has analyzed his audience. He shows his grasp of his subject. Africa is brought into the picture. The Christian education of the speaker is seen in his reference to Daniel 5:24–28. What a sharp sentence—"We know the age of European empire is at an end; not all Europeans know that yet." Note the liberal use of questions. The speech seems like a conversation between the speaker and the audience. The appeal of the speaker to the thinking of his audience is expressed in the phrase "conscious instruments."*

the age of European empire is at an end; not all Europeans know that yet. Not all Asians or Africans have been or are still aware that they must make themselves the conscious instruments of historic decision.

10. *See how words like* independence *and* colonial powers *run through the discussion. The paragraph is developed by examples. The speaker criticizes and then praises. The speaker exemplifies his principle of freedom of speech. He shows he is not afraid of the U.S.A. Yet the speaker attempts to be fair. What communist country would dare criticize Russia or Red China? Note the way the speaker varies his sentence structure. Confidence in freedom of discussion is expressed. Note such idiomatic English as "dovetail with its ideals." (The speaker taught English at the University of the Philippines and was on the editorial staff of many newspapers in the Philippines.) One of the glorious pages in American history is our country's magnanimity toward the Philippines. All Americans are proud of this record. The speaker does not want his audience to forget that the West is capable of such performance. The speaker reasons from example.*

10.   Political freedom has been won by many different means. The British surrendered power in Southern Asia because they knew they could no longer maintain it and were wise enough to base their action on reality. The French and Dutch had to be forced to the same conclusion. The United States has at times appeared to us lacking in consistency and vigor in upholding the right of non-self-governing peoples to independence. It has on some issues leaned heavily in favor of colonial powers and sometimes disheartened us because of its failure to make its actions dovetail with its ideals of equality and freedom. We think that this was more than regrettable; we think it has been unwise. Let it be stated in fairness, however, that uniquely among the colonial powers the United States in our case made a formal pledge of independence, fixed a date for it ten years in advance, and fully and honorably redeemed that pledge. True, we fought ceaselessly for our freedom and never gave up our struggle and we earned it when it came. But we of the Philippines have directly experienced the basic good faith of the United States in our own relationship and we feel that the principles upon which it was based will ultimately prevail.

11. *The speaker comes back to the importance of this conference. Note the imagination of the speaker. He is thinking along with his audience. Here is a warning*

11.   It is to be hoped, however, that this Conference will help remind all the Western powers that the issue of political independence for subject peoples

does not depend on their goodwill or slow access of wisdom or virtue. The age of empire is being helped into oblivion by the aroused will and action of people determined to be masters of their own fate. Those of us here who have already won our independence were only the initiators of this process. All the others, almost all now in Africa, stand at various points along their own roads to full self-determination. There is much, of course, one cannot readily foresee. But everything we know and understand about history assures us that whatever new travails the future holds, the old structure of Western empire will and must pass from the scene. Will it expire quietly and in dignity? Will it go out crashing violently? That will depend on many things. But the end is not in doubt.

12.   There are at least three things more to be said here about this matter of national political freedom.

13.   First, it is perilously easy in this world for national independence to be more fiction than fact. Because it expresses the deepest desires of so many people in the world it can be unscrupulously used as a shibboleth, as a façade, as an instrument for a new and different kind of subjection. I know that on this score there are violently different opinions in the world. I can recall how new nations like India, Indonesia and Ceylon were called puppets of imperialism when they were newly born to freedom. And of course, the Philippine Republic has been described by these same sources as a mere tool of the United States. On the other hand, there is the way some of us view the position of certain other coun-

to the Western Powers. The thought would meet ready acceptance by the assembled delegates. Again, the speaker has a magnificent grasp of history. He reveals his personal proof. Note the phrase "Age of empire." The speaker refers to specific sections of his audience. He is direct. Romulo is a prophet. He reasons from context. Like Edmund Burke, he has his eye on a larger audience than the one in front of him. (The speech was hailed in the U.S. Senate. Write to your Senator for a copy of the remarks on this speech.)

12.   Again note the brief transition paragraph. This is a good model for students of public speaking. Its organization is important. These transitions mark the subdivisions of the speech.

13.   Note how workmanlike the speaker is. He outlines his three main points and then takes up each one separately. The speaker does not mince words. He wants to warn against being deceived. This warning is one of the minor themes of the address. The speaker turns the tables on the critics and shows the power of the Philippines in their relation to the U.S.A. The speaker uses examples, but see how careful he is not to mention Russia and Red China by name. His loyalty to the U.S.A. is never in doubt. What a magnificent spokesman Romulo is for the West! What a bridge of understanding he creates! The faith of the U.S.A. in training its wards in the Philippines is justified in this illustrious speech. Note the specific mention of members of the audience—India, Ceylon, Indonesia. Note the skill of the speaker in using a figure of speech readily understood by the audience. Here is a com-

150 RHETORICAL ANALYSIS OF SPEECHES

mon ground. Note the thrust of the sentence "I think we ought to say plainly to each other when we think a puppet is a puppet." This is worthy of Churchill at his best.

tries which from our own perspective we consider as subservient to other powers. I wonder if in such countries you could read in the press or hear in the public speeches of their spokesmen anything resembling the open criticisms and other attacks that were common fare in places like India and the Philippines even before independence? I wonder if any of the spokesmen of these countries would ever speak as freely in criticism of the bigger country to which they feel friendly or allied as, say, we in the Philippines speak our minds about the United States? I am sure you will forgive my frankness, but in this land of the ingenious and artistic *wajang*, of the wonderful Indonesian shadow play and puppet shows, I think we ought to say plainly to each other when we think a puppet is a puppet.

14. *Note how many times* freedom *is repeated in this section. That is what he is talking about. The audience cannot escape it. This paragraph is developed largely by means of the question. The form is conversational. See how the speaker contrasts the totalitarian states with the democratic states. He repeats the idea of substituting a local oligarchy for a foreign oligarchy. See paragraph 35. How much more powerful the word* tyranny *is than* oligarchy. *See how deeply the speaker probes, how he makes the audience see the menace of communism. The speaker is talking about choices. There is no doubt on which side he is. Romulo defines freedom from his own experience and observation. The audience knows the truth of what is said. Here are the words of an Oriental who has studied Western political science. How familiar these words, phrases and sentences are to us, but how strange they must sound in the ears of an Oriental audience.*

14. Secondly, is political freedom achieved when the national banner rises over the seat of government, the foreign ruler goes, and the power passes into the hands of our own leaders? Is the struggle for national independence the struggle to substitute a local oligarchy for the foreign oligarchy? Or is it just the beginning of the conquest of real freedom by the people of the land? Is there political freedom where only one political party may rule? Is there political freedom where dissent from the policy of the government means imprisonment or worse? It strikes me that autocratic rule, control of the press, and the police state are exactly the worst features of some colonialist systems against which we have fought all our lives and against which so many of us are still fighting. Is this really the model of the freedom we seek? Or is it the free interplay of contending parties, the open competition of ideas and political views in the market place, the freedom of a man to speak up as he chooses, be he right or wrong? I know there are many possible answers to these questions. But for my part and for my people, may I say plainly that we regard the struggle for freedom as an unending, constant, unremitting demand upon us, that with all our acknowledged failings, faults, and weaknesses, we are seeking to build in our land a society in which the freedom of our Republic will truly become the freedom of every one of its citizens.

15.   Finally, in this world of contending great powers, the independence of the small or weak nation is at best a precarious and fragile thing. Obviously the ultimate greater freedom will lie in a greater coherence, a uniting of regional interests, in the creation of counterbalancing moral, economic and physical strength, in the greatest possible common action by all to avert the disaster of a new world war. Let us face squarely up to the fact that within the nation we can regain our self-respect and grapple with our local problems but that for the primary goals of economic transformation and well-being and peace, the nation no longer suffices. Western European man today is paying the terrible price for preserving too long the narrow and inadequate instrument of the nation-states in an epoch when nationalism, as such, can solve only the least of our problems and leaves us powerless to meet the more serious ones. We have to try to avoid repeating all of Europe's historic errors. We have to have the imagination and courage to put ourselves

15.   *The speaker refers to his outline— "Finally." He carries his audience with him. This is the third point under the second main division. The speaker warns his listeners that they had better stay together. History points the way. The speaker is not fighting old battles. He calls his audience to the 20th century conflicts. Note the long sentences, which are still easy to follow. Here is the political scientist speaking. The speaker has observed and read widely and has drawn conclusions. Note the "we" sentences. The speaker identifies himself with his audience. He is persuasive. Note the emphasis upon independence and interdependence. He has a vision of the world to be. Note the rhythm of such phrases as "precarious and fragile thing."*

in the forefront of the attempt to create a 20th-Century world based on the true interdependence of peoples.

16. *Note in the opening sentence of this paragraph the internal summary. The speaker refreshes the minds of his audience with his points and then states his second main theme, racism. This is the most explosive section of the address, yet notice how the speaker handles it. He is not a demagogue but a statesman. Read this section very carefully and note the persuasive techniques of the speaker. Racism is due to the weakness of the white man and yet all men are tainted with this same weakness. Note the use of such words as* searing, pernicious *and* virulent. *Read these sentences aloud and savor their rhythm. Note the use of example to make his point, the irrationality of racism. A less temperate speaker would have inflamed the passions of his audience; this would have been easy.*

16. I have said that besides the issues of colonialism and political freedom, all of us here are concerned with the matter of racial equality. This is a touchstone, I think, for most of us assembled here and the peoples we represent. The systems and the manners of it have varied, but there has not been and there is not a Western colonial regime, which has not imposed, to a greater or lesser degree, on the people it ruled the doctrine of their own racial inferiority. We have known, and some of us still know, the searing experience of being demeaned in our own lands, of being systematically relegated to subject status not only politically and economically, and militarily—but racially as well. Here was a stigma that could be applied to rich and poor alike, to prince and slave, bossman and workingman, landlord and peasant, scholar and ignoramus. To bolster his rule, to justify his own power to himself, Western white man assumed that his superiority lay in his very bones, in the color of his skin. This made the lowliest drunk superior, in colonial society, to the highest product of culture and scholarship and industry among the subject people.

17. *The speaker does not hesitate to use* racism *as his keyword for this section. Throughout this section the speaker is trying to combat the communist, who is trying to make capital out of racism. Note how valuable is Romulo's experience with the U.N. Cut this section at any point and it bleeds with the thought of racism. The speaker draws Africa into the discussion. Note the figure of speech "cuts." The speaker knows Western literature as well as*

17. I do not think in this company I have to labor the full import of this pernicious doctrine and practice. I do not think I have to try to measure the role played by this racism as a driving force in the development of the nationalist movements in our many lands. For many it has made the goal of regaining a status of simple manhood the be-all and end-all of a lifetime of devoted struggle and sacrifice. Today this type of Western racism survives in virulent form only in certain parts of Africa, notably in the Union of South Africa, but certainly in many other places as well on that vast continent. Against this every decent man on earth has to set his face. In the United Nations, the Asian and African states have again and again forced this issue on the unwilling attention of the other members. There we could see palpably the extent to which Western men have tried to become defensive about their past racist attitudes. Few of the Western countries were willing to go far enough in condemning the racial practices of the Government of the Union of South Africa. They have yet to learn, it seems, how deeply this issue cuts and how profoundly it unites non-Western people who may disagree on all sorts of questions. Again, we can only ~e that this Conference serves as a ˙ and yet jolting reminder to them 1at the day of Western racism is passing along with the day of Western power over non-Western peoples. Its survival in any form can only hang like an albatross around the necks of those many people in the West who sincerely seek to build a freer and better world.

Eastern. The reference is to Coleridge, "The Rime of the Ancient Mariner":

*Ah! Well a day! What evil looks
Had I from old and young!
Instead of the cross, the Albatross
About my neck was hung.*

Many of his audience have been educated in England and in schools where the English classics have been studied. The speaker wins attention by specific reference to the Union of South Africa. Again he is addressing Western nations over the shoulders of the delegates at Bandung.

18. No less than this can be said. But there is something more too. It is one of our heaviest responsibilities, we of Asia and Africa, not to fall ourselves into the racist trap. We will do this if we let ourselves be drawn insensibly—or deliberately—into any kind of counter-racism, if we respond to the white man's prejudice against us as non-white with prejudice against whites simply because they are white. What a triumph this would be

18. Here is the statesman, the philosopher, rather than the demagogue. The speaker reasons with his audience. He does not seek to inflame the passions. He persuades by warning of possible dangers. The doctrine of the dignity of man is repeated. Hate is a weakness in the white man. Racism is not a sign of strength. Racism would be a weakness in the colored man also. Is not the attitude born out of Christian charity? The speech is forensic and deliberative. Count the number of times the word responsibility *is repeated. What in-*

sight the speaker shows in proclaiming that the white man, through his weakness, has shown us how to be strong. Run through the sentences and note their variety of structure. The speaker is morally outflanking the white man.

for racism if it should come about. How completely we would defeat ourselves and all who have ever struggled in our countries to be free! There is no more dangerous or immoral or absurd idea than the idea of any kind of policy or grouping based on color or race as such. This would, in the deepest sense, mean giving up all hope of human freedom in our time. I think that over the generations the deepest source of our own confidence in ourselves had to come from the deeply-rooted knowledge that the white man was *wrong*, that in proclaiming the superiority of his race, *qua* race, he stamped himself with his own weakness and confirmed all the rest of us in our dogged conviction that we could reassert ourselves as men.

19. *The speaker secures interest by conflict—"Our quarrel." The speaker coins a word, "counter-racism." Note his understanding of the psychology of the motivation of man. Here is an appeal to reason rather than to passions. He reassures his audience. He refutes the communists. Note the memorable phrase "noxious nonsense." The speaker informs his audience on racial progress in the U.S.A. He knows the difference between all and some.*

19. Our quarrel with racism is that it substitutes the accident of skin color for judgment of men as men. Counter-racism would have us do the same: lump white men by their supposed r[...] grouping and govern our acts and re[...] actions accordingly. It is our task to rise above this noxious nonsense. We have the responsibility to remain aware that this kind of racist attitude has been the practice not of all white men, but only of some, that it flies in the face of their own profoundest religious beliefs and political goals and aspirations, that in almost all Western lands, and especially in the United States, the internal struggle against racism and all its manifestations has been going on steadily and victoriously.

20. *Here is persuasion by inclusion; we are all in the same boat. How can we condemn others for actions we ourselves are guilty of? The speaker knows the West*

20. We have the responsibility to acknowledge more than this; this business of racism, or other things like it, is an outcropping of one of many human

weaknesses that we all share. The racism of Western white man has played an especially prominent role in history because the Western man has associated it with the establishment of his great power over so many non-Western peoples. As such, it deserves the special and prominent place it must have in the thinking and feeling of everyone. But we must also soberly ask ourselves: is there a single society or culture represented in this Conference which does not in some degree have its counterpart of this kind of prejudice and ignorance? Where is the society in which men have not in some manner divided themselves for political, social and economic purposes, by wholly irrational and indefensible categories of status, birth, and yes, even skin color? It was a major part of the greatness of India's immortal leader, Mahatma Gandhi, that he devoted so much of his fruitful life of selflessness and sacrifice to a struggle against precisely this kind of thing in Indian life. Would that we all gave as much time to the mote in our own eye as we give to denouncing the beam in the eye of another!

as well as the East. No thoughtful man can disagree with his position. India with her untouchables comes to mind. The speaker gives each person in his audience an opportunity to examine himself. Each one can recognize himself in the speech. What he says is pertinent. The speaker persuasively points to a hero of India, Mahatma Gandhi. Note the Christian teaching, from Matthew 11:20.

21. Surely we are entitled to our resentment and rejection of white racism wherever it exists. But we are also called upon, as honest men who want to better *man's estate* wherever and whatever he is, to acknowledge that in degree we all suffer from the same sin of ignorance and immorality. I ask you to remember that just as Western political thought has given us all so many of our basic ideas of political freedom, justice and equity, it is Western science which in this generation has exploded the mythology of race. Let us not preserve stupid racial superstitions, which belong to the past. Let us

21. *"Man's estate" is again repeated. The speaker has a wise philosophy of man. As a world figure and scholar he sees the contribution of the West to the problems of political thought and racism. Note the persuasion of "Let us." The speaker is intent on giving a world view. The technique of "yes, but . . ." is used. This is the concluding paragraph in the section on racism. The speaker wants to gain the good will of his audience toward the West. Note such phrases as "stupid racial superstition" and "ugly disease." In the background of everything said is the shadow of communism.*

work to remove this ugly disease wherever it is rooted, whether it be among Western men or among ourselves.

22. *The speaker likes the figure of speech "all wrapped up." It smacks of American colloquial usage. Also see paragraph 32. The speaker uses three ways of getting across the idea—"the hub, the center, the heart." He carries his audience along with him. He marks out the path, "Lastly." Evidently the speaker believes the economic struggle is the most important. Perhaps this is why he has saved it until last. Read this paragraph aloud and sense the power of the ideas it expresses. His invention comes from experience, observation, reading, thinking and conversation.*

22.   Lastly, I have said that all of us here are concerned with peaceful economic growth. This brings us closest of all to the hub, the center, the heart of our common preoccupations, because the political forms and methods we seek and choose, the social ideas and ideals we embrace, are all wrapped up in the way in which we strive for *growth*. Economic growth, economic change, transformation of our backward and inadequate economies—these we all seek. These we *must* seek, else we stagnate and die. After all, it is precisely because the billion and a half people of Asia and Africa have begun in our time to strive for a better economic stake in life that most of us are here today. This is the great new overwhelming fact of this century. The *way* in which this is achieved will fix the shape of history for all future men.

23. *This paragraph is developed by cause and effect. Western colonialism is given much blame. The speaker cannot be blamed for favoritism. Note the short, driving sentences. Again it is "we." And note in the last sentence of the paragraph how he returns to his theme of freedom. The speaker knows his audience. He diagnoses their present condition and writes a prescription. The question is, can these needs be met by accepting communism? Communism means slavery. Communism does not permit its people freedom to act.*

23.   We all confront the staggering facts of our economic backwardness. This has been partly due to factors of climate, geography, and the stubborn survival of obsolete social patterns. But it has also in large measure and perhaps decisively been the result of patterns imposed upon us by Western colonialism. This heritage is the heaviest burden we carry with us into the new epoch of national freedom. The great masses of our people live in a state of rural poverty. We need to diversify our economies. We need to industrialize in accordance with our resources and needs. We have to win a more balanced place in the market places of the world. We have to do this in a manner that will effectively raise the standard of living of our people. These are the things we have fought for. These are the things that some of us here are still fighting for. For these things above all, we have needed to be free to seek our own way.

24. But let us not have too many illusions about national independence. We arrive in the world as nations in the middle of the 20th Century, not the 19th or the 18th. We have to strive to become *nations* in a time when history has already passed from the nation to larger units of economic and social coherence: the region, the continent, the world. It is a world as envisioned by Rabindranath Tagore "not divided into fragments by narrow domestic walls. . . ." The idea of national self-sufficiency served the Western world only for a short time as means of effective growth. Indeed, the great travail of the Western world, its conflicts, rivalries, and wars have derived in no small degree from the fact that the nation, as such, has outlived its usefulness as an instrument of progress. Not even the great powers of today can stand alone, much less newly emergent states weak in everything but the will to grow. In this 20th Century World the sober fact is that a purely national economy is an illusion. We cannot start where, say, England started two centuries ago. We have to make our places in a world that has already made tremendous advances technologically and where economic inter-dependence has become the key to effective economic development and growth.

24. *Not only does the speaker refer to Coleridge, but to Rabindranath Tagore, Hindu poet and musical composer. Long popular in India, he gained an international reputation and was awarded the Nobel prize in literature in 1913. Tagore spent some time in America at Urbana, Ill. The speaker is a prophet. He envisions one world. He does not want the Asian-African nations to revert to nationalism. Communism seeks to divide the world. Many of his audience know English history, so they would appreciate the example. Go through the address and underline the word illusion. The speaker wants his audience to think in terms of facts rather than illusions and myths.*

25. Considering the present state of the world, with its profound conflicts and insecurities, this may be viewed by

25. *The speaker calls the audience to the new world. He envisions a nuclear world. Note the style of "ugly, painful, and*

costly." Why not profit by the mistakes of the West? Again the speaker is using refutation. He argues for peace in order to bring about economic growth. The speaker plants dreams in the hearts of his listeners. He inspires them. He appeals to their imaginations. What is said applies directly to the present audience.

some as a crippling disadvantage. But in a very real sense, and a more hopeful sense, it is rather an advantage if we can but grasp it. It means that we need not go through the equivalent of the decades and centuries of ugly, painful, and costly development which occurred in most Western countries. It means that if circumstances favor it, we can make use of the most ultra-modern technologies to transform ourselves more rapidly, to make new and hitherto unforeseen use of our resources. Who knows yet what the new potentialities of nuclear power are going to mean for Asia and Africa? It is obvious that the real world we live in does not at this moment offer much promise of any early opportunity to find out. But here we have one of the real stakes we all share in preserving the peace, in creating international instruments which will put man to work for man's growth instead of his destruction.

26. *Note the topic sentence. See how every sentence is a restatement of this opening sentence. See how he begins with "The fact is . . ." three times. Again the background of the speaker with the U.N. shows up. Throughout his address he deals with propaganda myths and pure illusion, and in paragraph 38 he hits hard at "bookish dreams." All these nations are a part of the world. This appeal for world cooperation is the theme of Chester Bowles' "The Fourth Consensus" in Saturday Review, June 16, 1956.*

26.   Our fate is bound up with the fate of the whole world. National isolation, in any real sense, is an impossibility in our time, whether we think of an ideal world uniting its human and natural resources for the well-being of all, or the real world, deeply divided and groping its way to decisions that will in one way or another affect every person on earth. The fact is that we will need greater world coherence than we have now if we are to thrive. The fact is that the effective mobilization of world capital and resources will be absolutely vital to us in the process of mobilizing our own capital and our own resources. The fact is that these things will depend in great measure on the further course of the conflicts that now govern all world affairs. It is pure illusion to think that we can be independent of these big facts.

27. But this by no means leaves us helpless to act in our own interest. It does not mean that we have no choice but to leave the great decisions to others. Quite the contrary. *Quite the contrary, because it is precisely in our lands, in our continents, that the most important decisions are going to be made. And it is we who will make them, by what we do or by what we do NOT do in the coming years.*

28. It could be that Russia's bombs or America's bombs will determine the future shape of the world and the fate of humanity. If it comes to that the tragedy will be total: it will make all we may say or do here or anywhere else quite irrelevant. Reason will die and the survivors will move as best they can into a new epoch of savagery. But I do not think the great decisions will come that way. I think the shape of the world is going to be determined in large measure *by the way in which the peoples of Asia and Africa go about the business of transforming their lives and their societies.*

29. What do we want? How do we propose to seek it? These are the questions on which the fate of the world really turns. In not fully understanding this, many in the Western world commit their most tragic blunder. For our part, we of Asia and Africa have to face up squarely to the big choices that lie before us. We have to try to understand as clearly as we can exactly what they mean.

30. There are certain things in all our minds on this matter. We all want to the best of our power and wisdom to seek change in terms of the genius of our own various cultures and histories. We

27. *Again the debater realizes what is going on in the minds of his audience. He refutes the question. Note the oral style of "Quite the contrary. Quite the contrary. . . ." The speaker suggests that decisions made to go communistic will affect what is enacted on the international scene. These words are italicized for their importance. This is why he is speaking; he wants the nations to remain free to act.*

28. *The debater goes one step farther. There is fear of Russia, and fear of America. If bombs fall then this will happen; then there will be no need to worry. But—and the speaker comes back to his theme—Asia and Africa must themselves decide to transform their societies. Back of these paragraphs we must see the thinking of the speaker. If you nations join Russia, you will not be free to transform your lives. What is the problem? What is the solution? The solution must come from the people themselves. The solution depends on what the Asians and Africans want.*

29. *In order to persuade we must speak to people's wants, desires, concerns and needs. The speaker tells the audience to face up to what it really wants. The speaker wants his audience to be reasonable. If we know what we want, we may be able to choose it.*

30. *Romulo seeks to analyze the wants of his audience. Any speaker who will speak to wants will have attention. Romulo is an Asian. He can speak as one. Contrast with the West commands attention. The speaker presents choices, alternatives. He is thinking*

*with them. He details the wants. What a
powerful figure is "alien graft"! The audience will agree as to the wants. Read paragraph 40 as to what Romulo thinks his
audience wants.*

all want no more foreign exploitation of
our wealth for the benefit of foreign
interests. We do not want our future
development to turn out to be another
alien graft on our lives. We want this
development to raise the physical and
educational standards of our peoples.
What roads lead to these ends? How do
we begin to face up to these vast and
formidable tasks?

31.   *How can these wants be achieved?
Here is the problem-solution speech. He
eliminates the magic-wand theory. Human
values are appealed to. It is not economic
growth just for the sake of economic growth
but for the betterment of people. Note how
the speaker links greater freedom with material growth. This phrase "of the people"
takes on significance when he contrasts it
with government by the elite few, in paragraph 33. Note the repetition of the sentence form.*

31.   There is no magic wand or automatic formula to bring about social and
economic change. It means that we have
to assume our own heavy responsibilities. It means mobilizing people, mobilizing resources. It means great toil, flexi-
bility, adaptability, intelligence. But it
also means defining our goal. Is our goal
just so many new industries or factories,
new dams or bridges or transportation
systems? Or is our goal the betterment
and the greater freedom, through these
and other things, of the lives of the
people?

32.   *Romulo elaborates what is back of
his remark. This is a paragraph leading into
the two choices before the delegates: communism and democracy. The speaker shows
his knowledge of the history of the various
conferences. He is no newcomer. In the
coming paragraphs we find the climax of his
thinking. The speaker carries credibility.*

32.   This is no simple rhetorical
question. Wrapped up in it are all the
troubled issues of our times. And because according to the joint communique
of the Bogor Conference "the basic purpose of this Conference is that the countries concerned should become better acquainted with one another's point of
view," may I outline for you our views
on the possible choices open to us.

33.   *Have you ever read a better description of the communist state than this?
Read this aloud and see how the phrases
follow each other. This is a very carefully
written paragraph. Remember that Chou
En-lai of Red China is sitting in the audience. Is not the road that he describes the*

33.   There is one road to change
which some countries have adopted and
which offers itself to the rest of us as a
possible choice. This is the road which
proposes total change through total
power, through avowed dictatorship and

the forcible manipulation of men and means to achieve certain ends, the rigid control of all thought and expression, the ruthless suppression of all opposition, the pervasive control of human life in all spheres by a single, tightly-run self-selected organization of elite individuals. I know that an elaborate series of phrases and rationalization are often used to describe this system. But I am concerned not with propaganda myths. I am concerned with realities. I think we all have to be concerned with what this system offers and what it means.

one pursued by Red China? Again, the debater knows what is in the minds of his audience and he refutes the "propaganda myths." Myths versus realities is one of the minor themes of the speech. Here is a good example of thinking in terms of semantics. The words and myths do not match the facts.

34. Does the road to greater freedom really lie through an indefinite period of less freedom? Is it for this that we have in this generation raised our heads and taken up the struggle against foreign tyrannies?

34. Here is a paradox. Repeat these questions and give them their power. The foreign tyranny of this paragraph leads into the next paragraph.

35. Has all the sacrifice, struggle and devotion, all been, then, for the purpose of *replacing foreign tyranny by domestic tyranny?*

35. Is not this question as incisive as that of Patrick Henry? "Is life so dear, or peace so sweet as to be purchased at the price of chains and slavery?" In paragraph 33 we had a description of domestic tyranny.

36. Do we fight to regain our manhood from Western colonial rulers only to surrender it to rulers among ourselves who seize the power to keep us enslaved?

36. This paragraph is a restatement of the idea of paragraph 35. Enslaved is a powerful word. Note the rhythm of these questions.

37. Is it true, can it be true, in this vastly developed 20th Century, that national progress must be paid for with the individual well-being and freedom of millions of people? Can we really believe that this price will, on some dim and undefined future time, be redeemed by the well-being and freedom of the yet unborn?

37. Read paragraph 31 again and see how it ties in with the thought of paragraph 37. It is the freedom of the people. The speaker confounds his audience with this question. He challenges the thought of the communists in his audience. These four paragraphs support the assertion by restatement.

38. *The speaker gives the answer of the communists to this question. Note how he ridicules the answer. What a descriptive phrase is "withering away of the state." He has studied communism. Even the communists have given up this myth. The minor theme of illusions and myths comes in. This is a good example of a paragraph developed by stating a principle. The speaker knows communist propaganda. The debater refutes the claims of the communists. He appeals to human experience. Remember that Patrick Henry appealed to the lamp of experience. The figurative language of the speaker again shows his power—"roots itself more and more deeply."*

38.   The philosophers of this system have answered this question through their doctrine of the so-called withering away of the state. But the rulers who have established their power in real life and not in the realm of bookish dreams have abandoned this tenet of their faith. We have had ample opportunity to witness over more than a generation now that this kind of power, once established, roots itself more and more deeply, gets more and more committed to perpetuating itself. Moreover—and the whole logic of human experience throws its weight into the scale—this system of power becomes inherently expansionist. It can not accept the premise of peace with opponents outside its borders any more than it can make peace with opponents inside its borders. It seeks and must seek to crush all opposition, wherever it exists.

39. *Again we have a fine example of the imagination of the speaker. He paints pictures. He makes you see, hear, smell and feel action. Remember the pro-communists were listening to this. The neutralists were there too. Here is a warning. Note such descriptive words as* crush, strewn, sweet-smelling, clangs—*all evocative. The policeman is the symbol of the total state. What thought and experience is in this last sentence! Recall how the top communists in Russia have destroyed each other. Is not this paragraph worthy of the rhetorical skill of a Winston Churchill?*

39.   This road is open before many of us. The gateway to it is strewn with sweet-smelling garlands of phrases and promises and high sentiment. But once you march through it, the gate clangs behind you. The policeman becomes master and your duty thereafter is forever to say aye. Even those who enjoy the role of mastery must know that this system devours its own.

40. *These last two paragraphs are the peroration. The speaker has been leading up to these. Note the "super-imperialism, super-barbarism, super-power." How effective the climax of the sentence "or, we must add, Moscow" is! How this sentence must have struck home! The enemies are not only London, Paris, The Hague, Washing-*

40.   No, my friends, I don't think we have come to where we are, only to surrender blindly to a new super-barbarism, a new super-imperialism, a new super-power. We do not want leaderships in our countries subservient to foreign rulers, be they in London or

Paris, The Hague or Washington, or, we must add, Moscow. I think our peoples want to worship the Almighty and live in accordance with His laws, to better their lot, to educate themselves and their children, raise themselves from the degradation of want and disease and misery, by holding up their own heads and acting freely to achieve these great and difficult aims by their own free means in partnership with similarly dedicated people everywhere in the world.

ton! Nehru and Chou En-lai thought they had this conference in their pockets. Official Washington looked upon it as a stage for communist propaganda. Here is a friend of the West, a friend of Democracy, changing the complexion of the whole proceedings. In paragraph 29 Romulo asked "What do we want"? The rest of this paragraph is an attempt to answer that question. Have you ever read a better description of democracy?

41. That is the freedom of the democratic way of life. That is the freedom we want all the peoples of Asia and Africa to enjoy. That is the freedom that President Ramon Magsaysay of the Philippines had in mind when he authored the Pacific Charter which enshrines the dignity of man, his well-being, his security, his progress, his nation's right to self-determination. The Philippine Delegation is here not only to reiterate the ideals of that Charter but to underscore in this Conference that it is the sense of the Filipino people that such right of self-determination includes the right of nations to decide exclusively by themselves their ability to assume the responsibilities inherent in an independent political status. This is the time for Asia and Africa to reassert this principle and serve notice to the world that only by its unqualified acceptance by everyone can there be peace and justice for all mankind.

41. *The Philippines are an example of democracy. Note the mention of the President, Ramon Magsaysay. Personalities always command attention. The speaker does not stand alone. He represents a nation. The last paragraph echoes the idea of man's dignity, man's estate. In this paragraph there is an echo of the main themes of the address, self-determination, independent political status. The final sentence calls for action. Note the cadence of the final phrase. (In a recent election President Magsaysay won 7 out of 8 Senators. The President had been criticized for being too pro-American.) Note the appeal for co-operation. This is an application type of conclusion. The speaker wants action. Again there is the appeal of "togetherness." Here is the answer to communism.*

THE RIGHT TO VOTE [1]

Equal Standards for All

President LYNDON BAINES JOHNSON

Delivered to a Joint Session of the Congress of the United States of America, Washington, D.C., March 15, 1965.

ROBERT J. KLEBERG, a Congressman from Texas, took Lyndon Baines Johnson with him as his secretary to Washington in December, 1931. While in Washington, Johnson attended Georgetown Law School. He remained with Kleberg until 1935, when he was appointed State Director of the National Youth Administration of Texas, a position he held until 1937. He resigned that year to run for the House of Representatives from the Tenth Congressional District. In a special election necessitated by the death of Congressman James P. Buchanan, Johnson was elected from a field of ten candidates on April 10, 1937. He ran for the Senate in 1948 against former Governor Coke Stevenson, whom he beat in the second primary by the slim margin of 87 out of one million votes. Johnson's skill as a parliamentarian was perfected during eight years as Majority Leader in the Congress. Many think he is one of the most skillful, if not *the* most skillful, ever known there.

Of special interest to the student of public speaking is the active part Johnson took in forensics both as a student and as a teacher. He attended Southwest Texas State Teachers College in San Marcos

---

[1] *Vital Speeches*, Vol. XXXI, No. 12, April 1, 1965, p. 354.

(near Stonewall, Texas, where Johnson was born on August 27, 1908). In April, 1924, his senior year in high school, Johnson and 14 other students from Johnson City journeyed to San Marcos to take part in the district meet of the Texas Interscholastic League. Johnson and his partner won third place in debate. At his graduation exercises he read the class poem.

Running out of cash to complete his college education, he accepted an offer to become principal of Welhausen Ward School in Cotulla at the end of his sophomore year. The Welhausen School had been opened two years earlier for Latin-American children. This teaching experience provided him with a vivid illustration for his speech on "The Right to Vote."

Returning to San Marcos with money enough to complete his college degree, he threw himself into the extracurricular life of his alma mater. He continued his interest in intercollegiate oratory and debate. He became editor of the college paper, and gave an indication of his future interests by playing college politics. William C. Pool tells us of his education along this line:

Campus politics was good experience for a future political leader like Lyndon Baines Johnson. Not only did he learn politics on a person-to-person basis; but, like so many *White Stars*, his college society, he learned parliamentary procedure as a member of the Harris Blair Debating Society, which was sponsored by Professor H. M. Green. He would divide the club into two groups telling one to take one side of a question and the other to take the other side. Then a resolution would be proposed. Perhaps it had no real practical purpose; but the two sides would battle back and forth, using all the parliamentary tricks they could think of to defeat or pass the resolution.[2]

In 1930, at the age of 22, Johnson took a position with the Sam Houston High School in the Department of Speech. A story is told about how he liked to win. He was congratulated by a fellow-teacher for the good sportsmanship exhibited by one of his students who had lost a debate. Johnson replied, "I'm not interested in how they lost. I'm just interested in how they win." Under Johnson's coaching Sam Houston High School won the city debate tournament, the first time this had happened. In the fall of 1930 Sam Houston was one of five senior high schools in the city, with a faculty of seventy and a student body of almost seventeen hundred. San Jacinto High School was the school to beat. In a citywide meet, representatives from Sam Houston won either first or second place in every event that they entered. Johnson has said that this year spent at Sam Houston was one of the happiest of his life.

The desire to win has motivated Johnson's life in Washington. He

---

[2] William C. Pool, *Lyndon Baines Johnson, The Formative Years* (San Marcos: Southwest Texas State College Press, 1965), p. 111.

made a conspicuous record as a Congressman and as a Senator. He was
in the right spot at the right time for Presidential nominee John F.
Kennedy to choose him as his running mate in order to swing the
South into his camp. He was Vice President from 1961 to 1963. He
succeeded to the Presidency on the death of John F. Kennedy. He won
again in his sweeping victory of 1964 and he found a Democratic
Congress ready to pass the backlog of old New Deal legislation. He
has been called "the ablest President of this century," "the most skillful Majority Leader ever known in the Congress," "political artist of
genuis," "one of the most powerful Presidents in the history of the
United States."

In his article, "A British Editor's Size Up of President Johnson,"
Michael Davie, Deputy Editor of "The Observer," London, England,
states that President Johnson is establishing himself as one of the most
powerful Presidents in American history:

Johnson had not long been in office before Washington became obsessed by
him. All Presidents, naturally, preoccupy the capital, but with Johnson it
was more than a preoccupation. Washingtonians assumed, to begin with,
that they knew all about him, since he had been around town for 24 years
as Congressman and Senator and three years as Vice President; but they
gradually became aware that he was an infinitely more mysterious, complex
and formidable character than they had realized. At the same time, the
capital observed Johnson's gradually establishing himself as one of the most
powerful Presidents in American history. Kennedy, toward the end of his
life, was running into a legislative impasse with Congress. . . . But Johnson
had scarcely settled in office before bills were coming out of Congress like
candy bars from a slot machine.[3]

To win he uses influence rather than argument. Like Lincoln, he
believes men are motivated by self-interest. He and his staff know
what a Congressman and his district need, where the Congressman is
weak and where he is strong, and in order to get votes they play upon
these self-centered interests. This is surely using Aristotle's definition
of rhetoric: finding every available means of persuasion in a given
case.

Here are a few of the titles of the President's speeches found in
Vital Speeches, speeches of high quality, ample evidence that belief
in the spoken word, which motivated him as a student and teacher,
still plays an important part in his political thinking: "U.S. Economic
Problems," December 15, 1964; "United States Vietnam Policy," April
15, 1965; "The Dominican Republic," May 15, 1965; "State of the
Union," February 1, 1966; "Vietnam," March 15, 1966; "A Stronger
NATO," April 15, 1966; "The Challenge of the Americas," May 1, 1966;

---

[3] Michael Davie, *U.S. News and World Report*, August 29, 1966, p. 41.

"The Need for Scholars," June 1, 1966; "Vietnam War," July 15, 1966; "United States Asian Policy," August 1, 1966.

In the September 10, 1966 *The New Republic*, we have an appraisal of President Johnson's speaking by T.R.B.:

You would never go out to hear him for Churchillian eloquence. Call it folksy, corny, anything you want, but he can create an intimacy with the normal crowd where he practically puts his hands on its shoulders and breathes in its face. . . . Some of the speeches have had high quality. We think they've been effective. He's gone on the offensive. He's grabbed headlines. Unfortunately for him, his style is poor for TV and radio; it sounds overblown; it doesn't travel well.

The speech "The Right to Vote" is one of high quality. Every student of public speaking can learn lessons in invention, arrangement, style and memory from it.

1. Mr. Speaker, Mr. President, members of the Congress, I speak tonight for the dignity of man and the destiny of democracy. I urge every member of both parties, *Americans* of all religions and of all colors, from every section of this country, to join *me* in that cause.

1. *In this opening paragraph note that the two themes are stated: the dignity of man and the destiny of democracy. Here is an application of the maxim, "First I tell them what I am going to tell them; then, I tell them; then, I tell them what I told them."*

Note in paragraph 72 the sentence: "For at the real heart of battle for equality is a deep-seated belief in the democratic process."

Note in paragraphs 19, 20, 21 and 22 the definition of dignity.

Note in paragraphs 5, 22, 71 and 72 the repetition of the theme "democratic process."

2. At times, history and fate meet at a single time in a single place to shape a turning point in man's unending search for freedom.

2. *In passing note the short paragraphs. Sometimes a single sentence is used as a paragraph. In fact, there are 37 single sentences used as paragraphs. This undoubtedly makes it easier for the speaker to read and grasp at a glance the meaning and bring out the thought by emphasis. In this paragraph we have a philosophy of history. Note the iambic stress in the order of the words.*

3. So it was at Lexington and Concord. So it was a century ago at Appomattox. So it was last week in Selma, Alabama.

3. *In this paragraph we have symbols of great connotation for Americans—The Revolution: Lexington and Concord; the Civil War: Appomattox. And then, in order to bring the matter down to the present, he uses Selma as a symbol.*

4.   *The speaker elaborates on the symbol of Selma. Note the title of the address, "The Right to Vote." Right becomes a keyword in the speech. Note the theme of American rights. The word* right *in one form or context or another is repeated 36 times. Note how the speaker goes from the general to the particular in referring to the death of the "man of God."*

4.   There, long suffering men and women peacefully protested the denial of their rights as Americans. Many were brutally assaulted. One good man—a man of God—was killed.

5.   *This paragraph is made up of three sentences: two sentences begin with "There is no cause. . . ." The third sentence is the contrast. Say these sentences aloud and note the oral style, the rhythm of the idea controlling each sentence. Pride is a motivating factor in our lives. The speaker indicates that no one can find satisfaction in what happened in Selma, where guns, police dogs and brutality were used. Note the structure of this paragraph. It is a favorite one of the writer of this speech. There are two negatives followed by an affirmative: There is no cause. . . . There is no cause. . . . But there is cause. . . . The word* America *or* American, *a term of identification, is repeated 28 times during the address.*

5.   There is no cause for pride in what has happened in *Selma*. There is no cause for self-satisfaction in the long denial of equal *rights* of millions of Americans. But there is cause for hope and for faith in our democracy in what is happening here tonight.

6.   *The arrangement of the words in this sentence shows care. Note the rhythm of the sentence, the rhythm of thought:*

For the cries of pain
and the hymns and protests
of oppressed people
have summoned into convocation
all the majesty of this great government—
the Government of the greatest nation
    on earth.

6.   For the cries of pain and the hymns and *p*rotests of o*pp*ressed *p*eople have summoned into convocation all the majesty of this great Government—the Government of the greatest nation on earth.

Throughout the address note how the speaker dwells upon the power of the United States. He praises what the audience is a part of. The idea of the strength of the United States is repeated in paragraph 62— "This great rich, restless country. . . ." In paragraph 67 he refers to the "Great Republic." In paragraph 94 he says, "The might of past empires is little compared to ours."

Note in the passage quoted the alliteration of "protests of oppressed people."

Throughout the address attention is given to the sound of words as well as to their meaning.

7. *Our* mission is at once the oldest and the most basic of this country—to *right* wrong, to do justice, to serve man.

7. *Glance through the address and pay attention to the mechanical construction of the sentences and paragraphs. Such a construction makes it easy for the speaker to use the teleprompter. This helps a speaker to make his address sound like talk. The speaker can grasp the thought and put the emphasis in the correct place.*

This sentence is reminiscent of Micah 6: "What doth the Lord require of thee, but to do justly, and to love mercy, and to walk humbly with thy God?"

Note the use of personal pronouns. The speaker includes the audience with his "Our." In this address we is used 33 times, our 43 times, you 15 times, I 53 times, us 10 times and my twice.

8. In *our* time *we* have come to live with the moments of great crisis. *Our* lives have been marked with debate about great issues, issues of war and peace, issues of prosperity and depression.

8. *Note how the speaker identifies the audience with what he is talking about. He is not afraid to repeat the word* great. *One of the stylistic devices of the address is the use of parallel structure:*

issues of   war and peace
issues of   prosperity and depression

9. But rarely in any time does an issue lay bare the secret heart of *America* itself. Rarely are *we* met with a challenge, not to *our* growth or abundance, or *our* welfare or our security, but rather to the values and the purposes and the meaning of our beloved nation.

9. *The appeal to love of country, to pride of citizenship, is a motive running deeply throughout the address. Note the reference to the "secret heart of America." The sentence structure found in this paragraph is used frequently throughout the address. It consists of three parts: Rarely are we met with a challenge, (1) not to our growth or abundance, (2) or our welfare or our security, (3) but rather to the values and the purposes and the meaning of our beloved nation. Note the emotional power of the phrase "our beloved nation."*

10. The issue of equal *rights* for American Negroes is such an issue.

10. *Here is the theme of the address restated. Here is an internal summary. Note the speaker does not say Negro but American Negroes. The word America, or American, is repeated 28 times. Here is common ground.*

11. *If the first ten paragraphs are the introduction, we now have the first point of the discussion, and that is that America has a purpose and that purpose is freedom for all. Here again is the familiar sentence structure of the three parts:*
(1) And should we defeat. . . .
(2) And should we double. . . .
(3) Then we will have failed as a people and as a nation.

11. And should *we* defeat every enemy, and should *we* double *our* wealth and conquer the stars, and still be unequal to this issue, then *we* will have failed as a people and as a nation.

12. *Again we have the Biblical tone and a direct quotation—Matthew 16:26. The implication is that the goal of America is freedom for every man.*

12. For, with a country as with a person, "What is a man profited if he shall gain the whole world, and lose his own soul?"

13. *Note how these four sentences build up to a climax. Note the short, incisive sentences. Here is a definition by negation.*

13. There is no Negro problem. There is no Southern problem. There is no Northern problem. There is only an American problem.

14. *This paragraph is an elaboration of the preceding one. If it is an American problem then Americans must solve it. The symbol* American *stands for unity.*

14. And we are met here tonight as *Americans*—not as Democrats or Republicans; *we're* met here as *Americans* to solve that problem.

15 and 16. *The audience is reminded of an historical fact. Note the polarization of the group around these phrases. Here is the cohesiveness factor. To stir up a response the speaker uses sentences that are engraved upon the minds and hearts of every American since childhood. The Declaration of Independence and memories of Patrick Henry are evoked. The philosophers in the audience might remember that John Locke, in his Essay* Concerning Human Understanding *(1690), enunciated the principle in his statement, "The liberty of man in society is to be under no other legislative power but that established by consent of the Commonwealth."*

15. This was the first nation in the history of the world to be founded with a purpose. The great phrases of that purpose still sound in every American heart, North and South:

16. "All men are created equal." "Government by consent of the governed." "Give me liberty or give me death."

17 and 18. *This is a paragraph designed to lead into the next. These phrases have been made alive through Americans giving their lives to make them come true. The phrase "and tonight" would stir up the response of the Dominican Republic and Vietnam.*

17. And those are not just clever words, and those are not just empty theories.

18. In their name *Americans* have fought and died for two centuries and

tonight around the world they stand there as guardians of *our* liberty risking their lives.

19. Those words are promised to every citizen that he shall share in the dignity of man. This dignity cannot be found in a man's possessions. It cannot be found in his power or in his position. It really rests on his right to be treated as a man equal in opportunity to all others.

19.   Here we have an echo of the first paragraph—dignity. There is further explication of these American concepts. Note again the use of the three sentences to expound an idea:
(1) This dignity cannot be found. . . .
(2) It cannot be found. . . .
(3) It really rests on his right. . . .
Here again is the stylistic device of the three: two negatives and a positive.

20. It says that he shall share in freedom. He shall choose his leaders, educate his children, provide for his family according to his ability and his merits as a human being.

20.   Here is further explanation of what these great phrases mean. Here is development by definition. What does "freedom" mean? The word freedom *is used in paragraphs 2, 21 and 65 also. Freedom is political, educational and economic.*

21. To apply any other test, to deny a man his hopes because of his color or race or his religion or the place of his birth is not only to do injustice, it is to deny America and to dishonor the dead who gave their lives for American freedom.

21.   Here is amplification by going from the less significant to the more significant. This paragraph is a summation of what has been said. The purpose of America will be denied and the lives of those who gave their lives will be dishonored. Note the beauty of the composition. Say it aloud and note how easily the phrases fall from the lips.

22. *Our* fathers believed that if this noble view of the *rights* of man was to flourish it must be rooted in democracy. The most basic *right* of all was the *right* to choose your own leaders.

22.   Note the identification in "Our fathers." The second part of the theme, destiny of democracy, is brought in here— "rooted in democracy." Political rights are the most important; with this right a man can secure the others.
The phrase "choose his leaders" is used as the development theme, appearing also in paragraph 20. The speaker is not afraid of repetition.

23. The history of this *country* in large measure is the history of expansion of that *right* to all of *our* people. Many of the issues of civil *rights* are very complex and most difficult. But about this

23.   Here the speaker brushes away all the debate over civil rights and states simply that what he is asking for is the right to vote.

there can and should be no argument: every *American* citizen must have an *equal right* to vote.

24. *The structure of this paragraph is, again, based on the idea of three:*
(1) *There is no reason. . . .*
(2) *There is no duty. . . .*
(3) *Yet the harsh fact. . . .*

24. There is no reason which can excuse the denial of that *right*. There is no duty which weighs more heavily on *us* than the duty *we* have to insure that *right*. Yet the harsh fact is that in many places in this country men and women are kept from voting simply because they are Negroes.

25. *The President supports his assertion that the Negro has been denied the right to vote by using facts: "Every device of which human ingenuity is capable has been used to deny this* right."
(A) *"The Negro citizen may go to register only to be told that the day is wrong, or the hour is late, . . .*

25. Every device of which human ingenuity is capable has been used to deny this *right*. The Negro citizen may go to register only to be told that the day is wrong, or the hour is late, or the official in charge is absent.

26. (B) *"And if he persists and, if he manages to present himself to the registrar, he may be disqualified because he did not spell out his middle name, or because he abbreviated a word on the application. And if he manages to fill out an application, he is given a test.*

26. And if he persists and, if he manages to present himself to the registrar, he may be disqualified because he did not spell out his middle name, or because he abbreviated a word on the application. And if he manages to fill out an application, he is given a test.

27. (C) *"The registrar is the sole judge of whether he passes this test. He may be asked to recite the entire Constitution, or explain the most complex provisions of state law.*

27. The registrar is the sole judge of whether he passes this test. He may be asked to recite the entire Constitution, or explain the most complex provisions of state law.

28. (D) *"And even a college degree cannot be used to prove that he can read and write. For the fact is that the only way to pass these barriers is to show a white skin."*

28. And even a college degree cannot be used to prove that he can read and write. For the fact is that the only way to pass these barriers is to show a white skin.

29. *The speaker uses restatement to support his assertion:*
"Experience has clearly shown that the

29. Experience has clearly shown that the existing process of law cannot overcome systematic and ingenious discrimination. No law that *we* now have on the books, and *I* have helped to put three of them there, can insure the *right* to vote when local officials are determined to deny it. In such a case, *our* duty must be clear to all of *us*.

existing process of law cannot overcome systematic and ingenious (here is an echo of the word ingenuity *from paragraph 25) discrimination. No law that* we *now have on the books, and* I *have helped to put three of them there, can insure the* right *to vote when local officials are determined to deny it. In such a case,* our *duty must be clear to all of* us."

This is a transitional paragraph. Having shown that the Negro cannot vote under the present laws, the President states that a new law is needed. Note the identification of the President with the subject—"I have helped to put three of them there."

30. The Constitution says that no person shall be kept from voting because of his race or his color. We have all sworn an oath before God to support and to defend that Constitution. We must now act in obedience to that oath.

30. *This would be II under discussion. The oath to support the Constitution is something all lawmakers have in common. See paragraphs 36, 40 and 43.*

The President summons the Constitution —here is an "argument from authority"—to his aid in preparing the way for what he is going to say. The subject is identified with the audience. The power of an oath is brought in for its persuasive effect. Aristotle refers to this as one of the non-artistic proofs. The five are: Laws, witnesses, contracts, tortures, oaths. (Rhetoric 1.15; Cooper, p. 80)

31. Wednesday, *I* will send to Congress a law designed to eliminate illegal barriers to the right to vote.

31. *The President is specific in what he is going to do. He prepares his audience for action. To persuade, a speaker must know what he wants.*

32. The broad principles of that bill will be in the hands of the Democratic and Republican leaders tomorrow. After they have reviewed it, it will come here formally as a bill.

32. *The President outlines the method of procedure.*

33. I am grateful for this opportunity to come here tonight at the invitation of the leadership to reason with my friends, to give them my views and to visit with my former colleagues.

33. *Note these factors:*
(1) *invitation (He is not an unwelcome guest.)*
(2) *reason with my friends (Here is a favorite phrase.)*
(3) *give my views*
(4) *visit with former colleagues*

34.   *Here the President is reasoning with his friends. He had intended to wait until tomorrow but he decided to submit the proposal to the clerks the same night. He is prepared to reason with his former colleagues in the Senate on the principal proposals of the legislation.*

The next four paragraphs (35, 36, 37 and 38) give the four main proposals:
  (1) *strike down restrictions in all elections*
  (2) *establish a simple, uniform standard*
  (3) *eliminate lawsuits*
  (4) *insure that properly registered individuals are not prohibited from voting.*

34.   I have had prepared a more comprehensive analysis of the legislation which *I* had intended to transmit to the clerk tomorrow, but which *I* will submit to the clerks tonight. But *I* want to really discuss the main proposals of this legislation.

35.   This bill will strike down restrictions to voting in all elections, Federal, State and local, which have been used to deny Negroes the *right* to vote.

36.   This bill will establish a simple, uniform standard which cannot be used, however ingenious the effort, to flout our Constitution. It will provide for citizens to be registered by officials of the United States Government, if the state officials refuse to register them.

37.   It will eliminate tedious, unnecessary lawsuits which delay the *right* to vote.

38.   Finally, this legislation will insure that properly registered individuals are not prohibited from voting.

39.   *The President continues his conciliatory tone. He welcomes suggestions. Is there not a note of humor in the aside?*

39.   *I* will welcome the suggestions from all the members of Congress—*I* have no doubt that *I* will get some—on ways and means to strengthen this law and to make it effective.

40.   *The President is conscious that he speaks against a wall of resistance. Here is the appeal to law—the Constitution. An*

40.   But experience has plainly shown that this is the only path to carry out the command of the Constitution. To

those who seek to avoid action by their national Government in their home communities, who want to and who seek to maintain purely local control over elections, the answer is simple: Open your polling places to all your people.

alternative is given: "Open your polling places." The speaker provides ways and means to attain the objective.

41.   Allow men and women to register and vote whatever the color of their skin.

42.   Extend the *rights* of citizenship to every citizen of this land.

43.   There is no constitutional issue here. The command of the Constitution is plain. There is no moral issue. It is wrong—deadly wrong—to deny any of your fellow *Americans* the *right* to vote in this country.

44.   There is no issue of state's rights or national rights. There is only the struggle for human rights.

41, 42, 43, 44.   These paragraphs elaborate and clarify the thesis. Here we have refutation by residues:
   There is no constitutional issue
   There is no moral issue
   There is no state's rights issue

45.   *I* have not the slightest doubt what will be your answer. But the last time a President sent a civil *rights* bill to the Congress it contained a provision to protect voting rights in Federal elections. That civil *rights* bill was passed after eight long months of debate. And when that bill came to my desk from the Congress for signature, the heart of the voting provision *had* been eliminated.

45.   The President shows his conviction and his confidence. He assumes that Congress will do as he asks. But he refers to history and points to the danger.

46.   This time, on this issue, there must be no delay, or no hesitation, or no compromise with *our* purpose.

46.   Here is determination and strength of will. Note the magic three: No delay, no hesitation, no compromise.

47.   *We* cannot, *we* must not refuse to protect the right of every *American* to

47.   Note   the   restatement—what   a powerful support of the thesis.

vote in every election that he may desire to participate in.

48. *Note the urgency in these paragraphs. The appeal is to do it now.*

48. And *we* ought not, and *we* cannot, and *we* must not wait another eight months before we get a bill.

49. *This paragraph serves as a clincher. The theme of 100 years is repeated in paragraphs 56 and 58.*

49. *We* have already waited 100 years and more and the time for waiting is gone.

50. *Here is an appeal for cooperation. The speaker is not demanding; he is pleading.*

50. So *I* ask you to join me in working long hours and nights and weekends, if necessary, to pass this bill.

51. *Back of this paragraph is not only Selma, but also Birmingham and the civil rights march on Washington. There has been much pressure on the President from Martin Luther King and other Negro leaders. Note the magic three again and the symbols used by the President: (1) conscience of a nation (see paragraph 70), (2) grave concern of many nations, (3) harsh judgment of history. Here is the question of right and wrong, the question of reputation—what will history think of us?*

51. And *I* don't make that request lightly, for from the window where *I* sit with the problems of our country *I* recognize that from outside this chamber is the outraged conscience of a nation, the grave concern of many nations and the harsh judgment of history on *our* acts.

52. *This is a summation of the previous discussion and a looking forward to what follows.*

52. But even if *we* pass this bill the battle will not be over.

53. *Selma as a symbol is repeated. All of America is involved. America is spoken three times.*

53. What happened in *Selma* is part of a far larger movement which reaches into every section and state of America. It is the effort of American Negroes to secure for themselves the full blessings of American life.

54. *The President widens his appeal. Note the figure of speech "crippling legacy of bigotry and injustice." Here is an appeal to the motive of power.*

54. Their cause must be *our* cause too. Because it's not just Negroes, but really it's all of *us*, who must overcome the crippling legacy of bigotry and injustice.

55.   And we shall overcome.

55.   *The President introduced the word* overcome *in paragraph 54 and here, like a repetition of the theme, he repeats the song of the Negro masses. He repeats this refrain in paragraph 63.*

56.   As a man whose roots go deeply into Southern soil, I know how agonizing racial feelings are. I know how difficult it is to reshape the attitudes and the structure of our society. But a century has passed—more than 100 years—since the Negro was freed.

56.   *When the speaker refers to the President of another party he stresses unity of desire, a national wish. Here the speaker reveals that he knows what he is talking about. He is speaking as a Southerner. This might be classified as reluctant testimony, and it comes with double force. Note the repetition of the "I know." Remember, in* Julius Caesar *Shakespeare has Antony say, "I am here to speak what I do know." The President has earned the right to speak on this subject. Compare this with paragraphs 88, 89, 90 and 91. The President again stresses the time lag of 100 years. This is repeated four times in the next few paragraphs.*

57.   And he is not fully free tonight.

57.   *Note the device of the short simple sentence. See paragraphs 10, 17, 42, 52 and 55. These sentences permit a speaker who is reading to emphasize.*

58.   It was more than 100 years ago that Abraham Lincoln—a great President of another party—signed the Emancipation Proclamation. But emancipation is a proclamation and not a fact.

58.   *Here we have a repetition of the "100 years." Here is the appeal to a witness —many historians think Lincoln to be the greatest President we have produced. Note also the definition by negation—"proclamation and not a fact."*

59.   A century has passed—more than 100 years—since equality was promised, and yet the Negro is not equal.

59.   *Observe the use of restatement to support his thesis of delay—"A century has passed. . . ."*

60.   A century has passed since the day of promise, and the promise is unkept. The time of justice has now come, and *I* tell *you* that *I* believe sincerely that no force can hold it back. It is right in the eyes of man and God that it should come, and when it does, *I* think that day will brighten the lives of every *American.*

60.   *Again we hear the same words: "A century has passed. . . ." Compare the opening of this paragraph with the preceding. Note the repetition, like the restatement of a theme or strain in a musical composition. Its style is reminiscent of the Psalms. It is antiphonal. He returns to his theme, that such action will free all Americans. This lifts the discussion to a higher level. All will benefit. See paragraph 7 for the use of the word* justice; *see paragraph 66 for* injustice *and, again, paragraph 70 for* injustice.

61.   *The paragraph is developed by the rhetorical question. The speaker widens his appeal. Do not do this for the Negro alone but do it for everyone. Note the figure of speech "scarred by fear," and the cadence of "hatred and terror."*

61.   For Negroes are not the only victims. How many white children have gone uneducated? How many white families have lived in stark poverty? How many white lives have been scarred by fear, because we wasted energy and our substance to maintain the barriers of hatred and terror?

62.   *Note the directness. This is no essay. This is direct communication: "And so I say to all of you here and to all in the nation. . . ."*
Observe the parallel structure: "all, (1) black and white, all, (2) North and South, (3) sharecropper and city dweller."

62.   And so I say to all of you here and to all in the nation tonight that those who appeal to you to hold on to the past do so at the cost of denying you your future. This great rich, restless country can offer opportunity and education and hope to all—all, black and white, all, North and South, sharecropper and city dweller.

63.   *The theme is now widened—poverty, ignorance, disease. He again defines by negation, a favorite rhetorical device. He repeats the three, this time changing the order for the sake of variety. And then comes the repetition of the theme that has so many overtones: "We shall overcome."*

63.   These are the enemies: poverty, ignorance, disease. They are our enemies, not our fellow man, not our neighbor. And these enemies too—poverty, disease and ignorance—we shall overcome.

64.   *The theme that all are involved is repeated. He is refuting any attitude of guiltlessness on any part of the audience. The President is careful not to point the finger at any one section.*

64.   Now let none of us in any section look with prideful righteousness on the troubles in another section or the problems of our neighbors.

65.   *Note the use of specific symbols. See how cities with the same initial sounds are linked together—Buffalo and Birmingham, Selma and Cincinnati—alliteration.*

65.   There is really no part of America where the promise of equality has been fully kept. In Buffalo as well as in Birmingham, in Philadelphia as well as Selma, Americans are struggling for the fruits of freedom. This is one nation. What happens in Selma and Cincinnati is a matter of legitimate concern to every American.

66.   *Note the use of the personal pronouns: us, own, our, us, our. There is a strong appeal to togetherness. Note the use*

66.   But let each of us look within our own hearts and our own communities and let each of us put our shoulder to the wheel to root out injustice wherever it exists.

67. As we meet here in this peaceful historic chamber tonight, men from the South, some of whom were at Iwo Jima, men from the North who have carried Old Glory to the far corners of the world and who brought it back without a stain on it, men from the East and from the West are all fighting together without regard to religion or color or region in Vietnam. Men from every region fought for us across the world 20 years ago. And now in these common dangers, in these common sacrifices, the South made its contribution of honor and gallantry no less than any other region in the Great Republic. And in some instances, a great many of them, more.

68. And I have not the slightest doubt that good men from everywhere in this country, from the Great Lakes to the Gulf of Mexico, from the Golden Gate to the harbors along the Atlantic, will rally now together in this cause to vindicate the freedom of all Americans.

69. For all of us owe this duty and I believe that all of us will respond to it. Your President makes that request of every American.

70. The real hero of this struggle is the American Negro. His actions and protests, his courage to risk safety, and even to risk his life, have awakened the conscience of this nation. His demonstrations have been designed to call attention to injustice; designed to provoke change; designed to stir reform.

of the familiar cliche "shoulder to the wheel."

67. *Here we have the longest paragraph in the address. There are 121 words here. This is a poem on patriotism. Note the symbols which stir emotion in the audience: "peaceful historic chamber," "Old Glory," "Iwo Jima," "Vietnam," "common dangers," "common sacrifices," "honor," "gallantry." This paragraph praises the South and its part in preserving the United States. Here is emotional proof.*

68. *The speaker restates his theme, that this is a problem that concerns the entire country. He uses the familiar symbols "Great Lakes to the Gulf of Mexico," but changes the next phrase to introduce variety: "from the Golden Gate to the harbors along the Atlantic." Usually the symbols are "from the rock-bound coast of Maine to California."*

69. *The speaker hammers home the idea that this is the duty of all Americans, and he presents it as a duty. Most reasonable people respond to and are persuaded by what they think of as duty. Note the force of "Your President." He does not let us forget that we are one with him; here is a powerful appeal to togetherness.*

70. *"His actions and protests, his courage to risk safety, and even to risk his life"—the theme now changes to emphasis upon the American Negro. This section praises the Negro but at the same time warns against violence. Law and order must prevail. Note the style: the Negro demonstrations have been designed: (1) to call attention to injustice, (2) to provoke change, (3) to stir reform.*

71. *In the first paragraph it was explicitly asserted that the dignity of man and the democratic process were the two themes. Now the President dwells on the latter.*

71. He has called upon us to make good the promise of America. And who among us can say that we would have made the same progress were it not for his persistent bravery and his faith in American democracy?

72. *Notice the antithesis in these sentences:*
"Equality depends, not on the force of arms or tear gas, but depends upon the force of moral right—
[Equality depends] not on recourse to violence, but on respect for law and order."
Here the President is repeating the idea that the Negro should obey the law.

72. For at the real heart of battle for equality is a deep-seated belief in the democratic process. Equality depends, not on the force of arms or tear gas, but depends upon the force of moral right— not on recourse to violence, but on respect for law and order.

73. *Back of this first sentence are many conferences with Negro leaders. The audience no doubt is thinking of these. In this paragraph the President seeks to persuade those who are antagonized by violence and by thwarting of the law. The next four paragraphs spell out the specific rights that must be preserved.*

73. There have been many pressures upon your President and there will be others as the days come and go. But I pledge you tonight that we intend to fight this battle where it should be fought—in the courts, and in the Congress, and in the hearts of men.

74. *Attention is called to the right of free speech and free assembly.*

74. We must preserve the right of free speech and the right of free assembly.

75. *Note in this paragraph the speaker's Texas manner of speech—*holler *instead of* yell.

75. But the right of free speech does not carry with it—as has been said—the right to holler fire in a crowded theatre.

76. *Again he emphasizes right to free assembly but gives the limitations.*

76. We must preserve the right to free assembly. But free assembly does not carry with it the right to block public thoroughfares to traffic.

77. *The right to protest is set in its proper context. The conviction of the President is evident in the words "I intend . . . as long as I am permitted to serve in this office." Here is no dictator.*

77. We do have a right to protest. And a right to march under conditions that do not infringe the constitutional rights of our neighbors. And I intend to protect all those rights as long as I am permitted to serve in this office.

78. We will guard against violence, knowing it strikes from our hands the very weapons which we seek—progress, obedience to law, and belief in American values.

79. In Selma, as elsewhere, we seek and pray for peace. We seek order, we seek unity, but we will not accept the peace of stifled rights or the order imposed by fear, or the unity that stifles protest—for peace cannot be purchased at the cost of liberty.

80. In Selma tonight as in every— and we had a good day there—as in every city we are working for a just and peaceful settlement. We must all remember after this speech I'm making tonight, after the police and the F.B.I. and the marshals have all gone, and after you have promptly passed this bill, the people of Selma and the other cities of the nation must still live and work together.

81. And when the attention of the nation has gone elsewhere they must try to heal the wounds and to build a new community. This cannot be easily done on a battleground of violence as the history of the South itself shows. It is in recognition of this that men of both races have shown such an outstandingly impressive responsibility in recent days —last Tuesday and again today.

82. The bill I am presenting to you will be known as a civil rights bill.

83. But in a larger sense, most of the program I am recommending is a civil rights program. Its object is to open the city of hope to all people of all races,

78. *Then, to sum up his emphasis against violence, he restates his position for law and order as opposed to violence. This placates those who are antagonized by the actions of some Negroes.*

79. *Again Selma is used as the symbol of the current waves of protest. Note that we is repeated three times. Here is a phrase ("peace cannot be purchased at the cost of liberty") reminiscent of Patrick Henry: "Is life so dear, or peace so sweet, as to be purchased at the price of chains and slavery?"*

80. *Reference to the current struggle in Selma, in the phrase "and we had a good day there," drives home the urgency of the address. Here we have the introduction of a new phase of the subject.*

81. *"As the history of the South shows" —here the President shows knowledge of his audience. "Heal the wounds"—this phrase is reminiscent of Lincoln's phrase in The Second Inaugural, "to bind up the nation's wounds." There is a persuasive note of hope.*

82. *After a seeming digression he comes back to the basic purpose of the gathering, the presentation of a civil rights bill.*

83. *Here again is a phrase that Lincoln used: "But in a larger sense, we cannot dedicate. . . ." What the speaker is presenting is more than a bill: it is a civil rights*

program. *Note the figure of speech "to open the city of hope . . ." This figure may have been suggested by the Bible, in which we find many references to the city of God. Here, too, is strong determination: "And we are going to give them that right."*

because all Americans just must have the right to vote, and we are going to give them that right.

84. *This paragraph begins with "All Americans. . . ." The speaker is not afraid of repetition. Note the emphatic quality the second time it is said. Usually a speaker saying a thing for the first time makes an assertion; the second time it is for the sake of implication. Here the implication is that nothing is going to stop all Americans from having the privileges of citizenship.*

84. All Americans must have the privileges of citizenship, regardless of race, and they are going to have those privileges of citizenship regardless of race.

85. *This paragraph is reminiscent of the "Great Society" theme. The speaker opens up the idea of privileges. How can one enjoy such privileges? He spells out what is necessary to be able to enjoy them.*
    Note the fine figure of speech "clutches of poverty."

85. But I would like to caution you and remind you that to exercise these privileges takes much more than just legal right. It requires a trained mind and a healthy body. It requires a decent home and the chance to find a job and the opportunity to escape from the clutches of poverty.

86. *He dwells on the obverse of the idea he has been explaining:*
    trained mind—never taught to read or write
    healthy body—stunted from hunger
    decent home and a job and escape from poverty—hopeless poverty and welfare check

86. Of course people cannot contribute to the nation if they are never taught to read or write; if their bodies are stunted from hunger; if their sickness goes untended; if their life is spent in hopeless poverty, just drawing a welfare check.

87. *The ideas are put graphically— note the striking phrase "gates to opportunity." Throughout the speech there are many such well worn but meaningful expressions. Another such expression is "shoulder to the wheel."*

87. So we want to open the gates to opportunity. But we're also going to give all our people, black and white, the help that they need to walk through those gates.

87 to 93. *Here is one of the great passages of the address. This comes from the experience of the speaker. A picture is painted. Here is conviction born of long years of living with a problem. There is a vivid sense of personal observation and of strong dedication.*

88. My first job after college was as a teacher in Cotulla, Texas, in a small Mexican-American school. Few of them could speak English and I couldn't speak much Spanish.

89. My students were poor and they often came to class without breakfast and hungry. And they knew even in their youth the pain of prejudice. They never seemed to know why people disliked them, but they knew it was so because I saw it in their eyes.

90. I often walked home late in the afternoon after the classes were finished wishing there was more that I could do. But all I knew was to teach them the little that I knew, hoping that it might help them against the hardships that lay ahead.

91. And somehow you never forget what poverty and hatred can do when you see its scars on the hopeful face of a young child.

92. I never thought then, in 1928, that I would be standing here in 1965. It never even occurred to me in my fondest

88. *The speaker becomes involved in what he is saying. Personal experience reveals something of the values, the motivations of the speaker. Here is personal proof. Note how the scene is dramatized: scene, characters, action. The narrative element holds attention.*

89. *One is touched by the concern of the speaker for these unfortunates. The speaker widens his theme to include more than Negroes. Murray Kempton, in commenting on Theodore Sorensen, a speech writer for President Kennedy, points out that Sorensen's style did not suit President Johnson, for Johnson wanted a speech writer who knew the power of emotional proof. He says:*

After Mr. Kennedy died, Sorensen tried dutifully to fit his implements—it is too much to call them talent—as a speech writer to the new President's service. He failed, and not only, one thinks, because he had no heart for it, but because his inhibitions did not suit Mr. Johnson's taste. The President has said that he likes his words to be put in order for him by writers who can cry a little.[4]

90. *Here is a time picture. Here is an idea that was originally intense and that has been recalled frequently. The audience warms to a speaker with such sympathy for the downtrodden.*

91. *Such memories are the stuff that speeches and stories are made of. Observe the emotional tug of "young child."*

92. *The mystery of life is contained in this sentence. The odd turns of circumstance are brought out. The dates are con-*

[4] Murray Kempton, "Sorensen's Kennedy," *Atlantic Monthly,* Vol. 216, No. 4, October, 1965, p. 74.

trasted. Suppose the speaker had used the 1928 date in paragraph 88.

dreams that I might have the chance to help the sons and daughters of those students, and to help people like them all over this country.

93. *Determination and conviction factors are prominent in these two brief sentences. The speaker knows what he wants. He believes in his cause.*

93. But now *I* do have that chance. And *I'll* let you in on a secret—*I* mean to use it.

94. *Here is the appeal to the audience for their help, and a reminder of the speaker's self-esteem. Pride in belonging to the "richest, most powerful country which ever occupied this globe" is appealed to.*

94. And *I* hope that *you* will use it with *me*. This is the richest, most powerful country which ever occupied this globe. The might of past empires is little compared to *ours*. But *I* do not want to be the President who built empires, or sought grandeur, or extended dominion. *I* want to be the President who educated young children to the wonders of their world.

95. *Here, from paragraphs 95 through 100, we have a personal commitment. What a beautiful statement it is! Five sentences begin with "I want to be. . . ." Contrast and comparison, as in "taxpayers instead of tax eaters" and "helped to feed the hungry," sounds like the Bible. The speaker seeks to link up what he wants with the desires, wants and concerns of Congress and the people of the United States.*

95. *I* want to be the President who helped to feed the hungry and to prepare them to be taxpayers instead of tax eaters.

96. *". . . Who helped the poor" again has Biblical connotations. Here is the major theme of the address—"the right of every citizen to vote in every election."*

96. *I* want to be the President who helped the poor to find their own way and who protected the right of every citizen to vote in every election.

97. *The emotions are stirred by this religious appeal—". . . who helped to end hatred . . . and who promoted love . . ."*

97. *I* want to be the President who helped to end hatred among his fellow men and who promoted love among the people of all races, all regions and all parties.

98. *Here is a moving climax, with its allusion to war as the scourge of mankind. The critics of Vietnam and Santo Domingo must be on his mind.*

98. *I* want to be the President who helped to end war among the brothers of this earth.

99. And so at the request of your beloved Speaker and the Senator from Montana, the majority leader, the Senator from Illinois, the minority leader, Mr. McCulloch and other members of both parties, *I* came here tonight, not as President Roosevelt came down one time in person to veto a bonus bill; not as President Truman came down one time to urge the passage of a railroad bill, but *I* came down here to ask you to share this task with *me*. And to share it with the people that *we* both work for.

100. *I* want this to be the Congress —Republicans and Democrats alike— which did all these things for all these people.

101. Beyond this great chamber— out yonder—in 50 states are the people that *we* serve. Who can tell what deep and unspoken hopes are in their hearts tonight as they sit there and listen?

102. *We* all can guess, from *our* own lives, how difficult they often find their own pursuit of happiness.

103. How many problems each little family has. They look most of all to themselves for their future, but *I* think that they also look to each of us.

104. Above the pyramid on the great seal of the United States it says in Latin, "God has favored our undertaking." God will not favor everything that we do. It is rather our duty to divine His will. But *I* cannot help believe that He truly understands and that He really favors the undertaking that we begin here tonight.

99. *The speaker makes it clear that he came by invitation. Note how careful he is to mention the various leaders, and the name of Mr. McCulloch in particular. He draws upon the examples of President Roosevelt and President Truman for contrast and comparison. He comes to enlist support for a great cause. Here is a new note, "the people that we both work for." Here is persuasion at work: the thought that we are in this together.*

100. *He stays with the theme of the American public. The speaker directs the attention of Congress to their constituents. Here is another sentence beginning with "I want." But is not the rest also a want of the audience?*

101. *Note the respect in the phrase "great chamber." Note the phrase "out yonder," which is a part of his Texan style of speech. Again there is the appeal to think of the "people we serve." The speaker is aware of his television audience.*

102. *The phrase "pursuit of happiness" is another evocative phrase. We know others when we know ourselves. There is an apt reference to the experience of the audience.*

103. *Note the emotional tone of "each little family." The President becomes the spokesman of the people.*

104. *In this final paragraph, one wonders if the writer of this address is not the same speech writer who wrote the sentence for President Kennedy's inaugural, when he referred to the seal of the United States in the words "The eagle in the seal of the United States has two claws, one bearing arrows, the other an olive branch." The seal is a familiar symbol to the audience.*
Note the appeal to God. Religion and patriotism are fundamental emotional factors in our lives.

A RHETORICAL ANALYSIS
OF THE TECHNIQUES
OF PERSUASION IN THE
SPEECHES OF BRUTUS AND
ANTONY IN *JULIUS CAESAR,*
Act III, Scene ii [1]

FOR THE TEACHER and student of public speaking the tragedy *Julius Caesar* offers an excellent opportunity for the study of rhetorical persuasion. In this play Shakespeare subordinated poetry to rhetoric. How interesting it is that we even find a rhetorician, Artemidorus, in the cast. From the beginning to the end of the play the speeches are persuasive. Almost every character is trying to persuade someone else and sometimes even himself. For example, the people are persuaded by the tribunes not to honor Caesar. Brutus is persuaded by Cassius to lead the conspiracy. Brutus has a session with himself in which he talks himself into murdering Caesar. Brutus, against his better judgment, is persuaded by Portia to tell her what he is up to. Caesar at first listens to Calpurnia and decides not to go to the Senate, but Decius has the last word and gets him to go. Brutus attempts to persuade the people to support him and his cause. Antony gets the mob to mutiny. The climax of all this persuasion comes in the Forum scene, the turning point of the play.[2]

---

[1] Used by special arrangement with Penguin Books, Inc. From S. F. Johnson, ed., *The Tragedy of Julius Caesar* (Baltimore: Penguin Books, Inc., 1960).

[2] See G. B. Harrison, *Shakespeare's Tragedies,* Ch. 4, "Julius Caesar" (New York: Oxford University Press, Inc., 1952); H. H. Furness, Jr., *A New Variorum Edition of Shakespeare,* "The Tragedie of Julius Caesar" (Philadelphia: J. B. Lippincott Co., 1912).

In this analysis the speeches of Brutus and Antony in the Forum will be compared and contrasted from the point of view of a teacher of public speaking.

*Enter Brutus and [presently] goes into the pulpit,
and Cassius, with the Plebeians.*

Plebeians. We will be satisfied! Let us be satisfied!
Brutus. Then follow me and give me audience, friends.
   Cassius, go you into the other street
   And part the numbers.
5   Those that will hear me speak, let 'em stay here;
   Those that will follow Cassius, go with him;
   And public reason shall be renderèd
   Of Caesar's death.
1. Plebeian.   I will hear Brutus speak.
2. Plebeian. I will hear Cassius, and compare their reasons
10   When severally we hear them renderèd.
      [Exit Cassius, with some of the Plebeians.]
3. Plebeian. The noble Brutus is ascended. Silence!
Brutus. Be patient till the last.

Brutus faces an audience that wants to know why Caesar was murdered—"We will be satisfied!" Brutus attempts to meet this want.

Brutus chooses his audience. Those who prefer him will listen to him; those who prefer Cassius' style will go with him. Remember, Clarence Darrow chose his audience—a judge, rather than a jury, in the Loeb-Leopold trial. Antony had to take the audience as it was. Did the dictator-oriented stay to hear Brutus?

"Public reasons shall be rendered. . . ." Adlai Stevenson in the 1952 campaign said, "Let us talk sense to the American people." Hans J. Morgenthau (The New Republic, August 7, 1965, p. 17), in his article "Stevenson—Tragedy and Greatness," might have been writing about Brutus, who refused to take the steps to insure the completion of his

III, ii, 1 *will be satisfied* demand a full explanation   2 *audience* a hearing   4 *part* divide   7 *public reasons* reasons having to do with the general good (?) reasons in explanation to the public (?) 10 *severally* separately   12 *last* end of my speech

*deed. Morgenthau
says:*

*"In order to understand
the substance of
Stevenson's greatness,
we must remind our-
selves that there are
two ways in which to
be great in the pursuit
of power. The search
for power ordinarily
entails, at least in a
certain measure, the
sacrifice of the intel-
lectual and moral vir-
tues. It is in the nature
of the struggle for
power that the com-
petitors must deceive
themselves as they
deceive others. Those
who have chosen
power as the ultimate
aim in life must use
truth and virtue as
means to their chosen
end and discard them
when they do not
serve that end. The
prototype of this
power seeker is en-
dowed with what
Russell Kirk in a
contemporary refer-
ence has called 'a
canine appetite for
personal power.' He is
a Borgia or a Stalin,
the Machiavellian
prince, who will stop
at nothing to gain and
hold the power he
seeks. His greatness
consists in that single-
minded, ruthless pur-
suit of power, of which
lesser-and better men
are incapable. They
stop at some point on
the road to power,
distracted and re-
strained by the com-*

mon virtues of intellect and ethics."[3]

In a sense Stevenson was like Brutus: the devoted, consistent idealist. Brutus was not ruthless enough. He stopped on the road to power. He committed three errors: He might have murdered Antony, Caesar's friend. He might have refused to permit Antony to speak. He might have listened to Antony speak and offered a rebuttal, the invaluable rhetorical advantage of the last word. Morgenthau suggests that Stevenson was not ruthless enough.

13 Romans, countrymen, and lovers, hear me for my cause, and be silent, that you may hear. Believe me for mine

13. Brutus's speech is in prose. This is the only example in all of Shakespeare that is in prose. It emphasizes the mistake Brutus makes in speaking in a condensed and epigrammatic style. Such a style for other reasons is charming but is not favorable to persuasion, at least as the staple of discourse; its office is to give point and memorable quality to what is elsewhere amplified. "Not that I loved Caesar less, but that I loved Rome more"—the speech is futile. It does

---

13 *lovers* dear friends *my cause* i.e. the cause of freedom

[3] Reprinted by permission of *The New Republic,* copyright 1965, Harrison-Blaine of New Jersey, Inc.

*not grip the citizens.
They fail to under-
stand what Brutus is
talking about. For
after Brutus speaks
against the Caesar, the
dictatorial, type of
government, one of the
citizens cries out, "Let
him be Caesar."*

*13.   Facts, rea-
sons, opinions and
examples are materials
of proof. Brutus uses
none of these. He
makes assertion after
assertion without
proof.*

*The speech is care-
fully composed but it
is totally without feel-
ing and imagination.
No doubt he expected
Antony to speak with
equal moderation. He
does not attempt to
move the feelings of
his hearers to sym-
pathy with him, but
the speech is argu-
mentative and logical
throughout.*

*15.   Brutus does
not feel that he has to
persuade the audience.
It is as if they already
agreed with him. He
makes an appeal based
on personal proof—
". . . respect to mine
honor." It is a speech
of self-justification.*

15 honor, and have respect to mine honor, that you may
believe. Censure me in your wisdom, and awake your
senses, that you may the better judge. If there be any in
this assembly, any dear friend of Caesar's, to him I say
that Brutus' love to Caesar was no less than his. If then
20 that friend demand why Brutus rose against Caesar, this

*21.   The appeals
are to abstractions, to
patriotism—". . .
loved Rome more,"
and to freedom—
". . . live all free-*

is my answer: Not that I loved Caesar less, but that I
loved Rome more. Had you rather Caesar were living,
and die all slaves, than that Caesar were dead, to live all
freemen? As Caesar loved me, I weep for him; as he was
25 fortunate, I rejoice at it; as he was valiant, I honor him;

---

15 *have . . . honor* remember that I am honorable   16 *Censure* judge   17 *senses* reason

men." Contrast these appeals to those of Antony, who motivates the common man through personal gain and self-interest.

Love is one of the keywords of the play. In one form or another, it is repeated 13 times.

but — as he was ambitious, I slew him. There is tears for his love; joy for his fortune; honor for his valor; and death for his ambition. Who is here so base that would

26. *Brutus asserts that Caesar was ambitious but he offers no proof. He is convinced of his cause but does not convince others. Everyone needs a personal hero. Brutus seeks to establish himself as the personal hero of the common man.*

be a bondman? If any, speak; for him have I offended.
30   Who is here so rude that would not be a Roman? If any, speak; for him have I offended. Who is here so vile that will not love his country? If any, speak; for him have I offended. I pause for a reply.
    All. None, Brutus, none!

29. *Note the refrain, ". . . for him have I offended." This is a good oral style.*

35 *Brutus.* Then none have I offended. I have done no more to Caesar than you shall do to Brutus. The question of his death is enrolled in the Capitol; his glory not extenuated, wherein he was worthy; nor his offenses enforced, for which he suffered death.

35. *To placate the audience Brutus states that all the courtesies have been rendered the dead Caesar. He does not want to offend anyone.*

Enter Mark Antony [and others], with Caesar's body.

40   Here comes his body, mourned by Mark Antony, who, though he had no hand in his death, shall receive the benefit of his dying, a place in the commonwealth, as which of you shall not? With this I depart, that, as I

40. *Here Brutus attempts to prejudice*

---

29 *bondman* slave   30 *rude* barbarous   36 *shall do* i.e. if Brutus should so offend   *question of* considerations that led to   37 *enrolled in* recorded in the archives of   37–38 *extenuated* understated   38 *enforced* overstated   42 *place* i.e. as a free Roman

the audience against Antony by saying that he shall receive the benefits of Caesar's death. But, again, the phrase "as which of you shall not?" does not spell out such benefits except in an abstract way (i.e., freedom).

44. *Brutus calls upon his nobility of purpose again. He offers personal proof, and suggests his high-mindedness and patriotism.*

slew my best lover for the good of Rome, I have the
45   same dagger for myself when it shall please my country
to need my death.
All. Live, Brutus! live, live!
1. Plebeian. Bring him with triumph home unto his house.
2. Plebeian. Give him a statue with his ancestors.

49. *A real communicator would have listened to the remark "Let him be Caesar," and tried once more to point out that what he was trying to do was to get rid of the Caesar theory of government. He did not persuade this part of his audience. Antony, by contrast, makes short speeches and follows the reactions of his audience.*

3. Plebeian. Let him be Caesar.
50 *4. Plebeian.*   Caesar's better parts
Shall be crowned in Brutus.
1. Plebeian. We'll bring him to his house with shouts and
clamors.
Brutus. My countrymen —
2. Plebeian.   Peace! silence! Brutus speaks.
1. Plebeian. Peace, ho!

55. *Cassius believed that Brutus was making a mistake in permitting Antony to speak. Brutus also makes a mistake in departing and not listening to Antony. Here intellect and ethics interfere with the pursuit of power.*

55 *Brutus.* Good countrymen, let me depart alone,
And, for my sake, stay here with Antony.
Do grace to Caesar's corpse, and grace his speech

---

44 *lover* friend   49 *ancestors* (see note at I, ii, 159)   57 *Do
. . . speech* show due respect to Caesar's corpse and listen respectfully to Antony's speech

Tending to Caesar's glories which Mark Antony,

> **58.** *Brutus requests that the courtesies due the dead be observed. Brutus suggests what Antony should speak about—"Caesar's glories." But Antony, like a good debater, does not permit the opposition to tell him how to frame his speech or what his theme shall be.*

By our permission, is allowed to make.
60 I do entreat you, not a man depart,
    Save I alone, till Antony have spoke.   *Exit.*
1. Plebeian. Stay, ho! and let us hear Mark Antony.
3. Plebeian. Let him go up into the public chair.
    We'll hear him. Noble Antony, go up.

> **59.** *Antony speaks by permission. What effect will this have on the audience? Brutus was so sure of himself and of his cause that he was not afraid of what Antony would or could say. Brutus could have prevented Antony from speaking. This puts Antony in Brutus's debt. Antony did not take part in the assassination. He was a friend of Caesar. Afterwards he is one of the triumvirate that rules. Presumably he would like to get rid of the assassins. Who knows that they do not know too much? Who knows but that Brutus and the others may strike again —soon? If he can start a witch hunt, while preserving his own skin and appearing to speak well of those who purged Caesar, he may do several good jobs for himself at once. Antony was a distinguished person, a*

---

58 *Tending* relating   63 *chair* pulpit, rostrum   65 *beholding*
obliged

top man of the state.
Brutus must have had
his reasons for not
purging Antony.

65. *Antony pays
his respects to Brutus.
The audience has been
swayed to Brutus's
point of view and
Brutus is held in high
regard. Antony capi-
talizes on this high
regard.*

⁶⁵ *Antony.* For Brutus' sake I am beholding to you.
                    [Antony goes into the pulpit.]

66. *The Plebe-
ians, sometimes trans-
lated* Citizens, *are not
slaves or mercenaries.
They are presumably
interested in the wel-
fare of the state. These
Citizens are an impor-
tant part of the scene.
It is through them that
we get the feedback
and the emphasis.
Here we have a report
on the speech of Brutus
and its effect. Note
that the Third Plebeian,
who said, "Let him be
Caesar," does not make
any further remarks
about Brutus.*

4. Plebeian. What does he say of Brutus?
3. Plebeian.   He says for Brutus' sake
He finds himself beholding to us all.
4. Plebeian. 'Twere best he speak no harm of Brutus here!
1. Plebeian. This Caesar was a tyrant.
3. Plebeian.   Nay, that's certain.
⁷⁰ We are blest that Rome is rid of him.
2. Plebeian. Peace! Let us hear what Antony can say.

72. *These three
words—"You gentle
Romans"—recommend
him to the hearts of his
audience. His grace,
his magnetism and his
choice of the word
"gentle" have taken
his audience captive
before he has spoken
at any length.
Antony is aware of
the prestige of Brutus
with the crowd. Did
Antony hear Brutus's
speech? Or did he have*

Antony. You gentle Romans —
All.   Peace, ho! Let us hear him.

friends listen and tell him what Brutus said? Antony knows the audience is for Brutus. Naturally Antony cannot say at the beginning, "I am going to rouse you to hunt down Brutus." In 1960, in the U.S.A., the Democrats were careful not to say anything against President Eisenhower, who had a tremendous hold on the people's hearts. Antony must speak against a mind set developed by Brutus.

Antony. Friends, Romans, countrymen, lend me your ears;
 I come to bury Caesar, not to praise him.
75 The evil that men do lives after them;
 The good is oft interrèd with their bones.
 So let it be with Caesar. The noble Brutus
 Hath told you Caesar was ambitious.
 If it were so, it was a grievous fault,
80 And grievously hath Caesar answered it.

73. *Antony banishes suspicion and secures confidence. The opening is not antagonistic to the mind set developed by Brutus. Antony ingratiates himself with the audience by speaking of the "noble Brutus." Antony settles on the proposition he wishes to consider— "Was Caesar ambitious?" Note the conditional syllogism: "If it were so . . ." This is just the point. Was Caesar ambitious? The audience would have to agree that Caesar had paid well for his ambition if he were.*

 Here under leave of Brutus and the rest
 (For Brutus is an honorable man;
 So are they all, all honorable men),
 Come I to speak in Caesar's funeral.

81. *Antony admits his indebtedness to Brutus for permitting him to speak. Does this not mean that Antony has a free*

---

80 *answered it* paid the penalty

hand to say what he wants to say?

Here is the beginning of the refrain on which Antony will ring so many changes. The words will take on different meanings as Antony proceeds. The refrain is repeated 3 times.

In permitting Antony to speak we see a modern parallel in Nixon's agreeing to debate Kennedy against the advice of President Eisenhower. Douglas made a fatal mistake in debating Lincoln. Cassius advised Brutus not to let Antony speak.

85. *Antony identifies himself with Caesar. The audience can understand friendship. Antony so far has refused to attack Brutus. The average man can understand a friendship that is faithful and just. In contrast, Brutus murdered his friend.*

85   He was my friend, faithful and just to me;

86. *Antony takes the text of his speech from Brutus. The word* ambitious *is repeated 6 times during the scene.*

But Brutus says he was ambitious,
And Brutus is an honorable man.

88. *Antony begins to refute the thought that Caesar was ambitious. Caesar filled the treasury with ransoms*

He hath brought many captives home to Rome,
Whose ransoms did the general coffers fill.
90   Did this in Caesar seem ambitious?

---

85 *just* entirely reliable   89 *general coffers* public treasury

When that the poor have cried, Caesar hath wept;
Ambition should be made of sterner stuff.
Yet Brutus says he was ambitious;
And Brutus is an honorable man.

95 You all did see that on the Lupercal
I thrice presented him a kingly crown,

Which he did thrice refuse. Was this ambition?
Yet Brutus says he was ambitious;
And sure he is an honorable man.

100 I speak not to disprove what Brutus spoke,
But here I am to speak what I do know.

of captives. There is no graft here, no personal loot.

91. *No doubt many in his audience are poor. Caesar's concern for them will touch their lives. Antony does not let his audience forget that he is still questioning whether Caesar was ambitious, as Brutus had said he was.*

95. *There is an appeal to experience in the words "You all did see . . ." Here is a vivid example, a fact: that Caesar did not take the crown showed that he was not ambitious. Therefore Brutus's proposition falls.*

97. *He had no ambition for personal power. The reaching for the crown was supposed to be the reason for the murder.*

100. *Antony is still careful not to clash with Brutus. He repeats his refrain.*
Antony is not speaking to disprove what Brutus said but is speaking only what he knows. ". . . I am to speak what I do know." Here is a guidepost for all speakers: use of personal proof and personal knowledge.

102. *Antony makes an appeal to his audience to remember. A speaker always speaks to a pool of memory—perhaps the memory of past military conquests.*

You all did love him once, not without cause.
What cause withholds you then to mourn for him?

104. *Antony declares he is appealing to reason, not to passion.*

O judgment, thou art fled to brutish beasts,

105. *Antony now changes the pace and the tone of his remarks. He gives the audience a chance to shift mentally and physically so that it does not go to sleep, become fixed or hypnotized or float away into its own phantasy. A speaker must periodically rest his audience by changing his approach.*

105 And men have lost their reason! Bear with me.
My heart is in the coffin there with Caesar,
And I must pause till it come back to me.
1. Plebeian. Methinks there is much reason in his sayings.

109. *The speeches of the Plebeians show the effect of Antony's words. Here we see that the people are beginning to change their minds.*

2. Plebeian. If thou consider rightly of the matter,
    Caesar has had great wrong.
110 *3. Plebeian.*   Has he, masters?
    I fear there will a worse come in his place.
4. Plebeian. Marked ye his words? He would not take the
        crown;
    Therefore 'tis certain he was not ambitious.
1. Plebeian. If it be found so, some will dear abide it.

115. *Cicero has said that if you want the audience to weep you must weep yourself.*
   There is an incident in the career of Woodrow Wilson, in speaking for the

2. Plebeian. Poor soul! his eyes are red as fire with
115   weeping.

---

114 *dear abide it* pay a heavy penalty for it

*League of Nations,
when he was overcome
with emotion and
cried:*

*"As he spoke of the
dead boys in the graves
at Suresnes, Joe
Tumulty, standing in
the wings of the
auditorium, saw down
in the audience men
and women alike
reaching for handker-
chiefs to wipe their
eyes.*

*" 'There seems to me
to stand between us
and the rejection of
this treaty the serried
ranks of those boys in
khaki, not only those
boys who came home,
but those dear ghosts
who still deploy upon
the fields of France.'*

*"He halted. The
people looked at him
and he at them.*

*"The President of
the United States,
standing before an aud-
ience of some several
thousands of his fellow
citizens, was crying."*[4]

116 3. *Plebeian.* There's not a nobler man in Rome than
Antony.

4. *Plebeian.* Now mark him. He begins again to speak.

116. *Without
attacking Brutus
Antony has now won
over the audience to
his point of view—
"There's not a nobler
man in Rome than
Antony." The first part
of the speech is now
complete. He now pro-
ceeds to make Caesar
a national hero.*

4 Gene Smith, *When
the Cheering Stopped*
(New York: William
Morrow & Co., Inc.,
1964), p. 82.

118.   *Respect for Caesar's reputation is appealed to.*

Antony. But yesterday the word of Caesar might
      Have stood against the world. Now lies he there,
120   And none so poor to do him reverence.

121.   *Again we have a change of pace, a change of tone. Here is a musing recapitulation. He stirs up memories. He flatters his audience by calling them masters, as they are in a Republic. Having signalled to his audience thus that he is speaking again, he now hits them hard with a clarion exclamation: "O masters! If I were disposed to stir . . ." He thus disarms them.*

O masters! If I were disposed to stir
Your hearts and minds to mutiny and rage,

123.   *Antony still treads lightly in mentioning Brutus and Cassius. There is yet some respect left for them in the minds of the audience.*

I should do Brutus wrong, and Cassius wrong,
Who, you all know, are honorable men.
125   I will not do them wrong. I rather choose
To wrong the dead, to wrong myself and you,
Than I will wrong such honorable men.

128.   *Anything with a seal on it is a matter of curiosity. We want to know what is inside. Suspense, the uncertain, is introduced. He teases their interest by giving a hint as to what the will contains. Antony makes little or no appeal to patriotism or to freedom, as Brutus has done. Antony's appeal has to do with self-interest, with material possessions, with the regard that someone,*

But here's a parchment with the seal of Caesar.
I found it in his closet; 'tis his will.

---

120 *so poor* base enough   122 *mutiny* riot   129 *closet* study (?) cabinet for private papers (?)

*the great Caesar, had
for them—". . .
Caesar loved you."*

130 Let but the commons hear this testament,
     Which (pardon me) I do not mean to read,
     And they would go and kiss dead Caesar's wounds
     And dip their napkins in his sacred blood;
     Yea, beg a hair of him for memory,
135 And dying, mention it within their wills,
     Bequeathing it as a rich legacy
     Unto their issue.
     4. Plebeian. We'll hear the will! Read it, Mark Antony.
     All. The will, the will! We will hear Caesar's will!
140 *Antony.* Have patience, gentle friends; I must not read it.
     It is not meet you know how Caesar loved you.
     You are not wood, you are not stones, but men;
     And being men, hearing the will of Caesar,
     It will inflame you, it will make you mad.

130.   *Before An-
tony discloses what
is in Caesar's will, he
predicts to the crowd
how they will act when
he does tell them of its
contents. Here is
powerful use of sug-
gestion. He then flat-
ters them—"You are
. . . but men."*

145 'Tis good you know not that you are his heirs;
     For if you should, O, what would come of it?
     4. Plebeian. Read the will! We'll hear it, Antony!
     You shall read us the will, Caesar's will!

145.   *Note the
monosyllables. This
slows down the pace.
Say this line aloud and
note the effect.*

     Antony. Will you be patient? Will you stay awhile?
150 I have o'ershot myself to tell you of it.
     I fear I wrong the honorable men
     Whose daggers have stabbed Caesar; I do fear it.

149.   *Brutus had
asked Antony to re-
count the heroic events
of Caesar's life. In-
stead, he has brought
out the will. He uses as
an excuse for not read-
ing the will that it
would displease Brutus
and Cassius and the
others "whose daggers
have stabbed Caesar."*

     4. Plebeian. They were traitors. Honorable men!
     All. The will! the testament!
155 *2. Plebeian.* They were villains, murderers! The will!
     Read the will!

153.   *The audi-
ence answers "traitors"
—a word Antony has
been asking for. The
audience uses the term
"honorable men!" in*

---

130 *commons* plebeians   133 *napkins* handkerchiefs   141 *meet*
fitting that   149 *stay* wait   150 *o'ershot myself* gone further than
I intended

*scorn. It has finally
been completely won
over!*

*The purpose of
the second part of the
speech has now been
accomplished. It only
remains now for
Antony to get the
crowd to do his
bidding.*

157. *He has
worked up the crowd
to want to do his
bidding. The crowd
would not have lis-
tened to the will after
Brutus had spoken.*

Antony. You will compel me then to read the will?

158. *Antony
makes use of a visual
aid. Henry Ward
Beecher said that he
could not take up a
collection to free some
girl slaves unless they
were present in his
pulpit. This is drama.
First Antony shows the
mantle, then he shows
the body.*

Then make a ring about the corpse of Caesar
And let me show you him that made the will.

160. *Antony
comes nearer his audi-
ence at its request. He
wants to do as they
desire. Public speakers
in earnest like to be
one of the group; they
do not want to stand
off.*

160 Shall I descend? and will you give me leave?
All. Come down.
2. Plebeian. Descend.
3. Plebeian. You shall have leave. *[Antony comes down.]*
4. Plebeian. A ring! Stand round.
165 *1. Plebeian.* Stand from the hearse! Stand from the body!

166. *"Most noble
Antony!"—Antony wins
their regard.*

2. Plebeian. Room for Antony, most noble Antony!
Antony. Nay, press not so upon me. Stand far off.
All. Stand back! Room! Bear back!

169. *"If you have
tears . . ."—here is*

Antony. If you have tears, prepare to shed them now.
170 You all do know this mantle. I remember

---

165 *hearse* bier   167 *far* farther   168 *Bear* move   170 *mantle*
cloak (here toga)

The first time ever Caesar put it on.
'Twas on a summer's evening in his tent,

That day he overcame the Nervii.

Look, in this place ran Cassius' dagger through.
175 See what a rent the envious Casca made.

Through this the well-belovèd Brutus stabbed;
And as he plucked his cursèd steel away,
Mark how the blood of Caesar followed it,
As rushing out of doors to be resolved
180 If Brutus so unkindly knocked or no;
For Brutus, as you know, was Caesar's angel.

appeal to emotion. "This mantle"—here is a symbol. Man is a symbolic animal. Symbols evoke memories. Antony paints pictures with words—" 'Twas on a summer's evening in his tent. . . ." Note the contrast and comparison: the mantle then and the mantle now.

173. *Nervii was one of Caesar's greatest victories.*

174. *Now Antony makes bold to name each one of the conspirators who ran the dagger into Caesar. He calls Casca "envious," and he calls Brutus the "well-belovèd."*

The assembly which Antony harangues is composed entirely of citizens and veterans of Caesar's army. To the citizens these words say, "See, that Caesar who has delivered you from your fears, who has given safety to your wives and children."

176. *Antony still will not speak ill of Brutus but lets the events speak for themselves. Antony lets the audience judge the actions of what a man did to his dear friend.*

173 *Nervii* a tribe defeated in 57 B.C. in one of the most decisive victories in the Gallic Wars   175 *envious* malicious   179 *be resolved* learn for certain   180 *unkindly* unnaturally and cruelly   181 *angel* 'darling,' i.e. favorite who could do no wrong

All men can under-
stand friendship. Here
is the meanest of crea-
tures: the one who
stabs his best friend.
All men can under-
stand ingratitude. It
was Brutus's stab that
killed Caesar.

185.   *Here, for the*
first time, Antony uses
the word "traitor."
More than the thrust
of the traitor, it was
the ingratitude of the
killer that overcame
Caesar. All men can
understand this "mar-
ble-hearted fiend."

188.   *Now Pom-*
pey and Caesar are
somehow connected as
martyrs for Rome,
although just a few
weeks ago the crowd
had celebrated the
defeat of Pompey by
Caesar.

190.   *Here is the*
appeal to "together-
ness." This is some-
thing that the speaker
and the audience share.

195.   *Here is the*
subtle suggestion that
"you have seen noth-
ing yet." The speaker
goes from climax to
climax. Again Antony
uses the word "trai-
tors." He amplifies by

Judge, O you gods, how dearly Caesar loved him!
This was the most unkindest cut of all;
For when the noble Caesar saw him stab,

185   Ingratitude, more strong than traitors' arms,
       Quite vanquished him. Then burst his mighty heart;
       And in his mantle muffling up his face,

Even at the base of Pompey's statue
(Which all the while ran blood) great Caesar fell.

190   O, what a fall was there, my countrymen!
       Then I, and you, and all of us fell down,
       Whilst bloody treason flourished over us.
       O, now you weep, and I perceive you feel
       The dint of pity. These are gracious drops.

195   Kind souls, what weep you when you but behold
       Our Caesar's vesture wounded? Look you here!
       Here is himself, marred as you see with traitors.
       1. Plebeian. O piteous spectacle!

---

183 *most unkindest* cruelest and most unnatural   188 *base* ped-
estal   *statue* (trisyllabic)   192 *flourished* swaggered and bran-
dished its sword in triumph   194 *dint* impression   *gracious* full of
grace, becoming   195 *what* why   196 *vesture* i.e. the mantle
197 *marred* mangled   *with* by

going from the less significant to the more significant.

199. *"O noble Caesar!"—it has been "O noble Brutus!" "O noble Antony!" Now it is "O noble Caesar!" But in line 68 it was "This Caesar was a tyrant."*

2. Plebeian. O noble Caesar!
200 *3. Plebeian.* O woeful day!
4. Plebeian. O traitors, villains!
1. Plebeian. O most bloody sight!

2. Plebeian. We will be revenged.
[All.] Revenge! About! Seek! Burn! Fire! Kill! Slay!
205 Let not a traitor live!

203. *Revenge is a common theme in Elizabethan dramatic literature.*

Antony. Stay, countrymen.
1. Plebeian. Peace there! Hear the noble Antony.

206. *Antony seeks to slow down the mob, in order to play his trump card.*

2. Plebeian. We'll hear him, we'll follow him, we'll die with him!

208. *Note the climax—"hear," "follow," "die." "Stay, countrymen" provides identification. The citizens begin to swing over still more to Antony.*

Antony. Good friends, sweet friends, let me not stir you
210 up
To such a sudden flood of mutiny.
They that have done this deed are honorable.

210. *Notice the epithet "sweet." This is one of the most common adjectives in all of Shakespeare. See also line 224: "sweet Caesar's wounds."*

What private griefs they have, alas, I know not,
That made them do it. They are wise and honorable,
215 And will no doubt with reasons answer you.
I come not, friends, to steal away your hearts.
I am no orator, as Brutus is,
But (as you know me all) a plain blunt man
That love my friend; and that they know full well
220 That gave me public leave to speak of him.

213. *Antony still effaces himself. He says he cannot understand why this deed was done. He will not accuse the murderers. He points out that they are not answerable to him but to the audience. He holds the*

---

204 *About* to work   206 *Stay* wait   213 *private griefs* personal grievances   220 *public . . . speak* permission to speak in public

*crowd in check in order
to fan them into a still
higher rage. Antony
suggests that the mur-
derers had private
reasons. He touches
the imagination of the
crowd. What did they
personally expect to
gain from the murder
of Caesar? We all like
humility in a speaker;
when Antony says, "I
am no orator, as Brutus
is," he plays down his
own power. Antony
recommends himself to
his audience by saying
that he is a "plain
blunt man." But his
speech shows him to be
anything but plain and
blunt. He is not
sophisticated, as Brutus
is. One of the common
denominators of emo-
tion is love. Is he not
saying, too, that if
these friends had
thought that he had
the power of speech
they would not have
given him leave to
speak? Antony wants
the crowd to believe
that he is not taking
advantage of the situa-
tion. His motives
should seem above
reproach.*

221. *Here is a
description of what the
effective speaker
should have as equip-
ment. Note that he*

221   For I have neither writ, nor words, nor worth,
      Action, nor utterance, nor the power of speech
      To stir men's blood. I only speak right on.
      I tell you that which you yourselves do know,

---

221 *writ* a written-out speech (most editors emend to *wit,* i.e.
invention, which accords with the rest of the list of qualities of a
good orator that follows)   *words* fluency   *worth* stature as a
public figure, authority   222 *Action* skilful use of gesture   *utterance* good delivery   223 *right on* straight out, just as I think it

225 Show you sweet Caesar's wounds, poor poor dumb
mouths,

says he has no prepared speech. He has no vocabulary. He has no worth, no stature, no reputation. Here is, however, a principle of public speaking which all speakers should observe—"I tell you that which you yourselves do know." Henry Ward Beecher, the greatest preacher of the 19th century, claimed he did not learn how to preach until he started using the "you all knows." The speaker must get on common ground. He must identify with his audience. (See Yale Lectures on Preaching, 1st Series [New York: Ford and Co., 1872], p. 11.)

And bid them speak for me. But were I Brutus,
And Brutus Antony, there were an Antony

226. *Here is an enthymeme, an abridged syllogism based on probability. Aristotle said this was one of the two forms of proof. The other is example, and Antony has used examples. If Antony were Brutus, he could ruffle up your spirits. Antony is no Brutus. Therefore, Antony cannot ruffle up your spirits.*

Would ruffle up your spirits, and put a tongue
In every wound of Caesar that should move
230 The stones of Rome to rise and mutiny.
All. We'll mutiny.
1. Plebeian. We'll burn the house of Brutus.
3. Plebeian. Away then! Come, seek the conspirators.

228. *But Antony has already "put a tongue in every wound of Caesar."*

---

228 *ruffle up* stir to rage

233. *Again Antony pulls in the reins. He wants to prod the crowd still further.*

Antony. Yet hear me, countrymen. Yet hear me speak.
All. Peace, ho! Hear Antony, most noble Antony!
Antony. Why, friends, you go to do you know not
235   what.

236. *Antony reminds the crowd that they do not yet have the proper motivation to do what they propose. You really do not know why Caesar deserved your loves. Here is the trump card—the will. Here is the document, the mention of which in line 128 turned the crowd against Brutus; but they have still not heard it. The crowd is inflamed already but what will they do when they hear the details of the will?*

Wherein hath Caesar thus deserved your loves?
Alas, you know not! I must tell you then.
You have forgot the will I told you of.
All. Most true! The will! Let's stay and hear the will.

240. *Anything with a seal on it arouses interest and curiosity.*

240 *Antony.* Here is the will, and under Caesar's seal.
        To every Roman citizen he gives,

242. *Note the difference in the speech of Brutus (which was abstract) and the speech of Antony (which is concrete). Note the appeal to self-interest and the desire for property—75 drachmas. Brutus promises freedom; Antony promises personal gain. It is as if Antony had studied motivational research. Antony is a hidden persuader.*

        To every several man, seventy-five drachmas.
        2. *Plebeian.* Most noble Caesar! We'll revenge his death!
        3. *Plebeian.* O royal Caesar!
245 *Antony.* Hear me with patience.
        All. Peace, ho!
        Antony. Moreover, he hath left you all his walks,

---

242 *several* individual *seventy-five drachmas* about $30 to-day
244 *royal* nobly munificent 247 *walks* (see note at I, ii, 155)

He knows the realities of human motivation behavior. How vague Brutus's promise is when compared with Antony's. Brutus said, "Mark Antony, who, though he had no hand in his death, shall receive the benefit of his dying, a place in the common-wealth, as which of you shall not?" There is no detail here as there is in Antony's speech.

His private arbors, and new-planted orchards,
On this side Tiber; he hath left them you,
250 And to your heirs for ever — common pleasures,
To walk abroad and recreate yourselves.
Here was a Caesar! When comes such another?

248. *Antony calls attention to Caesar's love of the common people by citing the emperor's estate left as a park for their use. Note the use of the question and of his contact with the audience.*

1. *Plebeian.* Never, never! Come, away, away!
We'll burn his body in the holy place

253. *Antony gets the response he wants. The audience is moved to action.*

255 And with the brands fire the traitors' houses.
Take up the body.
2. *Plebeian.* Go fetch fire!
3. *Plebeian.* Pluck down benches!
4. *Plebeian.* Pluck down forms, windows, anything!
                      Exit Plebeians [with the body].

255. *From an attitude in line 68, " 'Twere best he speak no harm of Brutus here" and "This Caesar was a tyrant," Antony has swung the attitude to, "And with the brands fire the traitors' houses."*

260 *Antony.* Now let it work. Mischief, thou art afoot,
Take thou what course thou wilt.

260. *Antony has moved the crowd to*

---

248 *orchards* gardens   250 *common pleasures* public parks   254
holy place where the most sacred temples were in Rome   258
Pluck down wrench loose, tear out   259 *forms* long benches
windows shutters   260 *work* have its full effect

*do his will. He has
persuaded the crowd,
which was his aim.
They will do his work
for him.*

*Contrast Brutus's
speech with that of
Antony. In one we
have abstractions, in
the other concrete-
nesses. Brutus is so
high-minded that he
does not realize he did
not get his message
across to the audience.
Brutus is so sure of
himself that he does
not even stay to listen
to Antony's funeral
speech.*

*Antony's speech
takes into account
the needs, wants
and desires of his
audience. The repeti-
tion of words, phrases
and sentences in dif-
ferent settings subtly
changes the meanings.
There is appeal to
sentiment, affection,
gratitude and self-
interest. Brutus, in
contrast, makes little
contact with his audi-
ence. Antony gets into
their minds and hearts.*

*Brutus, in a sense,
prepared the audience
for Antony by making
the audience hostile
to him. Yet, a speaker
might fight better with
an antagonistic audi-
ence than with an
indifferent one.*

*Antony, or an ac-
complice, must have
listened to the pre-
vious speech for the
three points that
Brutus made: (1) that*

*Caesar was ambitious;
(2) that his murder
was a good deed for
the sake of Rome; and
(3) that the murderers
are therefore honor-
able men. As a good
debater Antony must
destroy the effect of
each of these
three ideas.*

COLLECTIONS OF SPEECHES

Arnold, Carroll C. and Ehninger, Douglas, *The Speaker's Resource Book* (Chicago: Scott, Foresman and Company, 1961)

Baird, A. Craig, *American Public Addresses: 1740–1952* (New York: McGraw-Hill, Inc., 1956)

Berquist, Goodwin F., Jr., *Speeches for Illustration and Example* (Chicago: Scott, Foresman and Company, 1965)

Black, Edwin and Kerr, Harry P., *American Issues: A Sourcebook for Speech Topics* (New York: Harcourt, Brace & World, Inc., 1961)

Brandt, Carl G. and Shafter, Edward M., *Selected American Speeches on Basic Issues* (Boston: Houghton Mifflin Company, 1960)

Brigance, William Norwood, *Classified Speech Models* (New York: F. S. Crofts & Co., 1928)

Byron, B. G. and Coudert, F. R., *America Speaks* (New York: Modern Eloquence Corporation, 1928)

Copeland, Lewis, *World's Great Speeches* (New York: Dover Publications, Inc., 1957)

Harding, S. B., *Select Orations Illustrating American History* (New York: The Macmillan Co., 1924)

Hastings, William T., *Man Thinking: Representative Phi Beta Kappa Orations, 1915–1959* (Ithaca: Cornell University Press, 1962)

Hurd, Charles, *Treasury of Great American Speeches* (New York: Hawthorn Books, Inc., 1959)

Lindgren, Homer D., *Modern Speeches* (New York: F. S. Crofts & Co., 1930)

Linkugel, Wil A., Allen, R. R. and Johannesen, Richard L., *Contemporary American Speeches* (Belmont, Calif.: Wadsworth Publishing Co., Inc., 1965)

O'Neill, J. M., *Models of Speech Composition* (New York: The Century Co., 1922)

Parrish, W. M. and Hochmuth, M., *American Speeches* (New York: Longmans, Green & Co., Inc., 1954)

Peterson, Houston, *World's Great Speeches* (New York: Simon and Schuster, Inc., 1965)

Representative American Speeches, Published annually in *The Reference Shelf* (New York: H. W. Wilson Co.)

Wrage, Ernest J. and Baskerville, Barnet, *American Forum: Speeches on Historic Issues,* 1788–1900 (New York: Harper & Row, Publishers, 1960)

———, *Contemporary Forum: American Speeches on Twentieth-Century Issues* (New York: Harper & Row, Publishers, 1962)

DISCOGRAPHY*

Churchill, Winston, *I Can Hear It Now*   Col. KOL-7000

———, *Famous Wartime Speeches* (1-64)   2-Cap. TBO-2192

Eisenhower, Dwight D., *Inaugural Addresses,* '53, '57 (with Kennedy on reverse side)   Sp. Arts 827

Goldwater, Barry, *Your Family Is the Target*   Key-927

Great Debates of 1960, Presidential Campaign—Nixon, Kennedy (4-62)   3-Sp. Word A-26

Johnson, Lyndon Baines (4-64)   Sp. Word 164

———, *Voting Rights Speech*   Sp. Arts 915**

Kennedy in Germany (4-64)   Phi. PCC-210

Kennedy Speaks (4-64)   Harmonia 3005

MacArthur, Gen. Douglas, *Address Before Joint Session of Congress,* April 19, 1951   CMS 102

Pope John XXIII (9-63)   Mer. RM-200

Pope Paul VI, U.N. Address (1-66)   4-Sp. Arts 935/8

---

* See Schwann *Long Playing Record Catalog* (Boston: published monthly).

** This is the speech of President Johnson analyzed in this text.

Roosevelt, Franklin D., *Inaugural Addresses* (with Truman on reverse side)   2-Sp. Arts 825/6

Stevenson, Adlai, *Voice of the Uncommon Man*   MGM 4329-D

Play

Shakespeare, *Julius Caesar*, Cambridge Univ., Marlowe Soc.   3-Lon. 4334

———, Dublin Gate Theatre   3-Sp. Word A-15

———, (Richardson, Quale, Mills)   3-Caed. SRS-230

In addition to the listing given here, there are many other excellent collections of the spoken word on records. Consult the holdings of your college and community libraries.

EXERCISES

A

THE PROCESS OF COMMUNICATION

Give a book report on one of the following:

Berlo, David K., *The Process of Communication* (New York: Holt, Rinehart & Winston, Inc., 1960)

Boulding, Kenneth E., *Conflict and Defense* (New York: Harper & Row, Publishers, 1963)

Brembeck, W. L. and Howell, W. S., *Persuasion* (Englewood Cliffs, N.J.: Prentice-Hall, Inc., 1952)

Chase, Stuart, *Roads to Agreement* (New York: Harper & Row, Publishers, 1951)

Cherry, Colin, *On Human Communication* (Cambridge, Mass.: M.I.T. Press, 1957)

Garn, Roy, *The Magic of Emotional Appeal* (Englewood Cliffs, N.J.: Prentice-Hall, Inc., 1960)

Haney, William V., *Communication Patterns and Incidents* (Homewood, Ill.: Richard D. Irwin, Inc., 1960)

Hovland, Carl I., Janis, Irving L. and Kelley, Harold H., *Communication and Persuasion* (New Haven: Yale University Press, 1953)

Johnson, Wendell, *People in Quandaries* (New York: Harper & Row, Publishers, 1946)

Lee, Irving J., "Procedure for Coercing Agreement," *Harvard Business Review*, XXXII (January-February, 1954), pp. 39–45

Minnick, Wayne C., *The Art of Persuasion* (Boston: Houghton Mifflin Company, 1957)

215

Oliver, Robert T., *The Psychology of Persuasive Speech* (New York: Longmans, Green & Co., Inc., 1957)

Rogers, Carl and Roethlisberger, Fritz, "Barriers and Gateways to Communication," *Harvard Business Review*, XXX (July-August, 1952), pp. 46–52

Schramm, Wilbur, editor, *Process and Effects of Mass Communications* (Urbana, Ill.: University of Illinois Press, 1954)

Sherif, Muzafer and Hovland, Carl I., *Social Judgment* (New Haven: Yale University Press, 1961)

Topics for Speeches

1. Why We Need to Go to the Moon
2. Discount Houses and Fair Prices
3. Indoctrination and American Troops
4. Should a Government Conceal the Truth?
5. Cold Sweat vs. Hot Sweat
6. The Fifth Amendment
7. The Tyranny of the Extreme
8. College and Political Action
9. The Liberal Arts College
10. Communication for What?

B

PERSONAL POWER IN PERSUASION

1. Read Book I of Aristotle's *Rhetoric*.
2. What is your definition of intelligence?
3. What do you mean when you use the word *virtue?*
4. How do you explain good will?
5. Read Erwin D. Canham's "The Value of Self Criticism," *Vital Speeches*, Vol. XXVI, No. 5.
6. Contrast the personal power of Stephen A. Douglas and Abraham Lincoln.
7. Wherein did the power of Clarence Darrow lie?
8. Who are your idols in public life? Analyze your reasons.
9. Read and report on Wendell White, *Psychology in Living*, 3rd Ed. (New York: The Macmillan Co., 1955).
10. Contrast the personal magnetism of Eisenhower, Truman and Johnson.

Topics for Speeches

1. Romance vs. Sex Appeal
2. Profits Mean Jobs
3. The Population Explosion Is Here Now
4. Tax the Co-ops
5. Safety on the Highway
6. Truth Crushed
7. Man Is Incurably Religious
8. Commonsense and Nonsense
9. Automation and Unemployment
10. Conquest from Within

C

VOICE AND ACTION IN PERSUASION

1. Listen to a news broadcast over television and pay attention to the voice and action of the reporter. Tell the class about it.
2. Go to a movie and study the posture, gesture and voice of your favorite movie actor (or actress). Give a report in class.
3. Listen to a recording of one of Winston Churchill's speeches. Describe his use of voice to the class.
4. Bring a recording of one of Franklin D. Roosevelt's speeches to class and analyze the voice for the class.
5. Be able to give a discussion of the deaf and dumb language.
6. Be able to show, through voice and action, how words can be made to mean different things.
7. Read and be able to discuss the work of Gilbert Austin. Consult Lester Thonssen's *Selected Readings in Rhetoric and Public Speaking* (New York: H. W. Wilson Co., 1942).
8. Observe a speaker's platform manners and give a report to the class.

Topics for Speeches

1. How Speakers Annoy Me
2. Mannerisms of Well Known Speakers
3. Are Voice and Action Important?
4. Does Smoking Harm the Voice?
5. What TV Did to Richard Nixon
6. The Wooden Indian
7. The Vivacious Woman
8. The Delivery of the College Chaplain
9. What Did Demosthenes Mean by Action?

D

ANALYSIS OF THE AUDIENCE

1. Read H. L. Hollingworth, *The Psychology of the Audience* (New York: American Book Company, 1935).
2. What is meant by identification and polarization in audience motivation?
3. What is your system of beliefs in regard to the following: church, alma mater, athletics, education, politics, marriage, pre-marital sex?
4. What is the best way to motivate neutrals, partisans and opponents?

5. Read a speech in *Vital Speeches* and underline the uses of impelling motives.
6. Is tact the same as sincerity?
7. What do you think of compulsory arbitration?
8. What do we mean by collective bargaining?
9. What congregation problems does the average preacher have?
10. Analyze the average college classroom audience in public speaking.

Topics for Speeches

1. Public Speaking Is Applied Psychology
2. The Only Motive Is Self-Interest
3. Different Kinds of Crowds
4. Rabble Rousers
5. Billy Graham and 35,000 People
6. Homogeneous Audiences
7. Every Audience Is Different
8. Adaptation is the Key
9. Ways of Identification
10. The Sense of Values

E

THE ROLE OF THE OCCASION

1. Does the time of day affect the reaction of the audience?
2. Read Hitler's *Mein Kampf* on the importance of the occasion.
3. What factors go to make up the occasion?
4. How important is timing in speaking?
5. Do great occasions make great men?
6. Discuss the role of the occasion in politics.
7. Does the occasion have anything to do with the mood of an audience?
8. Does the speaker or the occasion shape the attitudes of the audience?
9. Discuss Whately's dictum that "He that is not open to conviction is not qualified for discussion."
10. What are the differences in these occasions: Decoration Day, The Fourth of July, Labor Day, Thanksgiving?

Topics for Speeches

1. The Land of the Free
2. Rebels Without Causes
3. The Heart Has Reasons of Its Own
4. The Soul's Invincible Surmise
5. The Lessons of Adversity
6. The American's Prejudices
7. Suburban Rot
8. Parents and Teen-Agers
9. Value Systems and Living
10. It Just Wasn't Our Day

F
THE SPEAKER'S IDEAS

1. Would you rather hear a speaker's own experience or an experience he has read about? Why?
2. Discuss Cicero's thought that he who does not know the past remains forever a child.
3. Where do your own ideas for speeches come from?
4. What is your reaction to ghost writers?
5. Do ideas determine the organization of a speech?
6. Why is the idea of a speech the most important part of the speech situation?
7. Of what value is a file for a speaker's ideas?
8. Discuss the part memory plays in shaping a speaker's ideas.
9. How can a speaker's powers of observation be sharpened?
10. What do you feel about the humorous handling of ideas?

Topics for Speeches

1. When the Going Gets Tough the Tough Get Going
2. America and the Far East
3. The American Mind
4. Nature, Man and God
5. The Friends of Man
6. Promises to Keep
7. What I Want Out of Life
8. My Inheritance
9. Hunting for Scapegoats
10. A Definition of Education

INDEX OF
RHETORICAL
TERMS

In each reference, the first number given is the page number; the number after the colon refers to the particular paragraph on that page (in the Shakespeare excerpt, references are to lines in the scene reproduced).

A

D

Debate, 87:16; 159:27
  brief, 96
Debater, 193:58
Definition, 63:5; 78:2
  development by, 23:47; 84:11; 119:27; 135:5; 171:20
  by negation, 83:9; 177:58
Degree, topic of, 17:12
Deliberation, 122:40; 153:18
Desire, appeal to, 159:29
Development by:
  cause and effect, 17:13; 18:17; 35:11; 43:42
  contrast and comparison, 114:9; 119:28; 121:35; 129:67;
    168:5; 187ff.
  definition, 23:48; 54:21; 63:5; 65:9; 163:41; 170:13
  illustration, 26:63; 27:71; 79:2; 85:12; 126:59; 197:91
  particulars and details, 20:30; 53:9; 91:20; 122:40; 123:46;
    148:10; 172:25; 185:99; 209:48
  presenting reasons, 16:6; 154:19; 156:23; 191:26
  quotation, 33:5; 53:14; 81:7; 87:15; 103; 135:4; 137:10; 138:11
Diction, 180:75; 185:101
Digression, 181:82
Direct style, 66:11
Directness, 50:6; 90:18
Diversity in unity, 139:15
Dramatic style, 88:17; 130:73; 202:158

E

Earnestness, 184:95; 202:160
Echo, 19:23; 19:26; 23:51; 52:13; 55:24; 68:14; 126:58
Economy of attention, 67:13
Emotional proof, 32:3; 50:7; 54:22; 152:16; 169:9; 183:91; 203:169
Emphasis:
  by repetition, 25:62; 120:30; 182:84
  by space, 118:22
Energy in style, 54:19
Enumeration, 50:9; 67:13
Enthymeme, 117:19; 207:266
Epigram, 125:55; 130:72; 140:16
Examples, historical, 114:8; 203:173
Experience, reference to, 7:13; 32:4; 81:7; 117:19; 177:55
Explanation as support, 86:14; 123:44; 128:65

F

Facts, 70:19; 114:7
Familiar, use of the, 81:6
Feedback, 194:66

W

Wants, appeal to, 54:18; 159:28; 160:30; 187ff.
Weeping with an audience, 199:15
Words:
   choice of, 35:13
   common, 16:6
   as echoes, 54:28
   exact, 16:11; 34:7
   as sounds, 80:4; 136:8; 162:39
   that cry, 183:89; 192:51; 194:72
   as transitions, 61:2; 81:6

Y

"Yes" response, 155:21
"You and I, " 32:1; 52:13
"You all knows, " 206:221